Jaco Dreyer, Yolanda Dreyer,
Edward Foley, Malan Nel (Eds.)

Practicing Ubuntu

D1592745

International Practical Theology

edited by

Prof. Dr. Chris Hermans (Nijmegen),
Prof. Dr. Maureen Junker-Kenny (Dublin),
Prof. Dr. Richard Osmer (Princeton),
Prof. Dr. Friedrich Schweitzer (Tübingen),
Prof. Dr. Hans-Georg Ziebertz (Würzburg)

in cooperation with the
International Academy of Practical Theology (IAPT),

represented by

Heather Walton (President) and Robert Mager (Vice-President)

Coordination of IAPT conference-volumes:
Constanze Thierfelder
(Herborn and Marburg, Germany).

Volume 20

LIT

Practicing Ubuntu

Practical Theological Perspectives on
Injustice, Personhood and Human Dignity

edited by

Jaco Dreyer, Yolanda Dreyer,
Edward Foley, Malan Nel

LIT

Cover image: Ms. Suzanne Potgieter, Pretoria.

This book is printed on acid-free paper.

Bibliographic information published by the Deutsche Nationalbibliothek
The Deutsche Nationalbibliothek lists this publication in the Deutsche
Nationalbibliografie; detailed bibliographic data are available on the Internet at
http://dnb.d-nb.de.

ISBN 978-3-643-90848-3

A catalogue record for this book is available from the British Library

© LIT VERLAG GmbH & Co. KG Wien,
Zweigniederlassung Zürich 2017
Klosbachstr. 107
CH-8032 Zürich
Tel. +41 (0) 44-251 75 05
E-Mail: zuerich@lit-verlag.ch   http://www.lit-verlag.ch
Distribution:
In the UK: Global Book Marketing, e-mail: mo@centralbooks.com
In North America: International Specialized Book Services, e-mail: orders@isbs.com
In Germany: LIT Verlag Fresnostr. 2, D-48159 Münster
Tel. +49 (0) 2 51-620 32 22, Fax +49 (0) 2 51-922 60 99, e-mail: vertrieb@lit-verlag.de

In Austria: Medienlogistik Pichler-ÖBZ, e-mail: mlo@medien-logistik.at
e-books are available at www.litwebshop.de

Contents

III. PRACTICING UBUNTU: INTERNATIONAL
PERSPECTIVES

Introduction: The spirituality of *ubuntu and becoming human*

"I was glad to hear that you were critical. For a moment I thought you were going to tell us that *ubuntu* is the answer," someone commented on Stewart Motha's paper on *ubuntu* at the University of South Africa in 2009.[1] Another called *ubuntu* a "dangerous notion." U.S. born South African scholar of value theory and moral, political and legal philosophy, Thaddeus Metz,[2] identifies three problems with *ubuntu*: it is vague, it over-emphasises collectivism at the cost of individual freedom, and it is anachronistic. However, from a jurisprudence perspective, Metz turns to *ubuntu* to rediscover the dignity of humankind and its capacity for community – a capacity that is destroyed by human rights violations. Can *ubuntu* be useful in today's post-industrial technological globalised world?

Ubuntu appeared in the Interim Constitution of South Africa (Act 200 of 1993), meant as "a historic bridge" from the colonial and apartheid past to a "future founded on the recognition of human rights, democracy and peaceful co-existence and development opportunities for all." In the final Constitution (Act 108 of 1996) it is absent.[3] For Ramose this exclusion means that the legal ideas of the indigenous peoples of South Africa are not reflected and that a truly South African constitution is yet to be born.[4]

In "the great Sutu-nguni family" of Southern Africa, being humane is regarded as the supreme virtue. This philosophy of life is called *ubuntu* or *botho*, the practice of being humane.[5] The essence of *ubuntu* is dignity. The Shona (from Zimbabwe) articulate it as: "I am because we are; I exist because the community

---

[1] Motha, Stewart. 2009. "Archiving Colonial Sovereignty: From Ubuntu to a Jurisprudence of Sacrifice." *Suid-Afrikaanse Publieke Reg / Public Law* 22: 297-327; esp. 303.

[2] Metz, Thaddeus. 2011. "Ubuntu as a Moral Theory and Human Rights in South Africa." *African Human Rights Law Journal* 2: 532-559.

[3] Gade, Christian. 2011. "The Historical Development of the Written Discourses on Ubuntu." *South African Journal of Philosophy* 30 (3): 303-329, esp. 31.

[4] Ramose, Mogobe. 2006. "The King as memory and symbol of African customary law." In *The Shade of New Leaves (Governments in Traditional Authority: A South African Perspective)*, edited by M.O. Hinz, and H. Patemann. Berlin: Lit Verlag, 351-374; esp. 366.

[5] Ngubane, Jordan K. 1963. *An African Explains apartheid*. London: Pall Mall Press; esp. 76.

exists."[6] *Ubuntu* is truly an African term, which denotes a bond of unity among people. Human beings only become truly human through relationship with others.[7] *Ubuntu* appears in written sources in South Africa as early as the nineteenth century. Initially it referred to "human quality" and was later "defined" as humanism, a philosophy, an ethic, and a worldview.

This book is a practical-theological contribution to the theoretical discussion on the philosophy, epistemology and ethics of *ubuntu*, and explores practices informed by "*ubuntu*-like values" (the words of Joyce Ann Mercer) both in the South African context and in others across the globe. The discussion demonstrates that *ubuntu* can indeed contribute to insights regarding humanity in a post-industrial globalising world.

The three sections of the book represent three perspectives on practicing *ubuntu*:

I Practicing *ubuntu*: Injustice, personhood and human dignity

II Practicing *ubuntu*: Local perspectives

III Practicing *ubuntu*: International perspectives

Pam Couture sets the scene. She relates *ubuntu* to the idea of *bumuntu* in the Democratic Republic of Congo and to human rights. Amid the looting of the land and the looting of bodies, *bumuntu* – which is about more than human dignity and worth, as it also has spiritual connotations – can be utilised to disempower evil and bring healing, wholeness and dignity to the people, both collective and individual.

Wentzel van Huyssteen, Friedrich Schweitzer and David Hogue create a paradigm for the reflections on *ubuntu*. Healing presupposes a returning to the self. How are we human? Van Huyssteen traces the evolutionary development of *Homo sapiens* to language and pro-sociality, "the capacity for seeing things from someone else's perspective" and "the capacity to alter the world" (p. 35). From *becoming human* to *being human* requires (religious) imagination and a sense of morality. Humans construct their own environment, which Van Huyssteen calls "niche construction."

Moving the idea of niche construction further, Friedrich Schweitzer explores how practical theology can engage with a world that increasingly denies the presence of God. The challenge is to find "effective ways for preaching and teaching

---

6   Drucilla, Cornell, and Karin van Marle. 2005. "Exploring Ubuntu: Tentative Reflections." *African Human Rights Law Journal* 5: 195-219; esp. 205.

7   Asike, Jude. 2016. "The Philosophical Concept of 'Ubuntu' as Dialogic Ethic and the Transformation of Political Community in Africa." *Ogiris. A New Journal of African Studies* 12, http://dx.doi.org / 10.4314 / og.v 12i sl.l, 7 of 16.

based on thinking in complementarity" (p. 51). Complementarity and the language with which we communicate would not be possible without symbolic imagination. Symbolic imagination is also the domain of theology. David Hogue explores the intersections between interpersonal neurobiology and theological anthropologies that embrace *ubuntu*-values. This includes notions of belonging, mutuality and reciprocity. Intersubjectivity, from the perspective of *"ubuntu*-theology," emphasises the centrality of these values to human identity.

South African contributions explore *ubuntu* from a variety of angles and contexts. Nadine Bowers Du Toit, from the context of the people of mixed race, uses their expression "ma se kind" (mother's child) to focus on personhood, family, identity and co-existence. These doubly disenfranchised people can claim not only an "alien dignity," but also the full dignity of being "God's children." Dignity and worth are not to be found in "people's view of themselves or others' view of them. It is rather 'imputed to us by the love of God,'" which provides a God-given agency (p. 61).

Johan Cilliers regrets that the current "new South Africa" has moved from *ntu* (the root for the word "human") to *into*, meaning "a thing." He compares a sermon of Dutch Reformed moderator Koot Vorster at the 1971 Republic Day celebrations during the heyday of apartheid with a sermon of Desmond Tutu three days before the first democratic elections in South Africa. Tutu's sermon begins with "Wow!" and ends with "Hey!" In religious imaginative symbolic terms *ubuntu* incorporates both *awe* and an *ethics of celebration*. Wilhelm Gräb also explores sermons of Desmond Tutu, for whom "there is no conflict between human rights' universal validity and the obligation of Christians to speak up for human rights out of their Christian belief" (p. 89).

Fritz de Wet, who was associate professor at the North-West University, South Africa, died tragically in a car accident in January 2016. In this book he relates *ubuntu* to practical theology as "lived life." A lived life is purposeful life, beautiful life, ethical life, dignified life, graceful life and connected life (p. 83).

Against the backdrop of Europe's challenge and hesitance to deal with uprooted refugees and migrants in a culture of hospitality (*Willkommenskultur*), Daniël Louw builds on Tutu's notion of "compassionate society." He relates the Kenyan spirituality of *ûtugi* to pastoral caregiving and the Christian tradition of hospitality.

For Vhumani Magezi *"ubuntu* is in flames" as present-day South Africa suffers on account of "colossal injustice and rampant corruption" (p. 112). He suggests that practical theology explores a "new *ubuntu*", infused with Christian values. An "*ubuntu* in transition," a "liminal *ubuntu*" will not shy away from reality.

Johann Meylahn distinguishes between *Ubuntu* and *ubuntu*, the latter being embedded in a specific historical political context. He explores discourses on

Ubuntu as a glocal phenomenon. If the kind of Christianity that dominates western thought is deconstructed, then Christianity and *Ubuntu* can be in harmony. Reading discourses on *Ubuntu,* not against or before, but *with* the Christian text, the Jesus event becomes the generic story of God becoming flesh in human history. To acknowledge the child as born-for-us means to carry one another and respect the other's world. South Africa is crying in so many places. It is time to carry one another out into the truly new SA. With his focus on leadership, Ian Nell also distinguishes between the spirit of *ubuntu* and western approaches. Humility and service are part of *ubuntu* leadership. If we take the "long road to *ubuntu* leadership" (p. 142) we can move beyond exclusive and gender-insensitive approaches.

Present-day South Africa is "threatened with disintegration" (p. 147). There is a growing spirit of self-interest. Roger Tucker and Maake Masango identify the "weakness of *ubuntu*" as that it represses individual consciousness and opinion. An "*ubuntu* ethic" can be used as a "manipulative tool" to avoid punishment and sanction illegal conduct by politicians and officials. They suggest a selective application of *ubuntu* in multi-cultural South Africa.

Scholars from outside South Africa explore the relevance of *ubuntu* for the global world. Lynn Bridgers draws a postcolonial parallel between South Africa and New Mexico. *Ubuntu* counterbalances the west's emphasis on individuality and separateness.

Hans-Günter Heimbrock and Trygve Wyller highlight the participation and belonging aspects of *ubuntu* in their exploration of the migration crisis in Europe with the influx of asylum-seekers, refugees and undocumented people. In practical theology subjectivity and relationality are not seen as opposites. *Ubuntu* can provide epistemological strength to research methodologies in practical theology theory.

Joyce Ann Mercer relates "*ubuntu*-like values" (p. 192) to the collective trauma following the anti-communist massacre (1965-1967). For reconciliation in Indonesia "a more adequate form of *ubuntu*-community in Indonesia is needed that honours the social body without the need to sacrifice individuals for its existence" (p. 202).

John Mohan Razu relates the Tamil concept of *Manithaneyam* to *ubuntu*. He points out that caste manifestations are "the highest form of apartheid" (p. 215). *Manithaneyam* expresses humaneness, the core of a common humanity. Although the constitution of India guarantees its citizens basic rights with regard to personhood, dignity and equality, those outside the caste still suffer gross indignity. Both *ubuntu* and *Manithaneyam* can become a working principle for exposing injustice and including people.

Evelyn Parker focuses on the health risks and hopelessness of young women subject to partner violence and potential HIV/AIDS infection. She proposes a "critical *ubuntu*" that is not, as is often the case, "suspiciously silent" (p. 218) about patriarchy and sexism. Critical *ubuntu* can inspire a vision for ecclesial practice.

Neil Pembroke links *ubuntu*, "organisational spirituality" and "Trinitarian theology." *Perichoresis* in the sense of mutual indwelling and love, is central to Trinitarian theology. Organisational spirituality is about finding meaning, purpose and personal fulfilment in work and developing one's potential. For Pembroke *ubuntu* and Christian theological views of the human correlate because the human person is created *imago Trinitatis* (p. 230).

Jeanne Stevenson-Moessner examines multiple identity politics in relation to personhood, human dignity and injustice. She relates this to children who are transplanted into a new cultural context and experience trauma and an identity crisis. "Dreaming *ubuntu*" can contribute to awareness and cultural sensitivity, and can offer possibilities of healing.

For Raymond Webb interconnectedness is constitutive of a person's "very identity." Where distributive justice is a legal responsibility, for social justice the solidarity of the human community is needed (p. 250). He identifies *ubuntu*-like values such as *subsidiarity* – that action and control be exercised at the lowest level possible – and *accompaniment* – that all have value and gifts to contribute to the wellbeing of the whole. *Ubuntu* advocates that "all voices are to be heard, all gifts used, every contribution matters, humility is in order" (p. 253).

I. PRACTICING UBUNTU: INJUSTICE, PERSONHOOD AND HUMAN DIGNITY

Human dignity, injustice and *ubuntu*: Living the metaphor of *bwino/bumuntu*/white lime in the Democratic Republic of Congo

Pamela Couture

Abstract

Looting civilians has long been outlawed in international law; rape became a war crime first in 1998. Looting and rape, however, have been rampant during the war and subsequent conflict in the Democratic Republic of Congo. A persuasive argument against looting and rape that is consistent with international law can be created from local norms. The concept of *bumuntu*, while analogous to human dignity, contains additional spiritual connotations that allows it to ground arguments against sexual violence within the logic familiar to civilians, local Mai-Mai militias and other combatants.

Introduction

Religious peace building in the Democratic Republic of Congo (DRC) – is it an oxymoron? The Congo is associated with titles such as *The Heart of Darkness* (Conrad 1999), *All Things Must Fight to Live* (Mealer 2008) and *Blood River* (Butcher 2007). My research since 2007 challenges such stereotypes. In *We Are Not All Victims*[1] I document the religious peace building of Luba-Congolese people who contradict this image. They lived ordinary lives during the war (1998-2002) and responded with extraordinary grace.

---

[1]   Under the working title of *Where's the Peace to Keep?* this project has been supported by: The Luce Foundation and the Lilly Endowment through the Association of Theological Schools; the United Methodist Committee on Relief; Dianne Schumaker, a private donor; the North Katanga Annual Conference through contributions. It is published under the title *We Are Not All Victims: Religious Peacebuilding in the Democratic Republic of Congo*, 2016, Lit Verlag. I thank Rene Sephton of Australia for directing me to Mutombo Nkulu-N'Sengha's dissertation and Congolese readers Dr. Boniface Kabongo, Dr. Guy Mande Muyombo, and Rev. Ilgha Monga Ilunga for comments on the draft of this article.

By addressing the issue of sexual violence in DRC, I risk perpetuating what I have tried to counteract. Congolese women, however, deserve my direct attention to this work of peace building. Does *bumuntu*, the Kiluba language cognate of *ubuntu* in South Africa and human dignity in North Atlantic thought, offer a resource to resist rape and sexual violence?

The Baluba linguistic groups inhabit southern DRC. They originated from the Upemba Depression between Lake Tanganyika and the Congo River about 1500 years ago and established an empire of kingdoms whose power increased until the late 19th century. The Baluba are now considered a meta-ethnicity with many variants of Luba languages (Roberts 1996, 59). The witnesses in my study speak Kiluba and call themselves Luba people.

Bumuntu bwino

Bumuntu incorporates the communal understandings of *ubuntu* but also envisions individual virtue. Luba-Congolese Mutombo Nkulu-N'Sengha describes *bumuntu* and the epistemology by which it is known, *bwino,* in his 2002 Ph.D. dissertation. The Luba sage who exhibits *bumuntu* has *mucina* (also spelled *mutyima*) *muyampe* – a good heart – and exhibits *bumuntu* through virtues such as "compassion, love, dignity, respect, integrity, righteousness, truth, honesty, generosity, a wisdom and intelligence, peacefulness, hospitality, and freedom" (Nkulu N'Sengha 2002, 133).

Bwino, the epistemology through which *bumuntu* is known, seeks "the highest and most holistic knowledge...a fruit of personal effort...using the power of the human mind." *Bwino* refers to "wisdom" and "conscience" and is focused on "human flourishing." The person of *bwino* has a kind of "knowledge that incorporates both ethical and esthetical qualities" and engages in "a disciplined search for truth about reality, direction and purpose." *Bwino* teaches that "the individual act of thinking is nourished by the knowledge of the community" (Nkulu-N'Sengha 2002, 138).

Bwino can be grounded in three Kiluba proverbs. *Mwana wipangala ye umvwa* ("a child who raises questions is the one who gains understanding and genuine knowledge"); *Kuboko kumo Kubunga ke kololanga* ("one single hand cannot comprehend things"); and, *Bwino bonso ke Bwino, Bwino kwikala ne Bantu* ("true knowledge consists in living in harmony with fellow human beings") (Nkulu-N'Sengha 2002, 133). *Bumuntu,* to be truly human, is to respect sacred life in oneself and in other creatures, or *kilemeka ne kulemeka bantu ne bintu bya Vidye* (Nkulu-N'Sengha 2002, 17). Boniface Kabongo distinguishes *bwino* as "capacity, knowledge and ability to perceive what is right, fair and normal" and *bumuntu* as "the way a human being lives or experiences peace in the community and social relationships" (Kabongo 2015). *Bumuntu* is never "speculative." It always begins in the suffering and joys of the people.

Looting as suffering

In Congo "looting" symbolises suffering. This injustice is introduced in the following scene from *We Are Not All Victims.*

The new bishop pondered the last seven years which had hastened Kamina's decline. In the 1980s Mobutu had plundered the wealth of the country for his personal gain, and the economy in Kamina had struggled. But most people still had enough to eat. Then in 1991 and 1993 Mobutu's soldiers at Kamina Military Base pillaged the city's business and agricultural base. Goats and chickens, the staple sources of protein, no longer roamed the townspeople's yards. Small businesses, the center of the barter economy, had closed. Transportation, by train to Lubumbashi or by bike around Kamina and the surrounding villages, had stilled. No hospitals had medicine. No schools had books. Only a few churches and a little food, mainly cassava and fish, remained. Under the influence of Arab slave traders, under the power of Belgian King Leopold's *Force Publique,* and then under Mobutu—*a Congolese life was a looted life.*

Many forms of looting, or pillage, define Congolese life. King Leopold II of Belgium plundered, killed and maimed the Congolese. Joseph Desire Mobutu extracted taxes and pocketed aid. Multinational corporations and other African nations developed illicit trade in natural resources. Rwanda's involvement in the conflict minerals and arms trade fueled the 1998-2002 war (UN 2012). According to Guy Mande Muyombo any feminist interpretation of war in Congo should include the rape of the earth.

The wars in the DRC are packaged in ethnicity but are first and foremost resources-based. By analogy, the DRC is being raped through illegal exploitation of its mineral resources. Mother Earth continues to be raped even when guns are silent. Once more women and children are the most affected. Women and the earth are both raped by individuals who are driven by greed and power. They are both in the quest of dignity, and the question that need to be raised is, "how do the Luba understand the need to care for the earth?" (Mande 2015).

Looting also defines people's lives on an intimate scale. When Rwanda and its allies invaded the Tanganyika District of North Katanga in 1998-2001, villagers buried their possessions and fled. The soldiers unearthed and stole their belongings. In rural areas food insecurity and hunger fueled the pillaging. In Mobutu's army soldiers fed themselves by extorting food from the local population. During the war, when Congolese soldiers' pay was delayed, they continued this practice. The local Mayi-Mayi militias, who arose to protect villagers from the threat of

Mobutu's army, also expected villagers to pay in food for their "protective" services. When the food supply ran low the militias looted what remained. Militias also looted crops during harvest. At military-style checkpoints militias required payment in food and goods from local business people, who then had nothing left to sell at the markets.

An auto-ethnographic interlude

I am a white American woman writing the stories of Luba-Congolese people. Despite my good intentions, am I not "looting" the Luba-Congolese heritage? Do *bumuntu* and *bwino* – the standard for judging this work–offer a methodological alternative to scholarly looting?

I launched the research at the invitation of North Katanga United Methodist Bishop Ntambo Nkulu Ntanda. Throughout, I sought to respect the human dignity of the community. "One hand clapping" truly "cannot comprehend things." The witnesses shaped the story by guiding me to observe customs of respect; by rendering stories in Kiluba, Kiswahili, and French into English; by soliciting participants whose stories "completed" those I was hearing; by arranging transportation, accompaniment and food, health care and medical evacuations; by filling in gaps in the stories via phone or skype; by responding to chapters; by identifying, and translating background documents; and by translating, deepening, correcting, and verifying people's memories of events.

In 2007 the Kamina women bestowed my Kiluba name – Inamizo – "mother of the nations without discrimination," reflecting what they perceived my method and creating an ideal that I have sought to live up to. So their soul or spirit – their *muya* – lives in our work.

Three primary questions shape the research: "How does your work contribute to peace in Congo?" "How does your religious belief inform your work?" and "What do you think of a white American woman writing this Congolese story?" The Luba people are storytellers. I learned a new writing craft – creative nonfiction – to animate their stories in their own voices. I chose literary devices best suited to communicate to a western audience the community's spirituality, emotions, actions, obstacles and achievements. Inevitably, my voice and imagination enter the text. Yet, "true knowledge consists in living in harmony with our fellow human beings." I measured my work by community participation and edification. In that way, my *mucina* – my "thinking heart" – lives in this book.

"A child who raises questions is the one who gains understanding and true knowledge." The primary research documents Luba-Congolese activities related to religious peace building. Now, I am analyzing a secondary theme: the Luba-Congolese experience of rape and sexual violence.

Rape and sexual violence

Rape and sexual violence are ultimate forms of looting. In DRC law "rape" is defined as a person introducing sexual organs or an object – sticks, knives or machetes – into a bodily orifice of a man or woman in coercive circumstances (Zongwe 2012, 37-57). The DRC accepts international law in this regard. Rape has social consequences for the victim. A person who discloses rape risks everything: personal dignity, social standing, community support, and physical health. I introduce rape in this scene from *We Are Not All Victims*. In the following, the Banyamulenge are Tutsi Congolese of Rwandan descent; the Mai-Mai are militias who follow tradition, believing they will be protected from harm, including bullets, by ritual washing.

The overstuffed sofa in the *payotte* of Bishop's concrete house in Kamina seemed to the woman like a billowy luxury after the hard, damp dirt of her makeshift hut in the bush. She sat side by side with Bishop, the plump cushion firmly cradling her body. She was comforted, but not comfortable. She could not look at Bishop; rather, her eyes were focused on the floor between her feet, where her toe traced a line of cement separating two large, shiny tiles...

As Bishop inclined his ear toward to woman seated by him, the sounds of Annual Conference faded from his hearing, replaced by her heavy breathing and occasional deep sighs.

"I am so glad to know that you are alive," Bishop murmured quietly. "Speak when you are ready."

She glanced at him briefly, then looked back at the tiles on the floor. "It began with the war of the Banyamulenge, near Kalemie. If they found a man, even if he is a baby, they will kill him. If they found a woman and she is pregnant, they will kill her. That is why we wanted the Mai-Mai movement, to protect the people from the Banyamulenge."

She stopped, rubbed her toe along the line of the grout once more. Bishop squeezed her hand but waited patiently, without speaking.

"We hadn't eaten for three days. I was walking from the village to town to find food. I didn't know that the Mai-Mai had set up a barrier on the path, and that they didn't want people to come to the barrier. The Mai-Mai came to fight with the Banyamulenge. Then they found me. They said, 'Why are you taking our path?' They did not care about my answer. They said, 'Put this woman in the house. We will fight, and then we will come and kill her.' But God is with his people. I was able to run away."

Bishop sat, a silent, reverent witness to the woman's story. But he wondered: Had she been molested? It happened to so many women. He did not want to ask, to breach her privacy. But she told him, almost as an aside.

"Now, I am a useless Congolese woman."

In the popular imagination, looting and rape are particularly associated with wars in Africa. Yet they have historically accompanied North Atlantic war also. Tuba Inal, in *Looting and Rape in Wartime: Law and Change in International Relations,* demonstrates that Europeans increasingly prohibited looting in conferences on international law in Brussels in 1874, The Hague in 1899 and 1907, and Geneva in 1949. But rape as a war crime dropped from the agenda. It was first prohibited nearly a century later (1998) during the United Nations Conference of Plenipotentiaries in Rome that established the International Criminal Court (Inal 2013, 28-58).

Inal's theory of change: Prohibiting looting and rape in war in the North Atlantic

Inal argues that ideas that contribute to normative cultural self-understandings and their codification in law create normative change. Three ideas in the 19th century – the belief in "progress," "the sacredness of private property," and "civilised peoples" – created a self-image among North Atlantic nations that crystallised the international sentiment against looting civilians during war. Although rape had dropped from the international agenda (Inal 2013, 59-91), in the latter half of the twentieth century, "norm entrepreneurs" successfully argued that men *could* control their behavior and that rape actually *is* a war crime (Inal 2013, 122-155). After women's rape camps developed in Yugoslavia and Rwanda, women's NGO's in Rome were able to create "normative shock" – framing the issue as: "massive violations of women, which people believed belonged to history, had returned to the 'civilised world' " (Inal 2013, 155-166).

Cultural self-image and international law, however, requires constant surveillance and revision. In the same year that Europeans agreed in Brussels on the protection of civilians from looting during war (1874), conferees in Berlin divvied "savage" Africa among themselves. The Berlin Conference gave King Leopold II of Belgium access to Congo to plunder ivory and rubber and perpetrate grievous violence toward local people. In 1909 British "norm entrepreneurs" Edmund Morel and Roger Casement revealed Leopold's excesses and connected the Congo case to Europe's conscience (Hochschild 1998, 177ff).

In a second irony, in the year the international community outlawed rape (1998), Rwanda invaded DRC and ignited an alleged epidemic of sexual war crimes (CEDAW 2000, 2006). Mai-Mai militias also perpetuated sexual violence. Few of these crimes have been prosecuted. In ICC trials arising from the DRC there was pressure to drop sexual charges against Germain Katanga and Nathieu

Ngudjolo Chui, and sexual charges were not admitted against Thomas Lubanga Dyilo, despite testimony about his crimes (Inal 2013, 183-184).

Could *bumuntu* be called upon to build the sense among Luba-Congolese that "rape is contrary to who we are" and, along with *ubuntu* and human rights, among African and international leaders that "sexual violence is not something we tolerate," so that incidents of sexual violence are reduced, and when they occur, are prosecuted?

Human dignity and *bumuntu*

The concept *bumuntu* and its translation "dignity" are only analogues. Both collect a constellation of ideas that intersect (Gada in McCrudden 2013, 484; McCrudden 2013, xx).

Philosophically, *bumuntu* highlights the person of wisdom and conscience. Human dignity *may* carry such overtones, but it also reflects ways that hierarchy is sustained or undermined: a "dignified" person of social standing may be recognised as honourable because of virtue, self-control and reputation; or a "dignified" socially humiliated person, such as a slave, may be able to maintain self-respect or "inner freedom" (Goos in McCrudden 2013, 86-89). In the last century dignity has come to suggest a democratic ideal of equal worth (McCrudden 2013, 8).

Theologically, *bumuntu* corresponds closely to this idea of human worth – every *muntu* is one of "God's children." Protestant and Roman Catholic reflections propose that human beings are made "in the image of God," with inherent value and mystery (Soskice in McCrudden 2013, 229-243). Theologians find dignity in relationship to the doctrine of the Trinity (Hanvey in McCrudden 2013, 209-228), eschatology (Walsch in McCrudden 2013, 249-258), and the sanctity of life (Beattie in McCrudden 2013, 259-274; Gushee in McCrudden 2013, 275-288).

In legal discourse *bumuntu* and human dignity feed rights-talk. Discussions of human dignity led to the 1948 Universal Declaration of Human Rights. Discussions of *bumuntu* led to the 1986 African Charter of Rights and Freedoms. The relationship between human dignity and rights-talk is contested (McCrudden 2013, 2-3). In the North Atlantic, John Milbank argues that human dignity should supplant the language of human rights because it is more cohesive and coherent (Milbank in McCrudden 2013, 189-205). Costas Douzinas argues that human dignity only retards the possibility of genuine revolution for oppressed peoples (Beattie in McCrudden 2013, 261-262). Conor Geary (in McCrudden 2013, 155-171) finds a necessary relationship between human dignity and human rights. Some turn to rights-talk as the language with legal power.

Some Africans reject human rights as western individualism, but Nkulu-N'Sengha grounds African appeals to individual rights in *bumuntu*. He argues that *bumuntu* supports human rights for women. Citing Congolese Catholic feminists Mutonkole Mpiana wa Kabole, Beya Mbuyi, and Tshibola Kalengayi, and the Ghanaian, Mercy Oduyoye, he argues that emancipatory women's traditions already exist in Luba tradition, such as women keeping their own names at marriage, naming God as mother, and practicing as priests within traditional religion (Nkulu-N'Sengha 2002). Annike Thiem warns that appeals to dignity may limit human rights for women. The concept of human dignity is invoked to resist extreme violence against women but may also reassert traditional gender roles. Women who take public positions, such as those envisioned in the United Nations Resolution on Women, Peace and Security (2000), may be called "undignified" and considered to be inviting sexual violence. The United Nations understands gender through binary assumptions of male and female, so leaves unaddressed violence against gay and lesbian, intersex, transgendered and queer-identified people. Can *bumuntu* then offer an ideational response to rape and sexual violence (Thiem in Duewell et al. 2014, 498-504)?

Bumuntu and human dignity diverge in terms of method and foundations. American and European writers on human dignity begin either in abstractions or in human experience. *Bumuntu* always begins in the sufferings and joys of the people. The North Atlantic discussion of human dignity seeks a correct definition. *Bwino* seeks integration and synthesis. In everyday speech Luba people turn to the next speaker to "*complete* me."

Western scholars such as Thaddeus Metz (in Duewell et al. 2014, 310-318) may root human dignity philosophically. Theologians ground it theologically. For Nkulu-N'Sengha, the philosophy of *bumuntu necessarily* grounds itself in Luba indigenous religion, in the people's understanding and experience of God. The Supreme Creator (*Vidye*) cares for the entire cosmos (*ntanda*). Human beings (*muntu*) are "God's cattle" or "God's children."

Might *bumuntu* and *bwino* offer an ideational power that human dignity alone does not? Can these ideas help to create a normative situation in which rape and other sexual violence are prohibited and violations punished?

Bwino, bumuntu, and white lime against rape and sexual violence

Congolese law prohibits rape, domestically and internationally. The DRC ratified the Universal Declaration of Human Rights in 1965 and the United Nations Convention on Elimination of All Forms of Discrimination Against Women (CEDAW) in 1986. DRC submitted country reports in 2000 and 2006, critiquing existing Congolese laws and documenting war-related sexual violence against women, children and men. In 2006 the Congolese Parliament enacted progressive legislation that specifies an *obligation* on the government to prosecute rape, offers *precise* definitions of rape, and *delegates* prosecution – according to Inal, these elements of law make it enforceable. The law has been publicised; in 2007 professional women in North Katanga who sought help in creating a program entitled "Stop Violence Against Women" owned copies of it. Yet prosecution, conviction and deterrence remain notoriously difficult (Zongwe 2012, 37-57). In Europe, ideation crystallised to form the law; in DRC, cultural ideation must catch up with law. The metaphor of "white lime", with *bwino* and a critical understanding of *bumuntu,* might provide a resource for cultural reimaging.

In Luba society white lime symbolises justice and access to the spirit world. At investiture the leader receives white lime as a symbol of the responsibility to keep the peace. If someone disrupts the peace, the leader judges whether the cause is just. Two commandments are central to Luba justice: "do not steal" and "do not take another man's wife." Luba tradition therefore already incorporates accessible norms to counter looting and some forms of rape.

White lime enters my interviews with three different nuances. First, Luba leaders exercised their responsibility for determining just causes for conflict when the traditional chiefs of Katanga welcomed Laurent Kabila who sought to overthrow Mobutu. Second, the white lime symbolises joy in community. Religious leaders who reconciled congregations torn apart by the war, used white lime as the symbol of reconciliation. When a young graduate returned to his village, his excited mother dusted him with white flour. Third, white lime is used by diviners who seek sacred guidance. White lime captures the symbolism of justice and humanity restored. Can this symbol of justice, joy, guidance, and harmony be integrated with *bumuntu* to symbolise resisting rape and sexual abuse?

Bumuntu suggests that the sage doubts conventional truths. Could common assumptions, such as that women gain true personhood *only* through marriage and motherhood, be questioned? The sage draws upon new ideas. It lies within Luba tradition to incorporate ideas from theology and international human rights discourse. The sage seeks harmony and can therefore create a vision that sexual coercion is contrary to the Luba sense of self and community.

The *bumuntu* paradigm, combined with the Christian understanding of *imago dei* and the Petrine understanding to "obey God rather than man," can be seen as a major source of Roman Catholic rebellion against Mobutu's state terrorism (Nkulu-N'Sengha 2002, 10). For Ilgha Monga Ilunga (2015), *bumuntu* is grounded in God's creation. The loss of *bumuntu* is conceptualised in Adam and Eve's fall from grace. Rapists who dehumanise others and victims of rape have lost *bumuntu,* which must be restored.

Many Luba-Congolese people integrate Christianity and traditional spirituality. Could Christian and indigenous religious discourses together provide norms that resist sexual violence and uphold the human rights of women, augmenting the conclusions of secular investigators, such as Kelly and Vanrooyen (2011, 30-31) of the Harvard Humanitarian Initiative, who often fail to account for Christian and indigenous traditions that infuse all aspects of paramilitary and military life and traditional governance?

My interviewees take for granted two aspects of traditional religion as part of their worldview: first, ancestors are respected and their guidance is sought; second, ceremonies and objects become "icons" or even "real presences" of spiritual power. Luba-Congolese Christian peace builders integrate these cultural knowledges.

Ancestors in indigenous religion compare to saints in Roman Catholic tradition, except that ancestors are recognised by the family and saints are canonised by the institution. The Vatican has allowed ancestors to be recognised in the Luba mass (Nkulu-N'Sengha 2015). Ancestors' virtue earns their souls residence in the village of ancestors (*Kalunga Nyembo*), rather than in the place of suffering (*Kalunga ka Musono*). Ancestors exhibited *bumuntu* – true personhood – in their lifetimes. Both men and women may become ancestors who offer guidance to the living. Mai-Mai leaders and recruits in my interviews always insisted that they sought the will of their ancestors before making decisions to attack, to resist, to enter peace processes, or to demobilise. Civilians believe that the military maintain these traditions. Can resistance to rape be built from within a logic that these soldiers and warriors recognise?

Rape, ambiguous gendering and the spirit world

Bumuntu answers Thiem's concern for protecting people without depending upon binary understandings of gender. The spirit world that intersects with the human world in traditional religion has its own ways of defying binary assumptions that do not easily translate into western categories of a sexual continuum.

It has been assumed that within Africa, marriage and motherhood provide women's primary means of gaining social respect and true personhood. But women's dignity has a strong spiritual component. Luba art reveals the intersection between the spirit and human world. Women are considered closer to the spirit world. Spirits reside in a woman's breasts. Spirits of the deceased can reside in living people in different ways. The Luba art historian Mary Nooter Roberts summarises the way spirits defy binary gender assumptions (Roberts 2013, 68-81). Traditionally, ancestral spirits could live in two elderly women who reside together. Among royalty, the spirit of a male king could reside in a woman after his death who becomes their living presence, a *mwadi*. The *mwadi* takes wives and rules the *mwadi's* villages independently of the successor king. I cannot say "his" or "her" village as there is no gender pronoun in Kiluba. Or, at investiture the king may have been required to engage in incest with his sister or niece. She becomes his successor if he is unable to rule. In this way, ambiguous gendering affirms human dignity and *bumuntu*.

Ambiguous gendering is also reflected in humiliation when men are raped in war. If this fact is known, they are shunned. A woman whose husband was sexually violated asks, "Is my husband a husband or a wife?" Raped men, like kidnapped women, are known as "bush wives" (Moore 2008; IRIN 2011; Zongwe, citing Gettelman 2009, 44; Storr 2011). Rape as a weapon of war shames families and communities by destroying their dignity. This war crime can only be deterred if it is not given that power. If the community upholds the *bumuntu* – and the dignity – of the victim, the crime is undermined.

Given the powerful connection of women with the spirit world, the production of ambiguous gender, and the role of spiritual objects in aggression and protection, what does rape mean? Does rape reflect a fear of these powers and become a weapon not only against human enemies but against their spirit worlds? Is wartime sexual violence genocide, not only of people's ethnicity but of their spiritual protection? If the spirit world and ceremonial washing can protect a militant from bullets, can they protect a rapist from the spirit of the raped person?

A spiritual response to rape

If rape in the wars among African nations and militia groups is aimed not only toward human beings but also toward spirits, then a spiritual response is required in order to create an ideational resistance to rape. White lime, *bumuntu,* and *bwino* might form the basis of an African feminist *practical spirituality* that correlates and negotiates between traditional and Christian faith. It would promote *bumuntu* as respect and worth, extended to women, men, girls, boys and ambiguously gendered persons and their spirit worlds. The approval of ancestors, appropriate rituals, and icons of spiritual power would be necessary. White lime, *bumuntu* and *bwino* have a power of ideation that human dignity, and even rights-talk, does not.

However, a spiritual response constitutes only one aspect of resistance to rape. Just as looting and rape walk hand-in-hand, so do the eradication of sexual violence and absolute poverty. Military wives at Kamina Military Base (interviewed in 2008) described how poverty nurtured sexual violence within the DRC military. Women whose husbands are deployed elsewhere have no access to their husbands' salaries. If they follow their husbands from military base to military base they have no family to rely upon should he become ill, die, or cannot provide. Some are driven to prostitution to acquire money for food. Some are harassed when they cultivate crops in the fields. Perpetrators are often not brought to justice because payments are offered to women, families, or the courts to keep silent. Very poor women take the payments. The work of development as part of religious peace building is necessary.

For Luba-Congolese people who have been shunned by their communities, and for women, men, girls and boys living within their communities, I pray that *Vidye*, the Great Spirit, may inspire a resurgence of *bumuntu*, and guide *muntu* to recognise that *bumuntu* may disempower rape and sexual violence. And if the Creator, Redeemer and Holy Spirit will it, may my spirit, as Inamizo, be a "norm entrepreneur" for this understanding of *bumuntu* from the village of the ancestors.

References

Butcher, Tim. 2007. *Blood River: A Journey to Africa's Broken Heart.* London: Chattus and Windus.

CEDAW country reports, Democratic Republic of Congo. 2000, 2006. http://www.un.org/womenwatch/daw/cedaw/reports.htm

Conrad, Joseph. 1999. *The Heart of Darkness.* New York: Penguin.

Duewell, Marcus, Jens Braarvig, Roger Brownsword, and Dietmar Mieth, eds. 2014. *The Cambridge Handbook of Human Dignity: Interdisciplinary Perspectives.* Cambridge: Cambridge University Press.

Hochshild, Adam. 1999. *King Leopold's Ghost: A Story of Greed, Terror, and Heroism in Colonial Africa.* Boston: Houghton Mifflin.

Ilunga, Ilgha Monga. 2015. Personal email correspondence.

Inal, Tuba. *Looting and Rape in Wartime: Law and Change in International Relations.* 2013. Philadelphia: University of Pennsylvania Press.

IRIN. 13 October 2011. "Rape as a Weapon of War Against Men." http://www.irinnews.org/report/93960/health-rape-as-a-weapon-of-war-against-men

Kabongo, Boniface. 2015. Personal email correspondence.

Kelly, Jocelyn and Michael Vanrooyen. 2011a. "Militias in the DRC Speak About Sexual Violence," *Forced Migration Review* 37: 30-31

Kelly, Jocelyn and Michael Vanrooyen. 2011b. Hope for the Future Again: Tracing the Effects of Sexual Violence on Families and Communities in the Democratic Republic of Congo Pamphlet. http://hhi.harvard.edu/sites/default/files/publications/hope-for-the-future-again.pdf

Mande Muyombo, Guy. 2015. Personal email correspondence.

McCrudden, Christopher, ed. 2013. *Understanding Human Dignity.* Proceedings of the British Academy 192. Oxford: Oxford University Press.

Mealer, Brian. 2008. *All Things Must Fight to Live: Stories of War and Deliverance in Congo.* New York: Bloomsbury.

Moore, Jina. 2008. "In Africa, Justice for Bush Wives," http://www.csmonitor.com/World/Africa/2008/0610/p06s01-woaf.html.

Nkulu-N'Sengha, Mutombo. 2002. "Foundations for an African Philosophy and Theology of Human Rights: Rethinking the Human Condition in Post-Colonial Central Africa (1965-1997)." Ph.D. dissertation, Temple University.

Nkulu-N'Sengha, Mutombo. 2015. Personal email correspondence.

Roberts, Mary Nooter. 2013. "The King is a Woman" in *African Arts* 23 (46): 68-81.

Roberts, Mary Nooter and Allen F. Roberts. 1996. *Memory: Luba Art and the Making of History.* Munich: Prestel-Verlag and New York: The Museum for African Art.

Roberts, Mary Nooter and Alison Saar. 2000. *Body Politics: The Female Image in Luba Art and the Sculpture of Alison Saar.* Los Angeles: UCLA Fowler Museum of Cultural History.

Storr, Will. 2011. "The Rape of Men: The Darkest Secret of War." http://www.theguardian.com/society/2011/jul/17/the-rape-of-men.

Zongwe, Dunia Prince. 2012. "New Sexual Violence Legislation in DRC: Dressing Indelible Scars in Human Dignity." *African Studies Review* 55 (2): 37-57.

The changing landscape of South Africa and implications for practicing *ubuntu*

R. Simangaliso Kumalo

Abstract

The ethical concept of *"ubuntu"* as used within the African context that refers to the humanness and almost divinity of human beings was unthinkable to the missionaries and the Europeans when they came to Africa. For them there was *no* value that could be learned from the African tradition and culture. Meanwhile the Africans viewed these strange people with suspicion especially as they sought to preach their Christian religion, which was contradictory to their worldviews of the Supreme Being, ancestors, sacrifices and the Spirits, the norms that held their understanding of humanity, creation and religion together. This chapter seeks to discuss the implications of practicing ubuntu in a constantly changing South Africa.

> *"The great powers of the world may have done wonders in giving the world an industrial and military look, but the great still has to come from Africa giving the world a more human face"*
> *(Steve Biko 1972, 27)*

Introduction

Confronted with the need to live together and make sense of the two cultures and religion, early thinkers had to learn to bring religion and culture into dialogue by bringing African culture and the teaching of the Church into dialogue, instead of maintaining an alienating distance between the two of them. An African worldview does not embrace separation between religion and culture, because people regard it as normal to practice their religion and culture daily. *Ubuntu* was an intentional and holistic non-compartmentalised ethical expression of both religion and culture, which in Zulu is referred to as *isikompilo*.

The concept of *ubuntu* gained religious, social and political recognition in the post-colonial and post-apartheid South Africa. Following the transition from apartheid to democracy, an interest in *ubuntu* as an ethical concept gained momentum when political leaders, theologians and other voices sought to find ways of moving the country towards reconciliation and nation-building. Jaco Dreyer argues that "The idea of ubuntu suddenly started to feature prominently in South African political, social, moral and religious discourses" (Dreyer 2015, 189).

This paper seeks to discuss practicing *ubuntu* in a constantly changing South African religio-cultural and political landscape. It is divided into five parts. First, I will postulate a working definition and key principles of *ubuntu* which will be accompanied by the theoretical lens of liminality. Second, I explore the contestations around the *ubuntu* ethic. Here I give an example of the dialogue between King Lobengula, the king of the Ndebele and Jesuit missionaries and the London Missionary Society (LMS) during the colonial era. Third, we look at *ubuntu* as a basis for a humanitarian ethic. Fourth, *ubuntu* will be interrogated as the basis for a confessional Christian ethic. Finally, I will offer a tentative suggestion of how the *ubuntu* ethic can be utilised in the contemporary South African changing landscape.

As an African of Nguni origin and from a Wesleyan theological background, the notion of *ubuntu* was part of my upbringing; I grew up with it and have also learned what outsiders think of it. Therefore, I can claim to have a reasonable amount of knowledge about it, both from the inside and outside. I have experienced both its strengths (such as hospitality, care, and community) and weaknesses (when fellow Africans have been brutal and nasty to one another). My aim is to interrogate its claims and relevance for our rapidly changing landscape. I approach this task both as a trained practical theologian drawing from my passion for reflecting on the work of the Church and as a conscientious African, who is passionate about the rich heritage of my culture.

Towards a definition of *ubuntu* and the liminality theory

The term *"ubuntu"* is a Zulu and Xhosa word for "humanness" meaning the positive attributes of being human such as the sense of belonging, selflessness, hospitality, sharing, humility and respect. It emanates from the term *umuntu* (Zulu), *umntu* (Xhosa), *umuntfu* (Swazi), *motho* (Sotho), *Vhuthu* (Xitsonga) when referring to human beings. The opposite of *ubuntu* is animalism, *ubulwane* which lacks these attributes.

The stem and essence of the term *ubuntu* is as old as the Bantu languages. The written version of the term is as old as 1846, but the oral one is much older and was based on oral tradition (Gade 2013, 330). As this paper is concerned about the practice of *ubuntu*, I would like to focus on *ubuntu* as an ethical concept rather than on its socio-cultural and political dynamics. Noting the fact that the whole of the human being is built on the foundation of *ubuntu*, Setiloane observed: "The whole African traditional life-style with its age-sets, rites of passage, several generations living together, is built on the principle 'You cannot be human alone'. *Motho ke motho ka batho (*Sotho for 'a person is a person through others')" (Setiloane 1986, 13).

Ubuntu is about life in a racially diverse society, it is not just central for the black people, but rather for people from different cultural backgrounds, who find themselves in the same space and context. It is also important to note that *ubuntu* refers to all humanity, not just black people or people of African descent.

From this perspective then *ubuntu* has not developed fully to become an operational societal reality in contemporary South Africa. There are impulses of it when people live in charity, reconciliation, forgiveness, hospitality, community, sacrifice etc., and we see this taking place in different communities. However, at the same time we see the opposite such as greed, anti-communal practices, brutality, violence, xenophobia, etc. Such experiences make *ubuntu* an ideal, a vision or a normative ethical concept, whose claims can be universal but is not always practiced or visible in real life situations even by the very communities that claim to have cultures whose foundation is *ubuntu*. In this sense *ubuntu* has continued to remain on the margins as an ideal, something with potential, but has not yet been fully realised. It functions as an "already-not-yet" phenomenon. We only see impulses of it here and there, but it has not yet been embraced fully at a communal or national level. This makes *ubuntu* to occupy what Victor Turner classifies as a "liminal" space. He describes this as the "stage of being between phases" (Turner 1969, 95). Although Turner's primary focus was on rituals, I see the concept of liminality as relevant for *ubuntu*, because it no longer occupies centre stage in many South African communities. Reuel Khoza observed that some Africans would like to claim that "it (ubuntu) runs in their veins" (Khoza 2013, 55); however, this claim is disputed by others. For instance Khayeni Khumalo argued: "People are not born with ubuntu, rather become abantu, beings with humanness. If you don't mould, nurture and inculcate ubuntu in people they can actually behave like animals" (Khumalo 2015).

The aforementioned contradictory claims by Khoza and Kabila seem to suggest that *ubuntu* occupies a "space of betwixt." Some persons argue for its existence in their communities whilst those who are victims of other African people's behaviour that is contrary to the culture of *ubuntu*, feel that it is not real, but it remains an ideal. Therefore, even here in South Africa *ubuntu* occupies a liminal space.

One critique of *ubuntu* has been its indifference to patriarchy with African society. As the foundation of African law, moral philosophy, and a religious expression, some scholars have argued that *ubuntu* is responsible for the perpetuation of a deeply-rooted patriarchy throughout the African continent. The values enshrined in *ubuntu* have also been used traditionally to promote discrimination that stand in opposition to the values that the South African constitution and Bill of Rights seek to promote (Keevy 2014, 77). This seems contrary to the very ideals and values that are embedded in the concept of *ubuntu* as expressed by people like Desmond Tutu. Magadla and Chitando observe that *ubuntu* embodies a complexity that allows it to be "owned by the perpetrators of gender violence as well as advocates of gender justice" and that "there is a space in which to claim and use *ubuntu* in order to advocate for the reinvention of violent masculinity" (Magadla and Chitando 2014, 190). These observations raise the questions about the understanding of *ubuntu* that should be incorporated in theology, and a critical approach that takes into account the struggle for gender equality.

I propose the following working definition: *ubuntu* is an ethic of collectively-shared and life-giving values such as relatedness, spirituality, respect, communality, hospitality, participation, sacrifice, interdependency and sharing for the benefit of the individual, community and the environment.

Ubuntu as a contextual and contested terrain: Lobengula, the missionaries and us

In thinking about my place as a black African theologian, an *umuntu* – who grew up being taught about *ubuntu* and how to demonstrate it in real life situations – I have been preoccupied with the fascinating story of King Lobengula's encounter with the Jesuit missionaries. A story is told that King Lobengula Khumalo of the Ndebele people based at Nyati (Matabeleland)[1] in Zimbabwe was confronted by first the Jesuit missionaries in 1879 who wanted to set up a mission station and work among his people. Lobengula had been told about the missionaries by his elders and how they brought with them foreign cultures and teachings that would obliterate the culture of his people, which exemplified *ubuntu*. His father uMzilikazi kaMashobane had earlier met with Robert Moffatt, a missionary of the London Missionary Society (LMS) (De Gruchy 1999, 63). Lobengula was more careful not to allow these missionaries to "pollute his people" with their teaching. In the book *Memories of Mashonaland* George Knight-Bruce, the Bishop of Mashonaland and a Jesuit records this conversation between the king and the missionaries:

The King asked Jesuit missionaries:

---

[1]   Matebele is a Sotho translation of Ndebele people. Matabeleland is land of the Ndebele.

"Where are your wives?"

The missionaries answered that they had no wives.

"Then where are your mothers?" the King asked again.

"We don't believe in having anything to do with mothers or wives," answered the missionaries.

"Then you can go," said the King;

"I don't want anyone to teach my people who does not believe in mothers and wives" (Knight-Bruce 1895, 2).

The Jesuits were allowed to stay but not to preach their bad religion. Soon after that the king was approached by missionaries of the London Missionary Society (LMS) for the same purpose. At the end, both groups of missionaries were allowed to stay as long as they served Lobengula's ambition of teaching industrial education to his people, be his advisors and intermediaries between him and the other whites, but not to preach their gospel that contradicted their people's culture. They were compelled to submit to his sovereign rule and, in return, he would protect them. Although he himself never converted to Christianity, he loved the missionaries "calling them the king's vessels that must not be broken."

It is said that the Jesuits and the LMS missionaries remained in Lobengula's territory and taught his people industrial education, without preaching the gospel for about fourteen years without getting any convert. However, on 23 January 1894, the British South Africa Company started a war with the Ndebele, which led to Lobengula's death. His people protected the missionaries "calling them the kings' vessels that must not be broken," and as soon as the war was over they called back the missionaries to teach them the gospel (De Gruchy 1999, 112). The missionaries resumed their work with more vigour and more Ndebele people became Christians. This story seems to suggest that, like most cultures in a globalised society, none is left untouched and when the winds of change have come, they cannot be stopped from changing one's cultures, no matter how much defence is established to protect them. Lobengula's quest to protect his culture and what was good in it should be celebrated as a bold act in an era when globalisation and technology are ushering in fast changing landscapes and threats to ethical values. What if Lobengula had managed to reject the Western missionaries and their colonising partners representing the British Crown? Would history be praising him for being a wise king who had a vision and foresight? Should contemporary Africans be more critical of the missionaries for having contributed to the obliteration of African culture including the "*ubuntu* ethic"?

There are five purposes that *ubuntu* served that can be extracted from a critical examination of King Lobengula's response to the missionaries:

1. *Ubuntu* ensured political stability within the family, clan or ethnic group under the leadership of a chief or king. It maintained loyalty to the community and to the leadership of the community. So it was the glue that bound the community together.
2. It ensured that resources could be shared amongst the people. People shared cattle, harvests etc. As a result, they could say that *nongenakomo* (even the one without cattle) eats meat.
3. It was meant to ensure security against other rival groups, which were a constant threat. So people would be friendly, give gifts and intermarry in order to avoid conflict and war. That is the reason most of the ethnic groups would encourage marriage between the royal families, so that they could be related and united. This gesture of hospitality was a pillar of *ubuntu* but it was there for a purpose, to ensure relationships, harmony and ultimately peace.
4. It also served the purpose of providing social cohesion. People were taught to behave in a homogenous way that followed certain norms and values that were common to all and were dictated by society. Each person was expected to respect these and if they deviated, they were labelled as devoid of *ubuntu*, *akanabuntu*, i.e., he/she lacks humanness. Society would frown upon that and the person would be ostracised by the rest of the community.
5. The king was also concerned that the new faith would encourage young people to neglect their mothers and their responsibility to get wives in order to grow the nation. By reflecting on it, Magirosa understood it as a demonstration of the traditional culture of the Ndebele, "the pride of the Matebele and their respect and love for women" (Magirosa 2015, 1).

King Lobengula's meeting with both the Jesuits and the Congregational Church missionaries, demonstrates that the king redefined *ubuntu*. For him *ubuntu* was not just an abstract idea that people held in their minds, but it was practical and performed in a tangible way. Lobengula's actions towards the missionaries invited genuine enculturation of Christianity. He welcomed a Christianity that got involved with people in real life situations and not one that created an alternative dysfunctional community, with values and an ethos that contradicted those that benefitted the broader society.

Ubuntu as a foundation for a practical humanitarian ethic

As observed above, *ubuntu* as an ethical concept is not exclusively Sub-Sahara African, but rather cuts across ethnic and cultural borders. It is about the acceptance of all people. People from different cultures practice some of the traits of *ubuntu* without naming them thus and others receive it on a daily basis. Mzamane noted: "Ubuntu is colour blind-in fact, it reaches out more to those of other colours who may feel like outsiders. It is a doctrine of universal acceptance based on common human traits; it breaks down barriers derived from the construction of self and otherness" (Mzamane 2009, 236).

For Desmond Tutu, *ubuntu* is a theological concept that invites us to be persons because of the *Imago Dei*. Our existence is bound to God's act of creation in an indissoluble way. Thus, humanity is the image of God, in community (Hailey 2008, 5). Tutu's understanding of *ubuntu*, according to Battle, offers a "corrective hermeneutic for Western salvation theology that focuses on the individual" (Battle 1997, 8). Thus, central to Tutu's theology is the *Imago Dei*. It is from this – and not our biological differences – that our value as human beings springs.

Ubuntu has been brought to the fore by scholars and leaders like Desmond Tutu, who argued that it could make a contribution to the development of democracy and nation-building in the new South Africa. In this sense *ubuntu* is retrieved from African culture to become an ethical concept concerned with the well-being and rights of human beings at a universal level, not just African. This suggests that there must be an amalgamation of African and Western thinking and values. When this is done, the concept of *ubuntu* gives us a possibility of combining the best elements of African culture with the best of Western thinking. Consequently, *ubuntu* has to be reimagined from a traditional and cultural concept that seems to have nothing to do with real life, to a universal ethical concept that can be engaged when people are faced with real concrete problems.

Ubuntu as a confessional basis for Christianity

A much less emphasised aspect of *ubuntu* is its essentially religious and even "theological" nature. *Ubuntu* and African ethics cannot be separated from religion, and in a sense, from theology. Benezito Bujo notes that "Although the human person stands in the centre of African morals, the position of God is distinctly emphasised" (Bujo 2009, 114). Hailey describes this as a "natural synergy between Christian values and Ubuntu" (Haily 2008, 5). Neville Richardson argues that traditional African ethics are "indistinguishable from religion, in that infringements are seen as damaging not only to communities, but also to the delicate harmony of the whole deeply religious order of the universe" (Richardson 2009, 134).

It is important to note that in our contemporary era, the meaning of *ubuntu* has shifted. People use it to name their companies, magazines, educational programmes. Even politicians use it now and again to justify programmes that at times have nothing to do with the concept (Dreyer 2015). So the term *ubuntu* now means different things to different people. That is why I propose that people who are concerned about the fundamental issues that face the world should re-fashion the concept of *ubuntu* so that it can help to promote well-being and communal development in order to reclaim and appropriate it to those issues and initiatives that give life.

Practicing *ubuntu* in a changing landscape

Christianity is the dominant religion in South Africa; therefore, it is shaping the majority of South Africans especially regarding their values, norms and traditions. From a practical theology viewpoint, the mission of the Church is to proclaim God's kingdom to become a reality in the world. This has to be done through a dialogical approach, meaning that it has to take into consideration the cultural ethics of the people such as *ubuntu*.

One of the biggest challenges that Africans – particularly South Africans – face is how to practice *ubuntu*, in a society that is emerging from centuries of colonisation and oppression. Tutu has argued that *ubuntu* could make a contribution to the development of democracy and nation-building in the new South Africa. It is significant that South Africans revisit *ubuntu* and retrieve the resources that can be gleaned from it in order to take the country forward. These sentiments were echoed by MaNjobe when he observed that: "As South Africans we must reclaim ubuntu, put emphasis on mutual understanding, appreciate differences, and tolerate diversity in the multi-cultural environment we live in. The ubuntu values we promote must sufficiently meet the challenges of reconciliation, reconstruction and development" (Mzamane 2009, 236).

Ubuntu should be re-conceptualised and appropriated as an ethical concept instead of a cultural practice, so that it can address key societal issues such as the lack of community cohesion, hospitality and sharing of resources, etc.

Redefining the ministry of the church

There is need to discover what constitutes the mission of the church in this changing landscape. The church has to embark on the journey of promoting life in its fullness. The challenge for the church is how to employ *ubuntu* in an environment that is hostile to it. When re-appropriating *ubuntu* for the contemporary era and its challenges we need to draw a clear distinction between its social and cultural and political reality on the one hand and its reality as an ethical concept on the other. This essay argues that it is the ethical understanding of *ubuntu* that is needed in a changing landscape rather than the socio, cultural and even political appreciation of it. The ethical concept of *ubuntu* is much closer and even similar to concepts in Christian ethics, thus making it easier for the Church to engage it missionally.

Communality and individuality

A key characteristic of *ubuntu* is that it creates a wholesome community for the individual to belong. An individual cannot and should not be made to live in isolation. Individual people are born by and into communities. They are also welcomed, nurtured and socialised by others; they are communal beings. In Zulu culture it is said that "Individuals cannot exist alone, they are because they belong" (Thorpe 1999, 116). People are communal beings. In African communities they even dismiss an unsocial, individualist person as a non-person, *awu akusiye umuntu lona* meaning that one is not a human being alone, because human beings get into full individuality when they are in communion with others.

One of the criticisms of *ubuntu* is that it undermines the significance and uniqueness of the individual. For such thinkers the individual must be protected from the domination of the community for them to grow to their fullest potential. However, such thinking fails to understand that the community exists to empower, enable, support and accompany the individual in their journey to a full humanity and potential.

The individual depends on the corporate group. Only in terms of other people does the individual become conscious of his/her own being, his/her own duties and his/her own privileges and abilities towards himself/herself and others (Who in Moore 1973, 65).

Tutu echoed the same sentiments, when he asserted that "we must be viewed through the lens of ubuntu, because 'we can be human only in community, in koinonia, and in peace' " (Battle 1997, xii).

The self does not exist first and on its own before entering into relationship; rather it exists in relationship with others and its environment. Shutte demonstrates that within this African concept of humanity, all humanity is perceived as a family, making the earth the "family home." God is not outside this earthly home, but "at its centre" (Shutte 2002, 21).

Hospitality

Hospitality is a very important characteristic of *ubuntu* because it calls for people to notice one another and care for each other so that no one leaves and dies in isolation. Moeahabo Moila defined African hospitality as "a very close fellowship of a group of people, friendly reception of others; and unity in spirit and purpose. It means love and common concern for each other" (Moila 2003, 1). Julius Gathogo takes the definition further by emphasising the role of giving: "African hospitality can be defined as the extension of generosity, giving, freely without strings attached. It is the willingness to help, to assist, to love and to carry one another's burden without necessarily seeking a reward for it" (Gathogo 2001, 1).

Moila notes the significance of hospitality for humanity: "Men must no longer be strangers who pass-by each other, but who can become fellow-citizens, who greet each other and smile at each other, but who carry the other's burden in compassion and who, in departing from each other say *sibonene*-we have seen each other" (Moila 2003, 1).

In a world often dominated by individualism, despair, cruelty and self-centeredness, the *ubuntu* vision of hospitality calls our attention to critical values such as community, caring, hope, and concern for others.

Conclusion

The main question addressed here is how to practice *ubuntu* in a rapidly globalising South Africa. There is a gap between the embrace of *ubuntu* as part of local culture and the reality of living *ubuntu* more broadly. The paper proposes moving *ubuntu* from the margins and state of liminality to contemporary realities in *ubuntu* informed developments and social change (Turner 1969, 45). Mathieu Deflem observed that "luminosity provides, observes and participates with an opportunity to reconsider their situation and undertake a revolutionary re-ordering of the official social order; including moral and legal rules, social structure, and individual roles" (Deflem 1991, 1). In spite of *ubuntu* being in a space of liminality with the challenges that we face in South Africa, we need to excavate it for insights and answers. New ways of thinking and articulating *ubuntu* are not just recovering traditions but rediscovering a treasured ethic. *Ubuntu* is one key ethical concept, foundation for an African worldview, that can be used in collaboration or even contestation with Western concepts (e.g., human rights) in the search for answers to improve the world. It is when we practice *ubuntu*, which brings in the human element into all the challenges faced, that we will take Africa to the next level of development, peace and democracy, where all human beings will live with dignity in a world thus "giving the world a human face" (Biko 1972, 27).

References

Asante, Molefi Kete. 1990. *Afrocentricity and Knowledge.* Trenton, NJ: Africa World Press. Battle, Michael J. 1997. *Reconciliation: The Ubuntu Theology of Desmond Tutu.* Ohio: The Pilgrim Press.

Barnett, Michael, ed. 2012. *Rastafari in the New Millennium.* New York: Syracuse University Press.

Biko, Steve. 1970. *I write what I like.* Johannesburg: Ravan.

Biko, Steve. 1972. "The Quest for a True Humanity." In *Essays on Black Theology,* edited by Mokgethi B.G. Mothlabi. Johannesburg: Golden Era Printers and Stationers.

Biney, Ama. 2014. "The Historical Discourse on African Humanism: Interrogating the Paradoxes." In *Ubuntu: Curating the Archive*, edited by Leonhard Praeg and Siphokazi Magadla Pietermaritzburg: University of KwaZulu-Natal Press.

Bujo, Benezet. 2009. "Is There a Specific African Ethic? Towards a Discussion with Western Thought." In *An Anthology of Comparative and Applied Ethics*, edited by Munyaradzi Felix Murove. African Ethics: Scottsville: University of KwaZulu-Natal Press.

Chitando, Ezra. 2008. "Religious Ethics, HIV and AIDS and Masculinities in Southern Africa." In *Persons in Community: African Ethics in a Global Culture*, edited by Ronald Nicolson. Scottsville: University of KwaZulu-Natal Press.

Deflem, Mathieu. 1991. "Ritual, Anti-Structure, and Religion: A Discussion of Victor Turner's Processual Symbolic Analysis." *Journal for the Scientific Study of Religion* 30(1):1-25.

De Gruchy, Steve. 1999. *Changing Frontiers: The Mission Story of the UCCSA.* Gaborone: Pula Press.

Dreyer, Jaco S. 2015. "Ubuntu: A practical-theological Perspective." *International Journal of Practical Theology*, 19 (1): 189-209.

Furman, Katherine. 2014. "Ubuntu and the Law: Some Lessons for the Practical Application of Ubuntu." In *Ubuntu: Curating the Archive*, edited by Leonhard Praeg and Siphokazi Magadla. Pietermaritzburg: University of KwaZulu-Natal Press.

Gade, Christian B.N. 2013. "The Historical Development of the Written Language of the Written Discourses on Ubuntu." *South African Journal of Philosophy* 30 (3): 303-329.

Gathogo, Julius. 2003. *The Truth about African Hospitality: Is there hope for Africa.* Mombasa: Salt Productions.

Gerloff, Roswith, ed. 2003. *Mission is Crossing Frontiers: Essays in honour of Bongani A. Mazibuko*. Pietermaritzburg: Cluster Publications.

Goba, Bonganjalo. 1973. "Corporate Personality: Ancient Israel and Africa." In *Black Theology: The South African Voice*, edited by Brian Moore. London: Hurst.

Hailey, John. 2008. "Ubuntu: A Literature Review." A Paper Prepared for the Tutu Foundation, London.

Keevy, Ilze. 2014. "Ubuntu versus the Core Values of the South African Constitution." In *Ubuntu: Curating the Archive*, edited by Leonhard Praeg and Siphokazi Magadla.

Khoza, Reuel. 1994. "Ubuntu Botho African Humanism: A Discussion Paper on Ubuntu as a Philosophy of Life and its Potential Application" Unpublished monograph.

King, Sharon Minor. 1999. "Reconciliation: the Ubuntu Theology of Desmond Tutu." *Journal of Religious Thought* 55 (2): 127-130.

Knight-Bruce, George Wyndham Hamilton. 1895. *Memories of Mashonaland*. London: Society for the Propagation of the Gospel in Foreign Parts.

Kumalo, Khayeni. 2015. Interview by Simangaliso Kumalo, 29 July. Pietermaritzburg, South Africa.

Lindhardt, Martin. 2015. *Pentecostalism in Africa: Presence and Impact of Pneumatic Christianity in Postcolonial Societies*. Leiden: Brill

Magirosa, Maidei. 2015. "Early African Resistance to Christian Missionaries." February 19. http://www.thepatriot.co.zw/old_posts/early-african-resistance-to-christian-missionaries/

Magadla, Siphokazi and Ezra Chitando. 2014. "The Self Become God: Ubuntu and the 'Scandal of Manhood'." In *Ubuntu: Curating the Archive*, edited by Leonhard Praeg and Siphokazi Magadla. Pietermaritzburg: University of KwaZulu-Natal Press.

Moila, Moeahabo Phillip. 2003. *Challenging Issues in African Christianity*. Pretoria: CB Powell Bible Centre, UNISA.

Mzamane, Mbulelo Vizikhungo. 2009. "Building a Society Using the Building Block of Ubuntu/Botho/Vhuthu." In *Religion and Spirituality in South Africa: New Perspectives* edited by Duncan Brown. Pietermaritzburg: UKZN Press.

O'Donovan, Leo J., ed. 1980. *An Introduction to the Themes and Foundations of Karl Rahner's Theology*. London: Epworth Press.

Oosthuizen, Gerhardus C. 1985. "Africa's social and cultural heritage in a new era." *Journal of Contemporary African Studies*. Special Jubilee Edition: 77-114.

Richardson, Neville. 2009. "Can Christian Ethics Find its Way and Itself in Africa?" In *African Ethics: An Anthology of Comparative and Applied Ethics*, edited by M.F. Murove. Scottsville: University of KwaZulu-Natal Press.

Richburg, Keith. 1998. *Out of America: A Black Man Confronts Africa*. San Diego: Hartcourt Brace.

Setiloane, Gabriel M. 1986. *African Theology: An Introduction*. Johannesburg: Skotaville.

Shepherd, Ben. 2003. *Kitty and the Prince*. Cape Town: Jonathan Ball.

Shutte, Augustine. 2001. *Ubuntu: An Ethic for a New South Africa*. Pietermaritzburg: Cluster Publications.

Taylor, John. 1965. *The Primal Vision. Christian Presence amid African Religion*. London: SCM Press.

Thorpe, Shirley A. 1991. *African traditional Religion*. Pretoria: University of South Africa.

Turner, Victor. 1969. *The Ritual Process: Structure and Anti-structure*. Chicago: Aldine.

Wallis, Jim. 2014. *The (Un)Common Good: How the Gospel Brings Hope to a World Divided*. Michigan: Brazos Press.

Williams, David T. 2013. *Ubuntu: A Relational Theology of Humanity*. Pietermaritzburg: Cluster Publications.

From human evolution to empathetic personhood: A bottom-up approach

J. Wentzel van Huyssteen

Abstract

This essay explores, from a philosophical point of view, whether Darwin's perspective on human evolution can contribute to a present-day understanding of "the production of personhood," that is to a constructive, holistic, notion of self and personhood. Answers to the question of what it means to be a self, a human person, can be found in the history of hominid and hominin evolution. The problem of human evolution and its broader impact on theological anthropology are considered by tracking some challenging contemporary proposals for the evolution of crucially important aspects of human personhood.

Introduction

My recent research has focused on one of the most salient shared problems today in the interdisciplinary dialogue between theology and the sciences, namely that of *human personhood*. In my Goshen Lectures (February 2015) the question was whether the history of human evolution might provide bridge theories to theological anthropology and thus to a positive and constructive way of appropriating Darwinian thought for a public, interdisciplinary Christian theology. In this essay, from more philosophical point of view, the question is whether Darwin's perspective on human evolution can help us move forward to more constructive, holistic, notions of self and personhood, and make more intelligible what anthropologist Chris Fowler calls "the production of personhood" (Fowler 2004). In the history of hominid and hominin evolution surprising answers to the question of what it means to be a "self," a human person, can be found (cf. Van Huyssteen 2006; 2009; 2010a; 2010b; 2010c; 2011; 2013). Key aspects of hominid/hominin evolution affirm what Darwin identified as crucial aspects of human distinctiveness, or human species specificity. The problem of human evolution and its impact on theological anthropology will be considered by tracking some challenging contemporary proposals for the evolution of crucial aspects of human personhood.

Do we still understand the idea, or rather the *fact* of human evolution in the same way as Charles Darwin and Neo-Darwinians did?

Rethinking Darwin on human evolution

Scholars from numerous fields address the question of what makes us human and what it means to be a "self." Multidisciplinary input is needed. The question not only about what distinguishes humans from their hominid ancestors, but also about which peculiarities give humans their "species specificity." One possibility is to distinguish between anatomical and behavioral differences (see Van Huyssteen 2006, 203; Lewis-Williams 2002, 96; Tattersall and Mowbray 2003, 298).

The meaning, markers, and justification of human identity and status have fluctuated over time. Generally, *language* was seen as a crucial marker (see Deacon 1997; Mithen 1996; Mellars 1989, 1991; Nobel and Davidson 1996; Tattersall 1998, 2002). Conceptions of defining humanness have lately shifted toward the capacity for *prosociality*. This and a propensity for *imitation* are shared with primates (see Cartmill and Brown 2012, 182). *Music* (Mithen 2006), *sexuality* (Sheets-Johnstone 1990), and *empathy* (De Waal 2006, 2009; Sheets-Johnstone 2008; Kirkpatrick 2005; Boehm 2012) are hailed as the foundation not only of language, social norms and morality, but also of symbolic and even religious behavior.

Another panhuman trait is the capacity for seeing things from someone else's perspective, generally known as *Theory of Mind*. Humans are disposed to an intuitive understanding of the motivations of others, even where these do not exist (Cartmill and Brown 2012, 182). This ability gives humans adaptively valuable insight into the intentions of friends, enemies, predators, and prey. Both sadism and compassion are neurologically grounded in this disposition (Cartmill and Brown 2012, 182).

For Águstin Fuentes (2009) and Richard Potts (1996; 2012), the success of the humans' species can be attributed largely to their capacity to alter the world. Humans construct material items and create and navigate social and symbolic structures, space and place in a manner unequalled by other organisms. Human identity is interactively constructed by biological, behavioral, social, and symbolic contexts (Fuentes 2009, 12).

Some evolutionary anthropologists no longer find the distinction "Darwinian" and "Neo-Darwinian" useful for current evolutionary theories (Fuentes 2009, 12). Basic Darwinian theory prioritises *natural selection* and *sexual selection* as the prime factors in evolutionary change and adaptation. Natural selection is the process by which certain phenotypes (morphology and behavior) that are most effective at reproducing themselves (and their genetic basis or genotype) in a given environment, become more frequent in a population across generations. Sexual selection is the over-representation of specific phenotypes across generations as a result of mate choice and/or intrasexual competition. Traits that lead to the success of particular phenotypes are termed adaptations. These traits, and the individual possessing them, are deemed more "fit." "Fit" phenotypes strive for optimality and over evolutionary time become the majority (Fuentes 2009, 12).

Without discounting the role of natural and sexual selection, scientists are now expanding on Darwin's contributions. New trends emerge in evolutionary theory. Evolutionary anthropologist Christopher Boehm points out that, according to Darwin, potentially changeable environments are continuously acting on the gene pool with significant results for evolutionary development and even speciation (Boehm 2012, 3). At the heart of Darwin's project we already find what evolutionary biologists and anthropologists today call a process of *niche construction*: in an interactive process changeable natural environments act on variation in the gene pool. In this way gene pools were modified over generations.

Markus Mühling points out that both organism and environment function as cause and effect (Mühling 2014, 145). The traditional unidirectional character of evolutionary theory is hereby abandoned. Niche construction is not a fact of nature, readily explainable by classical Neo-Darwinism. It is rather an additional mechanism of evolution which operates at the same basic level as natural selection.

Niche construction is when an organism modifies the relationship between itself and its environment by actively changing factors in the environment and itself. Where classical Neo-Darwinism knows only one inheritance system, namely the *genetic system* in which the genetic pool alone transfers information over time, niche construction broadens Neo-Darwinism by adding another mechanism.

Eva Jablonka and Marion Lamb's call for a renewal of evolutionary theory. They argue for "evolution in four dimensions" rather than a focus on just the *genetic*. In addition to genetics as an important inheritance system, Jablonka and Lamb argue for three other inheritance systems that also have a causal role in evolutionary change. These are the *epigenetic*, the *behavioral*, and *symbolic inheritance* systems. Epigenetic inheritance[1] (Jablonka and Lamb 2005, 113) is found in all organisms, behavioral inheritance[2] (Jablonka and Lamb 2005, 180) in most,

---

[1] On a cellular level epigenetic differences are the consequence of events that occurred during the development of the cell. This determines which genes are turned on, act and interact. Though DNA sequences remain unchanged, cells do acquire information that they pass on to their progeny.

[2] Learning, a genetic capacity, is now also recognised as an agent of evolutionary change. Cultural evolution is complex, gradual and cumulative, involving several aspects of behavior.

and symbolic inheritance occurs only in humans (see Jablonka and Lamb 2005, 1-8; Fuentes 2009, 13). There is more to heredity than just genes. Some acquired information is inherited. Evolutionary change can result from instruction as well as from selection. This constructivist view moves beyond standard Neo-Darwinian approaches and acknowledges that many organisms transmit information via behavior. The acquisition of evolutionary relevant behavioral patterns can therefore also occur through socially mediated learning. Symbolic inheritance comes with language. The ability to creatively engage in information transfer can be complex and contain a high density of information. What makes the human species different and what makes us *human*, lies in the way in which we organise, transfer, and acquire information. The ability to think and communicate through words and other types of symbols makes humans a fundamentally different kind of niche constructor. Rationality, linguistic and artistic ability, moral sense and religiosity, are all facets of symbolic thought and communication (see Jablonka and Lamb 2005, 193-231).

Niche construction is a core factor in human behavioral evolution. A vast array of processes affects inheritance and evolutionary change. Natural selection can occur at multiple levels and is not the only or main driver of change (Fuentes 2009, 16).

Crucial to symbolic behavior is the ability of *imagination*. According to Fuentes (2014, 1; cf. Mithen 1996), understanding religious imagination – and, I would add, the evolution of the moral sense – can be aided by investigating the role of the evolutionary transition between *becoming human* and *being human*. In order to understand the emergence of the moral sense and of religion, interdisciplinary points of connection across explanatory frameworks outside of just one specific set of explanations of religion and of any one specific religious tradition should be found (see Fuentes 2014; Van Huyssteen 2006; Stosis 2009, 315-317).

Human evolution and imagination: From symbol to metaphysics

In my book, *Alone in the world: Human uniqueness in science and theology*, I argue from an evolutionary point of view for the *naturalness of religious imagination* (Van Huyssteen 2006, 93). The question would then be *how* such imagination, as part of a niche constructive system, emerged over the course of human evolution. From a broader view of evolution that includes extensive, interactive niche construction, one can say that *Homo sapiens sapiens* had a hand in making itself. Águstin Fuentes (2014) first argues that a distinctively human way of being in the world includes the capability of metaphysical thought as a precursor to religion; secondly, the role of niche construction, systemic complexity, semiotics, and an integration of the cognitive, social, and ecological in human communities during the Pleistocene (roughly two and a half million years to twelve thousand years ago),[3] should be recognised.

In the archeology of personhood and evolution across the Pleistocene, an increasing complexity in the way humans interface with the world, becomes evident (cf. Fuentes 2014, 9). Over the last 400,000 years there has been a dramatic increase in the complexity of culture and social traditions, tool use and manufacture, trade and the use of fire, as well as enhanced infant survival and predator avoidance, increased habitat exploitation, information transfer via material technologies. These are tied directly to a rapidly evolving human cognition and social structure that require increased cooperative capabilities and coordination within human communities.

Regarding the *future* of human evolution one should not see humans as the ultimate niche constructors. This would deny that humans can be succeeded by others in niche construction activity. Humans are rather relatively ultimate niche constructors, that is, relative to the known history of evolution (cf. Mühling 2014, 163). To call ourselves *ultimate niche constructors* also denies the possibility that something similar could take place elsewhere in the universe. Since contingency is part of niche construction as a free, dynamic process of evolution, humans cannot assume that they have control of over the process.

The emergence of language and a theory of mind with high levels of intentionality, empathy, moral awareness, symbolic thought and social unity are only possible in a cooperative and integrated social system, combined with enhanced cognitive and communicative capacities as a core adaptive niche. Fuentes includes an analysis of *compassion* (Fuentes 2014, 10). This can be traced even further back to the deep evolutionary roots of empathy and attachment (Van Huyssteen 2014; cf. Kirkpatrick 2005; Sheets-Johnstone 2008; Hrdy 2009, 82). Imagination is a key part of the human niche. It also explains, in part, why our species succeeded while other hominins became extinct. For Fuentes, genus *Homo's* capacity in the late Pleistocene era for imagination and giving meaning to the world underlie and preceded the ability to form a metaphysics (Fuentes 2014, 11). This ability facili-

---

[3] The transition from *becoming human* to *being human* can be understood better by a broad assessment of hominin evolution over 6 million years ("Hominin" includes humans and species derived from the lineage that split with the chimpanzee lineage roughly 7,8 million years ago). The focus should be on the final transition from the archaic form of the genus *Homo sapiens* into the current form of *Homo sapiens sapiens*. The shift to a wholly human way of being in the current socio-cognitive niche, provides insight into how humans experience the world here and now. Fuentes suggests that the emergence of a distinctly human socio-cognitive and ecological niche to existing in a meaning-laden world can be connected to the emergence of an imagination that is capable of metaphysical thought (Fuentes 2014, 2). This process is connected to the success of humans as a species.

tates religious belief and an array of other symbolic and meaning-laden aspects of human behavior and experience which are not at the core of our current niche and lives. There is no single trait or particular environment that explain human evolutionary success. Imagination and a landscape infused with multifaceted meaning, are part of the toolkit.

Interdisciplinary theology and the idea of personhood

Understanding cooperation, empathy, compassion, the use of materials, symbols and ritual, and the semiotic landscape in which humans exist(ed), contributes to the analysis of what it meant to become human. This is an interdisciplinary process. Insights gained from fossil and archaeological records, as well as from behavioral, neurological, and physiological systems, provide clues as to how humans perceive and experience the world. This creates the possibility for an imaginative, potentially metaphysical, and eventually religious, experience of the world (Fuentes 2014, 17), which leads to a better understanding of the propensity for religious imagination and the reality of religious experience in *Homo sapiens sapiens*. This does not argue that religion has an adaptive function. It rather argues that neither religion nor religiosity could have suddenly appeared fully blown. A search for structures, behaviors, and cognitive processes that could facilitate the eventual appearance of such patterns in human beings, is therefore useful.

For Christian theologians this provides an exciting bottom-up view of the complex way in which God has shaped and prepared our species to be physically, mentally, and spiritually "ready" for faith. This makes my original intuition that there is a naturalness to human imagination, also religious imagination (Van Huyssteen 2006) and that this facilitates engagement with the world in ways that are distinct from other animals (also closely related hominins) even more plausible. According to Águstin Fuentes this provides an addition to the toolkit of inquiry, both for evolutionary scientists and interdisciplinary theologians who attempt to reconstruct the historical path to humanity (Fuentes 2014, 18).

The idea that religious imagination might not be an isolated faculty of human rationality, but that mystical or religious inclinations are a universal attribute of the human mind, has been much discussed recently. Shantz (2009), for example, has offered a plausible account of religious experience and religious ecstasy, not only as a significant feature of the apostle Paul's life, but arguing for the epistemological relevance of religious experience. Interpretations of the *imago Dei* have varied throughout the history of Christianity (Van Huyssteen 2006). Interdisciplinary theologians are challenged to rethink what human distinctiveness might mean for the human person, a being that has emerged biologically as a center of embodied self-awareness, identity, and moral responsibility. This notion of self or personhood, when reconceived in terms of embodied imagination, symbolic propensity, and cognitive fluidity, *will enable theology to revision its notion of the imago Dei as emerging from nature itself*. This idea does not imply superiority or a greater moral value over other animals or earlier hominins. In this kind of interdisciplinary conversation theology can help to broaden the scope of "human distinctiveness" or the notion of self or personhood. *Homo sapiens* are not only distinguished by their embodied brain, by mental cognitive fluidity expressed in imagination, creativity, linguistic ability, and symbolic propensity. Real-life, embodied persons of flesh and blood humans are also prone to hostility, arrogance, ruthlessness and cunning. They are inescapably caught between "good and evil," the experience of which lies beyond the empirical scope of the fossil record, and therefore of science (Van Huyssteen 2006, 325). The evolutionarily developed body is the bearer of human distinctiveness. This embodied existence includes the reality of vulnerability, sin, tragedy and affliction.

Theologically speaking, the idea of the human person, emerging from a complex evolutionary history by means of niche construction, leads to an inclusive notion of the *imago Dei*. The "image of God" must be predicated of all humans. According to Genesis all are created in the image of God. This is not reserved for those with particular abilities or qualities, or denied to those with limitations, handicaps or deficits. For Jessica Bratt this approach not only extricates the *imago Dei* from the exclusive union of male and female (to which it was confined to some degree by Karl Barth's relational interpretation), but also makes it available for those are not in a relation with others (Bratt 2005). The *imago Dei,* for theologian Wolfhart Pannenberg, is neither a quality such as reason or self-consciousness nor only relationality. It is the disposition towards transcendence and fellowship. Therefore, the image of God is present also in those who, for instance, live in vegetative states, are mentally or physically handicapped, sociopathic, or otherwise prevented from functioning in ways typical of most humans (Van Huyssteen 2006, 141).

Philosopher Roger Scruton, in his work, *The Face of God* (2012), expands Ricoeurian ideas of "self" to include the "religious self" and ultimately God. Being present to another as a person is radically different from being in the vicinity of a thing. The former is radically intersubjective. When the other is acknowledged as another, a range of reciprocal, morally charged relations is implied. The human spheres of family, neighbourhood, and church are the consequence of the capacity for first person relations and typically human patterns of behavior, affect, and judgment. These distinguish human persons from animal existence.

For Scruton, the question as to what it means to be a person in a world of objects, is preliminary to the question about what and where God is (Scruton 2012, 172). This actually answers the question whether God is a person or not:

if we are indeed, as Genesis teaches, created in the image of God, then human nature *and* human community are instances of God's presence in the world. The personhood exhibited in the human face reflects the "face of God." Scruton hereby creates the possibility for a bottom-up theological anthropology. God's presence in the world is discoverable only if one attends to the nature and the significance of human community. There the face of God, in the person of Jesus Christ, has been made present.

This is Scruton's answer to materialism and scientism: the qualities of human personhood and of God as a person cannot be explored as mere objects. It makes clear what God is *not*: God is not mysterious and supernatural, but is present through Jesus Christ in the faces of others. Scruton rejects a dualism of self and body. He saves the mystery of human consciousness from those who would reduce it to biology and neuroscience (Holloway 2012, 1).

This has implications for the question of God's presence in the world. Through the objectifying eyes of science, it is impossible to see the place, time, or events that can be interpreted as showing God's presence. God disappears from the world when addressed with the "why" of explanation. So also do human persons disappear from the world when only neurological explanations are given of their acts (Scruton 2012, 45). Maybe, after all, God is a "person" like us, whose identity and will are bound up with God's nature as a subject. Maybe God can be found in the world when we cease to invoke God with the "why" of causality, but address God with the "why" of reason and understanding instead. For Scruton the "why" of reason and understanding is from "I" to "you" (Scruton 2012, 45).

Scruton concludes this line of thinking by stating:

You can situate human beings entirely in the world of objects. In doing so you will in all probability reduce them to animals whose behaviour is to be explained by some combination of evolutionary psychology and neuroscience. But then you will find yourself describing a world from which human action, intention, responsibility, freedom and emotion has been wiped away: it will be a world without a face. The face shines in the world of objects with a light that is *not* of this world – a light of subjectivity. You can look for freedom in the world of objects and you will not find it: not because it is not there, but because it is bound up with the first person perspective, and with the view from somewhere of the creature who can say 'I' (Scruton 2012, 49).

This is not a simplistic distinction between "interpretation" and "explanation," but opens the door to true interdisciplinary reflection on the human person and the person of God. Scruton distinguishes between the "why" of science (searching for *causes*), the "why" of reason (searching for *arguments*), and finally the "why" of *understanding* (searching for meanings that could be inaccessible to causal thinking and rational argumentation; Scruton 2012, 68). Though all of these levels of thinking have their place in theology and in theological anthropology, the comprehensive "why" of understanding clears the way for the powerful role of aesthetics in coming to grips theologically with uniquely human experiences such as suffering, tragedy, guilt, redemption, and beauty. For Scruton this happens especially through the Christian Eucharist (Scruton 2012, 20). This is why the meaning of the sacrament is easy to experience, but difficult to explain, unless explained through a work of art such as the German composer Richard Wagner's drama *Parsifal*. In the quest for understanding the religious self and community, aesthetics takes its place alongside other dimensions of theology and the sciences. Its unique task is to probe what can never be fully probed only by the natural, human, or social sciences. In this sense one can move from human evolution to empathetic personhood while developing a bottom-up approach to theological anthropology.

References

Barnard, Alan. 2012. *Genesis of Symbolic Thought*. Cambridge: Cambridge University Press.

Boehm, Christopher. 2012. *Moral Origins: The Evolution of Virtue, Altruism, and Shame.* New York: Basic Books.

Botha, Rudolf. 2011a. "Inferring Modern Language for Ancient Objects." In *The Oxford Handbook of Language Evolution,* edited by Maggie Tallerman, and Kathleen Gibson, 303-312. Oxford: Oxford University Press.

Botha, Rudolf. 2011b. "Constraining the Arbitrariness of Exaptationist Accounts of the Evolution of Language." *Lingua* 121: 1552-1563.

Botha, Rudolf. 2012. "Protolanguage and the 'God particle.' " *Lingua* 122: 1308-1324.

Botha, Rudolf, and Martin Everaert, eds. 2013. *The Evolutionary Emergence of Language: Evidence and Inference*. Oxford: Oxford University Press.

Botha, Rudolf, and Martin Everaert. 2013. "Introduction: Evidence and inference in the study of language evolution." In *The Evolutionary Emergence of Language: Evidence and Inference*, edited by Rudolf Botha and Martin Everaert, 1-17. Oxford: Oxford University Press.

Bratt, Jessica. 2005. "Wolfhart Pannenberg: Imago Dei as Gift and Destiny." Unpublished paper, Princeton Theological Seminary.

Cartmill, Matt, and Kaye Brown. 2012. "Being Human Means that 'Being Human' Means Whatever We Say it Means." *Evolutionary Anthropology* 21:183.

Clottes, Jean, and David Lewis-Williams. 1998. *The Shamans of Prehistory: Trance and Magic in the Painted Caves*. New York: Harry N. Abrahams.Deacon, Terrence. 1997. *The Symbolic Species: The Co-Evolution of Language and the Brain*. New York: Norton.

De Waal, Frans. 2006. *Primates and Philosophers: How Morality Evolved*. Princeton, NJ: Princeton University Press.

De Waal, Frans. 2009. *The Age of Empathy: Nature's Lessons for a Kinder Society*. New York: Three Rivers Press.

Donald, Merlin. 1991. *Origins of the Modern Mind: Three Stages in the Evolution of Culture and Cognition*. Cambridge, MA: Harvard University Press.

Donald, Merlin. 2001. *A Mind so Rare: The Evolution of Human Consciousness.* New York: W.W. Norton.

Fowler, Chris. 2004. *The Archaeology of Personhood: An Anthropological Approach.* London & New York: Routledge.

Fuentes, Agustin. 2009. "A New Synthesis: Resituating Approaches to the Evolution of Human Behaviour." *Anthropology Today* 25 (3): 12-17.

Fuentes, Agustin. 2010. "On Nature and the Human: Introduction," and "More Than a Human Nature." *American Anthropologist: Vital Forum* 112: 512-521.

Fuentes, Agustin. 2012. *Race, Monogamy, and Other Lies They Told You: Busting Myths about Human Nature.* Berkeley, CA: University of California Press.

Fuentes, Agustin. 2014. "Human Evolution, Niche Complexity, and the Emergence of a Distinctly Human Imagination." *Time and Mind: The Journal of Archaeology, Consciousness and Culture* 7 (3): 241-257.

Gregersen, Niels. 2003. "The Naturalness of Religious Imagination and the Idea of Revelation." *Ars Disputandi: The Online Journal for Philosophy of Religion* 3, http://www.arsdisputandi.org/.

Hefner, Philip. 1998. "Biocultural Evolution and the Created Co-Creator." In *Science and Theology: The New Consonance,* edited by Ted Peters, 174-188. Boulder, CO: Westview Press.

Holloway, Richard. 2012. Review of Roger Scruton's *The Face of God.* In *The New Statesman,* http://www.newstatesman.com/books/2012/03/face-go-gifford-lectures.

Hrdy, Sarah. 2009. *Mothers and Others: The Evolutionary Origins of Mutual Understanding.* Cambridge, MA: Harvard University Press.

Ingold, Tim. 2010. "What is a Human Being?" *American Anthropologist: Vital Forum* 112 (4): 512-521.

Jablonka, Eva, and Marion Lamb. 2005. *Evolution in Four Dimensions: Genetic, Epigenetic, Behavioural, and Symbolic Variation in the History of Life.* Cambridge, MA: MIT Press.

Kirkpatrick, Lee. 2005. *Attachment, Evolution, and the Psychology of Religion.* New York & London: The Guilford Press.

Kearney, Richard. 2004. *On Paul Ricoeur: The Owl of Minerva.* Aldershot: Ashgate.

King, Barbara. 2007. *Evolving God: A Provocative View on the Origins of Religion.* New York: Doubleday.

Lewin, Roger. 1993. *The Origins of Modern Humans.* New York: Scientific American Library.

Lewis-Williams, David. 2002. *The Mind in the Cave: Consciousness and the Origins of Art.* New York: Thames and Hudson.

Marks, Jonathan. 2010. "Off Human Nature." *American Anthropologist: Vital Forum* 112: 512-521.

Mellars, Paul. 1989. "Major Issues in the Emergence of Modern Humans." *Current Anthropology* 30 (3): 349-385.

Mellars, Paul. 1991. "Cognitive Changes and the Emergence of Modern Humans in Europe." *Cambridge Archeological Journal* 1 (1): 63-76.

Mithen, Steven. 1996. *The Prehistory of the Mind: A Search for the Origins of Art, Religion, and Science.* London: Thames and Hudson.

Mithen, Steven. 2009. *The Singing Neanderthals: The Origins of Music, Language, Mind, and Body*. Cambridge, MA: Harvard University Press.

Mühling, Markus. 2014. *Resonances: Neurobiology, Evolution and Theology: Evolutionary Niche Construction, the Ecological Brain and Relational-Narrative Theology*. Göttingen: Vandenhoeck & Ruprecht.

Newlands, George. 2004. *The Transformative Imagination*. Aldershot: Ashgate Press.

Newlands, George. 2006. *Christ and Human Rights*. Aldershot: Ashgate Press.

Noble, William, and Iain Davidson. 1996. *Human Evolution, Language and Mind: A Psychological and Archeological Inquiry*. Cambridge: Cambridge University Press.

O'Brian, Matthew. 2012. Review of Roger Scruton's *The Face of God*. *First Things*, Nov. 2012. http://www.firstthings.com/article/2012/11/scrutinizing-the-sacred.

Olding-Smee, John, Kevin Laland, and Marcus Feldman. 2003. *Niche Construction: The Neglected Process in Evolution*. Princeton, NJ: Princeton University Press.

Potts, Richard. 1996. *Humanity's Descent*. New York: Morrow.

Potts, Richard. 2012. "Environmental and Behavioral Evidence Pertaining to the Evolution of Early *Homo*." *Current Anthropology* 53 (6): 299-317.

Ricoeur, Paul. 1992. *Oneself as Another*. Chicago, IL: University of Chicago Press.

Ricoeur, Paul, and Peter Homans. 2008. "Afterword: Conversations on Freud, Memory, and Loss." In *Mourning Religion*, edited by William Parsons, Diane Jonte-Pace, and Susan Henking, 221-238. Charlottesville, VA: University of Virginia Press.

Robinson, Andrew. 2010. *God and the World of Signs: Trinity, Evolution, and the Metaphysical Semiotics of C.S. Pierce*. Leiden & Boston, MA: Brill Publishers.

Ruse, Michael. 2012. *The Philosophy of Human Evolution*. Cambridge: Cambridge University Press.

Schrag, Calvin. 1992. *The Resources of Rationality: A Response to the Postmodern Challenge*. Bloomington, IN: Indiana University Press.

Scruton, Roger. 2012. *The Face of God: The Gifford Lectures 2010*. London & New York: Continuum.

Shantz, Colleen. 2009. *Paul in Ecstasy: The Neurobiology of the Apostle's Life and Thought*. Cambridge: Cambridge University Press.

Sheets-Johnstone, Maxine. 1990. *The Roots of Thinking*. Philadelphia, PA: Temple University Press.

Sheets-Johnstone, Maxine. 2008. *The Roots of Morality*. University Park, PA: The Pennsylvania State Press.

Stosis, Richard. 2009. "The Adaptationist-Byproduct Debate on the Evolution of Religion: Five Misunderstandings of the Adaptationist Program." *Journal of Cognition and Culture* 9: 315-332.

Tattersall, Ian. 1998. *Becoming Human: Evolution and Human Uniqueness*. New York: Hartcourt Brace.

Tattersall, Ian. 2002. *The Monkey in the Mirror: Essays on the Science of what Makes us Human*. New York: Hartcourt.

Tattersall, Ian. 2011. "Origins of the Human Sense of Self." In *In Search of Self: Interdisciplinary Perspectives on Personhood*, edited by Wentzel van Huyssteen and Erik Wiebe, 33-49. Grand Rapids, MI: Wm. B. Eerdmans.

Van Huyssteen, Wentzel. 2006. *Alone in the World: Human Uniqueness in Science and Theology.* Grand Rapids, MI: Wm. B. Eerdmans.

Van Huyssteen, Wentzel. 2009. "Interdisciplinary Perspectives on Human Origins and Religious Awareness." In *Becoming Human: Innovation in Prehistoric Material and Spiritual Culture,* edited by Colin Renfrew and Iain Morley, 235-252. Cambridge: Cambridge University Press.

Van Huyssteen, Wentzel. 2010a. "What Makes us Human? The Interdisciplinary Challenge to Theological Anthropology and Christology." *Toronto Journal of Theology* 26 (2): 143-160.

Van Huyssteen, Wentzel. 2010b. "When Were We Persons? Why Hominid Evolution holds the Key to Embodied Personhood." *Neue Zeitschrift for Systematische Theology* 52: 329-349.

Van Huyssteen, Wentzel. 2010c. "Coding the Nonvisible: Epistemic Limitations and Understanding Symbolic Behavior at Çatalhöyük." In *Religion in the Emergence of Civilisation: Çatalhöyük as a Case Study,* edited by Ian Hodder, 99-121. Cambridge: Cambridge University Press.

Van Huyssteen, Wentzel. 2011. "Post-Foundationalism and Human Uniqueness: A Reply to Responses" in *Toronto Journal of Theology* 27 (1): 73-86.

Van Huyssteen, Wentzel. 2013. "The Historical Self: Memory and Religion at Çatalhöyük." In *Vital Matters: Religion and Change at Çatalhöyük,* edited by Ian Hodder, 109-133. Cambridge: Cambridge University Press.

Van Huyssteen, Wentzel. 2014. "From Empathy to Embodied Faith: Interdisciplinary Perspectives on the Evolution of Religion." In *Evolution, Religion, and Cognitive Science: Critical and Constructive Essays,* edited by Fraser Watts,. and Léon Turner, 132-151. Oxford: Oxford University Press.

Welsch, Wolfgang. 1996. *Vernunft: Die zeitgenössische Vernunftkritik und das Konzept der transversalen Vernunft.* Frankfurt a.M: Suhrkamp Taschenbuch.

Wildman, Wesley. 2009. *Science and Religious Anthropology.* Farnham: Ashgate.

Wuketits, Franz. 1990. *Evolutionary Epistemology and its Implications for Humankind.* Albany, NY: SUNY Press.

"From human evolution to empathetic personhood": A systematic theology approach and its meaning for practical theology – A response to J. Wentzel van Huyssteen

Friedrich Schweitzer

Abstract

This contribution is a response to Wentzel van Huyssteen's "From human evolution to empathetic personhood." It discusses van Huyssteen's views from the perspective of practical theology in three different respects: first, in terms of evolutionary theory as a background for practical theology; second, by applying the concept of "constructing evolutionary niches" to the understanding of the praxis of practical theology; and third, following a major interest of practical theology and Christian education, by discussing possibilities for making van Huyssteen's view of evolution and theology understandable to people in the church and beyond. These considerations and analyses are seen as a contribution to the interdisciplinary dialogue between systematic theology and practical theology. The emphasis is on interdisciplinary cooperation rather than on unilateral processes of reception. Both disciplines should emerge from such dialogues with new impulses and ideas.

It is a great honour to be given the opportunity to respond to the chapter of such a first-rate theologian and theorist. In this case, it is also a personal pleasure for me because I first met Wentzel van Huyssteen almost 20 years ago at Princeton Theological Seminary. Moreover, I have been following at least some of his many publications that I cherish as very stimulating and useful for my own work in practical theology and religious education, especially concerning the theological understanding of evolutionary theories in the tradition of Charles Darwin.

It was only for the present occasion, however, that I intentionally considered the question of what van Huyssteen's very impressive and well-informed work and analysis from systematic theology – as represented by his article in this volume – may mean for practical theology. In other words, my response to his chapter is an interdisciplinary exercise which, for the most part, will focus on practical theology as the recipient of results from another theological discipline. In doing so, however, I will also point out a number of questions arising from practical theology that might be of interest to systematic theology. Interdisciplinary work should not be limited to processes of unilateral reception but should be reciprocal in the sense of a dialogue from which all disciplines involved emerge with new impulses and ideas. This understanding implies that I consider practical theology as a theological discipline that has more to offer than the attempt of putting research results from other disciplines into practice.

What then can van Huyssteen's presentation on human evolution and personhood mean for practical theology? In the following, I want to suggest three interdependent levels on which van Huyssteen's results can be taken up in practical theology.

I start out with the statement that, in my understanding, contains van Huyssteen's basic intention: "the history of human evolution as such might provide us with important bridge theories to theological anthropology and thus to a positive and constructive way of appropriating Darwinian thought for a public, interdisciplinary Christian theology" (p. 34).

Here, van Huyssteen refers to the possibilities of constructively using Darwinian ideas in theology in general. For practical theology, this might mean that we could or should place our discipline in a new comprehensive interdisciplinary matrix – the matrix of research on human evolution. In many ways, however, this suggestion may not sound very plausible. In the present, practical theology is mostly in dialogue with the social sciences and with theories of culture that avoid all evolutionary assumptions. Yet upon further reflection, at least from a European perspective, this suggestion of including evolutionary theories clearly resonates with classical approaches to practical theology, such as Schleiermacher's understanding of the discipline (Schleiermacher 1850) or Hegelian versions of practical theology. Such approaches to practical theology tended to view this discipline within the parameters of human history and evolution, for example, by relating it to the developing unification of nature and reason, which was their way of describing the path to true humanity. Moreover, such views can not only be found in positions of the 19th century but they have strongly influenced contemporary thinkers like Jürgen Habermas (cf. Habermas 1981), and through him, some strands of practical theology in many countries as well. In other words, suggesting that practical theology should not limit its interdisciplinary relationships to the social sciences and to theories of culture might in fact remind our discipline of its own origins and encourage it to consider anew the possible importance of an interdisciplinary dialogue with evolutionary theories. The matrix or framework offered by evolutionary theories can remind practical theology of the wider horizon in which the praxis addressed by it has to be considered. Compared to this horizon, an exclusive focus on the individual level but also on congregations or even on societal questions must appear too narrow. We certainly cannot simply go back to the times of German 19th century idealism. Yet, at least in some respects, the dialogue with modern evolutionary theory may offer a viable alternative. At the same time, such attempts at broadening the theoretical scope or background of practical theology must also remain mindful of practical theology's particular strength that lies in its attention to the always concrete circumstances of individual and social life that so often tend to be overlooked by large-scale theories – a critical remark that I will further pursue in the following.

In order to make more concrete what an evolutionary approach could mean for practical theology, I refer to an example that is addressed in van Huyssteen's chapter and that also plays a role in my own work. For this purpose, I refer to the work of social evolutionist Michael Tomasello, director of the Max Planck Institute for Evolutionary Anthropology in Leipzig, Germany. Just as van Huyssteen points out that "seeing things from someone else's perspective" and to develop a "Theory of Mind" (p. 35) makes humans human, Tomasello holds that it is the capacity of perspective taking that is unique to the human (cf. Tomasello 1999). His tenets are based on empirical studies and experiments with chimpanzees and young humans. Yet, they have far-reaching implications for understanding human personhood in general as well as the work of practical theology. Could it make sense then, for example, to investigate the question of how the praxis studied by practical theology is related to the foundational human capacity of perspective taking? If there should indeed be a meaningful relationship between both, what does this mean for the understanding of practical theology?

In my own work, taking the perspective of the other is viewed as an aspect of process and ability in the context of interreligious learning (cf. Schweitzer 2014). The ability to take the perspective of the religious other can be considered a basic presupposition for interreligious communication as well as for mutual respect (cf. Selman 1980). In this case, practical theology aims at strengthening people's abilities for perspective taking. Following van Huyssteen's suggestion, it may make sense to ask if the interest in perspective taking could and should be broadened so that perspective taking would be understood as one of the basic concepts of practical theology altogether. If perspective taking does indeed refer to one of the most fundamental characteristics of human existence distinguishing it from other forms of life, fostering the respective ability can be called a key task in all fields of practical theology, in theory as well as in praxis.

The question about the praxis of practical theology leads to my second set of considerations in response to van Huyssteen's chapter. In my view, van Huyssteen's presentation offers practical theology important possibilities for understanding the practice of practical theology in a new sense, again by introducing a background from evolutionary theory but also in a more specific sense. If I am correct, according to van Huyssteen, we should now consider practice as part of "niche construction." The core quote here is: "what evolutionary biologists and anthropologists today are calling a process of niche construction: in a remarkable interactive process potentially changeable natural environments were, and are, acting continuously on variation in the gene pools of populations, and in this way gene pools were modified over generations" (p. 36).

In this case, the relationship between evolution and human praxis is interactive. The activity of "niche construction" is part of evolution but it also influences evolution: "*niche construction* itself is in fact seen as an additional mechanism of evolution working at the very same basic level as natural selection" (p. 36). In other words, "*Homo sapiens sapiens* is a species that had a hand in making itself" (p. 37). What makes humans human is dependent upon the "niche" that the humans themselves have constructed or, to be more precise, that the humans have been able to co-construct together with the environment. In my understanding this implies that this "niche" must also be continuously protected and maintained, and that it should possibly and intentionally be developed further in order to support the human or even humane character of the life of this species.

How should practical theology respond to this offer of becoming a "niche constructing discipline"? In discussing this question it should be clear from the beginning that this use of the term "niche" means something quite different from the traditional criticism of certain kinds of religion or theology that are accused of accepting or pursuing a "niche existence." Making do with such a "niche existence" is equivalent to not facing up to the challenges of the present but of withdrawing into a corner where such challenges might be escaped. This would certainly not be an attractive prospect for practical theology.

However, van Huyssteen's use of the term "niche" has nothing to do with backward strategies for hiding from the evolutionary drift. Instead, an evolutionary "niche" is what opens up new evolutionary possibilities through the effects of a particular environment that is constructed.

In the case of the human, this environment is closely tied to special developments, like the development of imagination and of a moral sense. According to van Huyssteen, this imagination includes religion – in fact, so much that van Huyssteen seems to come quite close to making religion the unique characteristic that makes humans human, and therefore, to viewing religion as the true cause for human flourishing: "More importantly, within this evolutionary context one can now envision a distinctive imagination as a core part of the human niche that ultimately enabled the possibility of metaphysical thought. It is ultimately this component of our human niche as our way of being in the world, that is the central aspect of our explanation for why Homo sapiens has flourished while all other hominins, even members of our own genus, have all gone extinct" (p. 38).

While this conclusion flows quite naturally from van Huyssteen's argument, it is at this point that practical theology would press for clarification and for a more concrete understanding.

Firstly, we should consider the ambivalence of religion. What kind of religion should practical theology try to nourish? Certainly not any kind of religion. Yet what would be the criteria that practical theology should use in this case? Secondly, what exactly would be the "niche" practical theology is trying to build and to maintain or to enhance? Are we talking about the church as the true niche? Or do we have to think about the symbolic ecology in general? Thirdly, what exactly are the principles upon which this "niche" should be based? Is the general reference to the symbolic sense and the imagination enough or do we have to become more specific by including principles like justice for characterizing an adequate niche? Would this imply that there are different human "niches" competing with each other? Or that there are at least competing and contradictory principles used for "niche construction" in line with certain interests? If it is true that the "niches" constructed by humans are shaping them, such questions are indeed of prime importance. Fourthly, what are the practical forms of living and acting in which "niche" adequate principles can find their embodiment? For practical theology it is not enough to become aware that humans owe their existence to an evolutionary "niche." Practical theology needs clear perspectives for its praxis. I have to leave these questions unanswered here. To develop adequate answers would require further work on practical theology's understanding of "niche construction."

My third consideration builds on van Huyssteen's paper, but also goes beyond it. Here, I focus on yet another core task and interest of practical theology, namely the question of how the combination of evolutionary theories and theological views of the human can become a common Christian understanding beyond the academy. Phrased differently, how can van Huyssteen's views be made available to the general public? This question refers to a core interest of practical theology. At the same time, it reminds all theological disciplines of their educational commitments and tasks.

From general debates as well as from our own empirical research, it seems that faith in God the creator continues to lose its credibility. This is not only true for scientists but especially for so-called common people. In our recent survey with confirmands in nine European countries, we found that even among the 14 years old confirmands who register for confirmation, there is no majority in favor of this faith any more. In Germany, for example, it is only 46% of the confirmands who affirm that God created the world. In other countries, for example in Sweden, the respective figure is down to about 20% of the confirmands (cf. Schweitzer et al. 2015, 367). In other words, most young people in central and northern Europe seem to be lacking the ability to combine evolutionary theories and faith in God the creator.

This is, of course, no objection to van Huyssteen's aims, which I understand to point to some kind of cooperative complementarity between science and religion. Yet my observations raise the additional question of how people can become aware or even convinced of this cooperative complementarity. Traditional religious teaching and preaching does not seem to be successful in this sense. To quote again from our study on confirmands: the number of those in agreement with creation faith actually does not rise during confirmation time (cf. Schweitzer et al. 2015, 375). The percentage at the end of confirmation time is the same as it was at the beginning, which implies that a minimum of approximately one year of teaching with these adolescents does not result in any kind of reconciliation between religion and science. One could of course say that this is where the task of systematic theology ends and where practical theology has to come into the picture. Yet as we know, such easy division of labor between the theological disciplines has never worked very well. Designing effective ways for preaching and teaching based on thinking in complementarity should be a task shared by both, systematic theology and practical theology – maybe another way of "niche construction."

One interesting model for this task actually comes from a cooperative project between the psychology of religion, physics, and theology. A group of researchers in Switzerland found that the decisive step towards thinking in complementarity as they call it, hinges upon the distinction between thinking about objects in the world and thinking about thinking or thinking about different ways of thinking (Reich 2002). We can also call this the ability of meta-thinking. Consequently it is this ability for which practical theology should strive in preaching and teaching because it is needed to enable one to reconcile evolutionary thinking and theological anthropology.

Van Huyssteen ends his paper by referring to the difference between the " 'why' of causality" and the " 'why' of reason" or understanding. Practical theologians want to add to this the reference to people becoming able to make this distinction. The "niche" that van Huyssteen wants practical theologians to be aware of, must be such that it supports the development of this ability – maybe as another step in evolution through which not only an educational elite has the capacity of meta-thinking but indeed the population at large.

It seems, then, that dialogue between systematic theology and practical theology can be stimulating and quite useful, hopefully for both disciplines. Different disciplines add different perspectives to the understanding of the same object. Such differences should not be considered an obstacle for cooperation but as an important motive for entering the interdisciplinary dialogue.

References

Habermas, Jürgen. 1981. *Theorie des kommunikativen Handelns.* 2 vols. Frankfurt am Main: Suhrkamp.

Reich, Karl H. 2002. *Developing the Horizons of the Mind: Relational and Contextual Reasoning and the Resolution of Cognitive Conflict.* Cambridge & New York: Cambridge University Press.

Schleiermacher, Friedrich. 1850. *Die praktische Theologie nach den Grundsätzen der evangelischen Kirche im Zusammenhange dargestellt*, edited by Jacob Frerichs. Berlin: de Gruyter.

Schweitzer, Friedrich. 2014. *Interreligiöse Bildung: Religiöse Vielfalt als Herausforderung und Chance.* Gütersloh: Gütersloher Verlagshaus.

Schweitzer, Friedrich, Kati Niemelä, Thomas Schlag and Henrik Simojoki. 2015. *Youth, Religion and Confirmation Work in Europe: The Second Study.* Gütersloh: Gütersloher Verlagshaus.

Selman, Robert L. 1980. *The Growth of Interpersonal Understanding: Developmental and Clinical Analyses.* New York: Academic Press.

Tomasello, Michael. 1999. *The Cultural Origins of Human Cognition.* Cambridge, MA: Harvard University Press.

II. PRACTICING UBUNTU: LOCAL PERSPECTIVES

"Ma se kind": Rediscovering personhood in addressing socio-economic challenges in the Cape Flats

Nadine Bowers Du Toit

Abstract

The Afrikaans saying "ma se kind," means "mother's child." This is a colloquial term of the "coloured" (a contested term for mixed race) community in South Africa to reference anyone regarded as family (biological or otherwise). Despite such recognition of interconnectedness in this community, coloured identity is both highly contested and fragmented as result of apartheid ideology and policy (such as "forced removals"). This uprooting of families and communities and the resultant loss of identity and community, played a key role in the rise of gangsterism and other socio-economic issues in the "coloured" community. This paper explores ways in which a theological understanding of personhood could engage this community to rediscover its interconnectedness as a means of addressing the socio-economic challenges.

Introduction

I am a so-called "coloured" female and have recently chosen to move back to the outskirts of the Cape Flats where I grew up. The Cape Flats were a result of the Group Areas Act (1950) which led to the forcible removal of black and coloured people from the cities. In this essay I focus only on so-called "coloured" communities. The term "coloured" has a distinct meaning in South Africa. It is not used – as is the case elsewhere – to denote black people in general. It is also a highly contested term in the community itself. During the apartheid era many "coloured" people preferred to be identified as "black" (in solidarity with the liberation struggle) or termed themselves "so-called coloured" as they felt that they were "so called" by the apartheid state.

Adhikari describes them as a "phenotypically varied social group of highly diverse social and geographical origins." Their heritage can be traced to a diverse group of people who "had been assimilated into Cape colonial society by the late nineteenth century" (Adhikari 2005, 1). This includes Cape slaves from African and Asian origin, the indigenous Khoisan population and European settlers. For Hendricks it is disingenuous to simply identify "coloureds" as the "mixed race offspring of inter-racial liaisons": "coloured" identity is rather a complex historically located identity that stems from the processes of slavery, genocide, rape and perceived miscegenation. The identity construction has been cloaked by the perceived shame of illegitimacy and lack of authenticity that has to a large extent psychologically disempowered the bearers of the identity (Hendricks 2010, 118).

In light of the issues of identity and disempowerment – which are largely historically rooted – the focus here is on the restoration of personhood. The Afrikaans saying "ma se kind" ("mother's child") is a colloquial term used among the "coloured" (mixed race) community to refer to anyone regarded as family (biological or otherwise). The paper explores how the popularised notion of "ma se kind" can be engaged and reinvigorated through socio-historical, psycho-social, theological and lived experience perspectives.

The contested and complex nature of "coloured" identity in socio-historical perspective

The complex historically located identity of the "coloured" population is problematised by the fact that during the colonial era, which gave birth to growing race and ethnic stratification, coloureds as "mixed race" attempted to attain intermediate status and closer assimilation with European culture. "Coloureds", whose phenotypical (racial) characteristics were closer to that of white Europeans, enjoyed privileges that racially darker people did not (Petrus and Isaacs-Martin 2012, 92). "Race and ethnicity became a symbol not only of the inferiority of what would become coloured identity, but also of divisions within the coloured groups" (Petrus and Isaacs-Martin 2012, 92). In 1948 the Nationalist Party came to power and legalised segregation though acts such as the Population Registration Act (1950) that categorised race groups, and the Group Areas Act (1950) of which the aim was racially homogenous townships. These acts further entrenched the inferiority and negativity associated with the "in-between" nature of "coloured" identity (Petrus and Isaacs-Martin 2012, 93). It was further complicated by the proviso in the Population Registration Act that coloureds could apply to be re-classified as white. They would then enjoy the privileges associated with this race. Members of my own family applied to be re-classified and were forever lost to their families as they sought to establish new identities. This practice of what was colloquially referred to as "turning white" or "crossing the colour line" had ramifications for individuals, families and the community's self-understanding. "Consequently race and ethnicity came to symbolise not only the social inferiority of coloured identity, but its economic inferiority as well" (Petrus and Isaacs-Martin 2012, 94). Not being recognised as belonging to any group, and yet finding their origins in many groups (European/Afrikaner, Black African, Asian, indigenous), has resulted in what Turner calls a "liminal identity."

In terms of coloured identity and status the liminality of coloured culture symbolised incompleteness. In other words, the transitional position of coloured people meant that they were not fully human, but were trapped in an intermediate phase between apartheid – imposed binary oppositions such as non-human (as represented by the black African group) and fully human (as represented by the White group), uncivilised and civilised, belonging and not belonging (Petrus and Isaacs-Martin 2012, 96).

The Group Areas Act (1950) was one of the most hated of the apartheid legislation. "Coloured" people were forcibly relocated to residential and business districts on the periphery, which broke up long standing communities (Adhikari 2004, 3). This was also the case with black communities. In Cape Town the most well-known example among the "coloured" community was District Six. Prior to the Group Areas Act (1950) Cape Town was one of the most racially integrated cities in South Africa (Trotter 2009, 51).

The people were re-located to public housing complexes with few recreation facilities. They were placed far from the economic hub of the city. The effects were devastating.

Residents who had identified with particular neighbourhoods were dispossessed of them, deprived of their patrimony, sundered from their social networks, and forced to accommodate themselves to a new existence with strangers from other communities. In many ways they had to re-crate their sense of self and their social lives as their old networks were torn apart (Trotter 2009, 55).

According to Trotter "coloured" "memory production is driven by three moral intentions":

… to counter the government's rationale for Group Areas (counter memory), to compare the difficult present to an idealised past (comparative memory) and to commemorate their former communities with highly selective stories which honour their former homes, communities and identities (commemorative memory) (Trotter 2009, 56).

Trotter questions whether the nostalgia regarding the pre-removal era could be romanticising, but he does recognise the removals as mass social trauma (Trotter 2009, 72). People speak fondly of the communal spirit and social networks of the former communities and compare that to the fragmentation and violence of today (Trotter 2009, 61). One of the greatest social costs of the forced removals is the rise of gangsterism, which is rife on the Cape Flats (Kinnes 1996; Dixon and Johns 2001, 3; Cooper 2009, 2; Daniels and Adams 2010, 46, 47). Many "coloured" areas today are gang "hotspots." The social and economic exclusion of many "coloureds" (a community where levels of unemployment and poverty are high) in the Western Cape has resulted not only in youth joining gangs, but in some members of the communities turning to gang leaders to provide basic necessities (MacMaster 2007, 278).

The 1970's and 1980's saw the rise of renewed contention around the issue of coloured identity. This was precipitated by the emergence of the Black Consciousness movement, which "sought to promote black solidarity and self-reliance" (Adhikari 2005, 4). During this era politically conscious "coloureds" increasingly rejected the term "coloured" as a government categorisation meant to promote their "divide and rule" strategy (Adhikari 2005, 4; Petrus and Isaacs-Martin 2010, 94). "Coloured" theologian Allan Boesak in particular promoted the identity of "coloured" people as "black" as a means of resistance. The participation of "coloured" people in the ANC aligned United Democratic Front – and conversely "coloured" participation in the apartheid government sanctioned Tricameral parliament[1] – both resulted in the recognition of "coloured" identity as "a concession to apartheid thinking" (Adhikari 2005, 4). Nagel argues that "ethnic boundaries and thus identities are constructed by both the individual and group as well as by outside agents and organisations" (Petrus and Isaacs-Martin 2012, 94). This identity construction is particularly complex in the context of "coloured" identity (cf. Hendricks 2010, 118).

"Colouredness" in a post-apartheid context tends to be perceived as "not black enough, not white enough." This expresses the marginalisation that "coloureds" feel in a post-apartheid era and its "preferential allocation of resources to black Africans in the Western Cape when their needs as just as great" (Hendricks 2010, 117). In the more diversified economy of the past two decades the "coloured" working class cannot compete, which results in high levels of unemployment. They have the sense of being "stuck" on the wastelands of the Cape Flats, with little social or economic mobility. This, according to them, is rooted in affirmative action and Black Economic Empowerment (BEE) policies, which are "further advantaging (black) Africans at their expense" (Petrus and Isaacs-Martin 2012, 99). "[C]onsequently, in this context coloured identity is not only a symbol of continuing hardship for certain sectors, but also of regression, due to the perceived loss of status formerly enjoyed under apartheid" (Petrus and Isaacs-Martin 2012, 99). This view is echoed by Adhikari:

Not only has the new democratic dispensation brought with it a degree of freedom of association and possibilities for ethnic mobilisation inconceivable under white domination, but it has also undermined, even invalidated, some of the most basic assumptions and

---

[1]   This was a kind of "shadow" parliament, which allowed coloured and Indians supposed own representation. Many conscientised coloureds and Indians refused to give any support to what they regarded as another instrument of the apartheid regime.

practices that had underpinned coloured identity from the time it crystallised in the late 19th century. And with the racial hierarchy that had regulated social relations in white-ruled South Africa having broken down in important respects, intergroup relations have become more complex and expressions of social identity more fluid (Adhikari 2004, 167)

In the post-apartheid era possibilities for ethnic mobilisation and a reclaiming of the indigenous Khoisan identities have emerged. Former President Thabo Mbeki, in his "I am an African" speech, claimed "khoisaness" as part of his identity. However, this sentiment is not widespread in the African or "coloured" communities. Khoisan identities have been denigrated throughout colonial and apartheid history" (Ruiters 2009, 112). Mbeki's speech was a call to *ubuntu* – to a national identity that would bind all sectors of what Archbishop Tutu termed the "rainbow nation." Many "coloureds" have chosen to not identify with this national identity. In recent years some – especially the coloured elites – who once rejected the term "coloured" and preferred "black" or "so-called coloureds" have recently begun to reclaim the term "coloured" (Ruiters 2009, 113). Questioning and reconstructing their identities is an attempt "to move away from the negative representation of coloured identity" (Ruiters 2009, 110-111). Maybe this paper is in itself an attempt by a "coloured elite" to reclaim this notion.

Coloured identity through social and relative deprivation identity theory lenses

"Coloured" people in general continue to grapple with their identity and sadly "the issue of coloured identity is largely overshadowed by negative stereotypes of this identity" (Petrus 2013, 76). Due to the ambiguities arising from their history, "coloureds" have often been viewed as having no identity. This resulted in both coloured and other groups, stereotyping them in a negative manner. According to Petrus, "multiple meanings can be attached to this identity." He further notes that the hybrid nature of this identity has contributed significantly to the social, political and economic marginalisation many coloureds feel in a post-apartheid context (Petrus 2013, 76).

Mummenday and associates investigate the strategies used to cope with unfavourable group position or a negative social identity. They develop a hybrid model, combining Social Identity Theory (SIT) and Relative Deprivation Theory (RDT). According to SIT, "a disadvantaged or inferior position of one's own group leads to a negative social identity ... which triggers attempts to improve one's status position" (Mummenday et al. 1999, 230). This is evident historically in the racial re-classifying of some during the apartheid era in order to enjoy the privileges associated with "whiteness." More recently it is also evident in the attempts by the "coloured" elites to question and reconstruct their identity by reclaiming parts of their past (through identification with the Khoisan) or by re-claiming and redefining the term "coloured" from its negative past owners (the apartheid state). This is evident in "coloured's" memorialising of their past prior to the forced removals. They contrast the communal spirit and social networks of former communities with the fragmentation and violence of many current com-munities. These are perhaps strategies to improve their status position. However, in the history of the "coloured population," there is a complicated "in-group" and "out-group" dynamic. It is largely the elites who have had the power to claim and reclaim these identities in an attempt to enhance self-esteem (cf. Stets and Burke 2000, 225). An "in-group" of "coloured elite" is thereby re-inforced. " ... [T]he motivation behind this strategy is thought to be the desire to achieve, main-tain or enhance positive social identity. It is assumed that, by establishing positive distinctiveness for the in-group as a whole, its group members are establishing a positive identity" (Rubin and Hewstone 1998, 41).

Even when a group has low status, in-group identification (such as identifi-cation with a Khoisan identity or romanticised shared past) may result in greater commitment to the group and less desire to leave it, deny it or in this case dis-associate with it in favour of other identities such as "African" or "black" (Stets and Burke 2000, 226). Coloured street gangs symbolise the "continuing search for belonging, identity and rootedness" and they "function as symbols of resistance to externally imposed identities" (Petrus 2013, 77, 78). Gangs on the Cape Flats, therefore, provide a means for "coloured" youths to "adapt to their liminal status, and perhaps even to use it to their advantage by using their social (re) organisa-tion in the street gang to transcend the social limitations and boundaries of their communities" (Petrus 2013, 79).

Unlike Social Identity Theory (SIT), RDT argues that what really "matters is the perception of a negative discrepancy between one's own and another group's share of positive resources or positive outcomes, as well as the negative eval-uation of this discrepancy with its affective consequences" (Mummenday et al. 1999, 231). Contentment or resentment is largely based on a comparison of the preferred future with the current outcome in which one's group is seen to suffer deprivation relative to another group. This negative comparison between the ac-tual and referent outcome, may result in "mild forms of dissatisfaction with the status quo." This has always been the case with the "coloured" population and is reflected in the refrain "not black enough, not white enough." Both pre- and post-apartheid, many "coloureds" felt (and still feel) that they suffer deprivation relative to other groups. They believe that they have never fully benefitted from the socio-economic system. This leads not only to feelings of frustration and re-sentment, but also powerlessness (Webber 2007, 100). The social and economic power held by gangs in Cape Flats communities is often crippling to socially and economically vulnerable communities on the Cape Flats (Bowers Du Toit 2014, 3).

The debate around BEE (Black Economic Empowerment) and affirmative action policies further complicates matters. According to RDT, mild forms of dissatisfaction can worsen if the group feels that "... the procedures or instruments leading to this negative outcome were unjustified and that an alternative procedure could have caused more favourable outcomes" (Mummenday et al. 1999, 231). As fraternal deprivation increases, so too will the likelihood of collective strategies. "Hope" lies in the belief that future change is possible.

Reclaiming the notion of "Ma se Kind"

How a theological understanding of personhood in community speaks to issues of identity will now be considered. The manner in which some individual Christians and congregations are beginning to enact this within community, will be explored.

"God se Kinnes" and the notion of alien dignity"

There have been attempts – at least by the "coloured elites" – to move away from the negative stereotyping of the "coloured" identity. However, for the majority the largely negative stereotypes have resulted in marginalisation on social, economic and political levels in the new South Africa. This negative stereotyping is not only experienced from other groups, but has also been internalised.

"Coloured" practical theologian and former anti-apartheid activist, Dr. Llewellyn MacMaster, who has done significant research on gangsterism and the church's response, purposely wears a t-shirt with the words "God se Kinnes" (God's children) as a play on the phrase "Ma se kind." This is a significant message for people who have in many ways seen themselves as identity-less. An image of him wearing this T-shirt posted on social media elicited a surprisingly strong positive response from the largely "coloured" viewers who immediately identified the link between the two notions. Thielicke's notion of "alien dignity" (Thielicke 1966,165) emphasises that human dignity and worth are not to be found in people's view of themselves or others' view of them, but are "imputed to us by the love of God" (Koopman 2007, 180). Our worth as persons is not based on individual capacities, but is inextricably linked to God claiming us as God's own. So "coloured" people are worthy, because they are "God se Kinnes" (God's children). It is alien, because the source of dignity is God. It is also inalienable because it cannot be removed by any external event or person or structure. This alien dignity implies equality with all God's people and a renewed sense of relationality with God and others.

At this point it is important to note that not even the humblest, threatening and vulnerable state impacts negatively on our dignity. Because we have alien dignity we can be assured of special protection in the most threatening conditions and situations, the notion of alien dignity also implies that all people are equal, despite any diversity of role, social status, race, colour, class or sex. Alien dignity encourages us to accept diversity and affirm equality (Koopman 2007, 181).

This opens up the possibility for restored relationships with other population groups without getting "stuck" in the binary of "in-" and "out-groups", of "not black enough, not white enough." "Coloured" people are "enough" because of their identity being imputed by the love of God. This love of God is for all peoples, including "coloureds", who then belong and are interrelated to other groups by virtue of this claim. Although power relations between the race groups (as a result of apartheid history) cannot be discounted, the deep-seated inferiority complex of "coloureds" may find psycho-social "relief" in such a theological understanding. It can challenge their "fixedness" in the old racial hierarchy. Their multi-layered identity is thereby affirmed as they begin to understand that they were created for a life in relationship and that their identity reflects part of God's very own life in relationship as interdependent. However, in the term "ma se kind" lies the same negative possibility that Naude (2013, 246) notes with regards to *ubuntu*, namely that my brothers and sisters are only of my "own kind." A relational understanding of personhood opens up possibilities for faith communities to lead the way in challenging this notion to be broader, thereby providing opportunities to escape the binary and even embrace the "Africanness" of their own roots.

"Ma se kind": Reclaiming and reframing our stories

The notion of "ma se kind" ("my mother's child") is clearly a reference to fraternity/brotherhood/sisterhood within the "coloured" community – a kind of *ubuntu*. This sense of community was deemed to have existed before the forced removals. Even 40-50 years later people grieve for the loss of the social networks and communal spirit of their former communities. The social trauma resulted in the fragmentation of families and communities. Many were discarded on the wastelands of the Cape Flats and left there to fend for themselves while they possessed little social or economic mobility. This became the breeding grounds for gangs who provided the community and identity that "coloured" youths so desire. They also provided the them with the means to experience economic mobility through illicit activities such as drug running, robbery, prostitution and extortion. In a sense the forced removals made an already vulnerable group more vulnerable and seemingly powerless. However, despite the fact that fraternal deprivation has increased, so too are collective strategies for re-claiming our story increasing. Perhaps this can rebuild social capital – a resource sorely lacking on the Cape Flats (Calix

2014, 74). Transforming people begins "with helping people discover that their human dignity and identity are intrinsically related to God in Christ through his redemptive purpose in salvation history" (Bediako 1996, 8). This restoration of identity, "an opening up of our true self" (Anderson 1982, 84), allows the poor and marginalised to understand who they are (identity), their value (dignity) and through the restoration of these to understand that they have gifts which can contribute to both their own wellbeing and that of their community (vocation) (Myers 2001, 115). During the apartheid era, my father pastored a congregation in a Cape Flats community. This congregation contributed to building social capital in the community. Though its members were uneducated and held low-paying jobs, in the church community they were leaders. As a result of their renewed understanding of who they were in Christ, they became active in the broader community, assisting neighbours to obtain employment and sharing what they had with those who were struggling.

According to Relative Deprivation Theory hope lies in the belief that future change is possible. Perhaps what is required is what Brueggemann (1982) terms "prophetic imagination." Congregational leaders and Christian workers should take the lead in assisting communities to re-imagine how God sees them – not as a wasteland – but rather as fertile ground for future leaders and places of peace and prosperity. Here "coloured" people not only exercise counter, comparative or commemorative memory, but also use these to re-imagine or re-frame what their current communities could look like through God's eyes. A Christian worker from the gang-infested community of Mannenberg names his community "God's special possession" (Bowers Du Toit 2014, 11). His work focuses on empowering at risk youth to imagine a new future.

Restoring marred identity

It is largely the elites who have had the power to claim and reclaim these identities and enhance their self-esteem. In many ways "coloured" identity could be termed an "identity of denial." People are always seeking to escape the negative stereotypes. Those not belonging to this elite have little basis for understanding their self-worth. Many individuals suffer from a "marred identity" (Myers 2001, 115), believing that they have no value and little contribution to make. They lack the hope that they will ever escape their circumstances. The youth who are searching for identity are especially vulnerable to these feelings. It is exacerbated by the cycle of poverty which entraps Cape Flats youth, "which engenders further feelings of failure and rejection leading to low self-esteem, which in turn makes them vulnerable to searching for power and social recognition within a gang" (Bowers Du Toit 2014, 6; cf. Daniels and Adams 2010, 54).

In God's economy, however, not only the elite have the power to reclaim their identity as children of God – all are made in God's image and deeply valued. All can re-discover that their human dignity and identity are intrinsically linked to God in Christ.

I spoke at an "adoption service" in an informal settlement on the Cape Flats once. The aim was that adult members "adopt" younger members, mostly teenagers, as their "spiritual children." Many came from single parent households. Often their biological parents were not church members. One girl's mother was the owner of an illicit tavern. The "adoption" was to provide a mentoring structure in recognition of the worth and dignity of the young people.

The church's role does not end with youth who are susceptible to gangsterism, but should engage with gang members themselves to guide them to "appreciate or re-appreciate their God-given gift of personhood" (MacMaster 2007, 288).

Rediscovering God-given agency

The violence and socio-economic challenges of the Cape Flats are deeply disempowering. This lack of Shalom calls out for redemptive action. During the darkest days of our history, some "coloureds" identified with the Black Consciousness movement in their call for solidarity and self-reliance. These actions were a means of resistance to the strategies of the oppressive apartheid state. These actions in history suggest that, despite feelings of marginalisation and deprivation, the "coloured" people can, through the restoration of their identity and dignity, understand that "they have gifts that can contribute to both the wellbeing of themselves and their community" (Myers 2001, 115; cf. Sands 2010, 37). All human beings have been given stewardship over creation. In this manner they are imbued with God-given agency to act on behalf of the Shalom of the community. In recent years churches have engaged the issue the violence in their communities through peace marches, vigils and community "peace talks" with gang members. Churches stand at the forefront of 'taking back power' – they exercise their God-given agency (Bowers 2005, 187). One Faith Based Organisation has initiated a social entrepreneurship project to address the economic challenge of unemployment. This project takes the form of a bakery and coffee shop in the heart of one of the most violent and socio-economically deprived Cape Flats communities. Such small but faithful acts indicate that individuals and communities are re-discovering the *Imago Dei* as vocation.

Conclusion

The notion of "coloured" identity in South Africa is both a complex and painful. In many ways, it is an "identity of denial" with people trying to escape the negative stereotyping both from within and outside of the group. This has "psychologically disempowered the bearers of this identity" (Hendricks 2010, 118). The forced removals have had a devastating effect on this already affected group. Pre-forced removals "coloured" communities shared (and still share in some ways) a sense of community cohesion, with others as their brothers and sisters ("ma se kind"). This is perhaps a form of *ubuntu*. A theological exploration of personhood in community has shown that, through the re-claiming and re-orientation of individuals and communities, through theological anthropology practiced and taught by faithful faith communities in these contexts, hope can emerge.

References

Adhikari, Mohamed. 2005. "Contending Approaches to Coloured Identity and the History of the Coloured People of South Africa." *History Compass* 3:1-16.

Adhikari, Mohamed. 2009. "From Narratives of Miscegenation to Post-Modernist Re-Imagining: Towards Historiography of Coloured Identity in South Africa." In *Burdened by Race: Coloured Identities in Southern Africa*, edited by Mohamed Adhikari, 1-22. Lansdowne: UCT Press

Anderson, Ray. 1982. *On Being Human: Essays in Theological Anthropology*. Eerdmans: Grand Rapids.

Bediako, Kwame. 1996. "Theological Reflections." In *Serving the Poor in Africa*, edited by Tetsunao Yamamori, 181-192. Monrovia CA: Marc.

Bowers, Nadine F. 2005. "Development as Transformation: The Local Church in Lavender Hill as an Agent of Change in a Post-Carnegie II Context." DTh dissertation, University of Stellenbosch.

Bowers Du Toit, Nadine F. 2014. "Gangsterism on the Cape Flats: A Challenge to 'engage the powers'." *Teologiese Studies / Theological Studies* 70 (3). doi: 10.4102/hts.v70i3.2727

Bracken, Joseph. A. 2008. "Personhood and Community in new Context." *Horizons* 35 (1): 84-110.

Brueggemann, Walter. 1982. *Living toward a Vision: Biblical Reflections on Shalom*. New York: United Church Press.

Calix, Keith. R. 2013. "Wie is ek? Coloured Identity and Youth Involvement in Gangsterism in Cape Town, South Africa." Senior honours thesis, Stanford University.

Cooper, Adam. 2009. " 'Gevaarlike Transitions': Negotiating Hegemonic Masculinity and Rites of Passage amongst Coloured Boys Awaiting Trial on the Cape Flats." *Psychology in Society* 37 (2009): 1-17.

Daniels, Doria and Quinton Adams. 2010. "Breaking with Township Gangsterism: the Struggle for Place and Voice." *African Studies Quarterly* 11 (4): 45-57.

Dixon, Bill and Lisa-Marie Johns. 2001. "Gangs, Pagad and the State: Vigilantism and Revenge Violence in the Western Cape." *Violence and Transition Series*, Centre for the Study of Violence and Reconciliation. http://scholar.google.co.za/scholar?q=Dixon+%26+Johns+2001&btnG=&hl=en&as_sdt=0%2C5

Hendricks, Cheryl. 2005. "Debating Coloured Identity in the Western Cape." *African Security Review* 14 (4): 117-119.

Kinnes, Irvin. 1996. "The struggle for the Cape Flats." In *Now that we are Free: Coloured communities in a democratic South Africa*, ed. Wilmot Godfrey James, Daria Caliguire and Kerry Cullinan, 16-20. Cape Town: IDASA.

Koopman, Nico. 2007. "Some Theological and Anthropological Perspectives on Human Dignity and Human Rights." *Scriptura* 95: 177-185.

MacMaster, Llewellyn M. 2007. "Social and Economic Emasculation as Contributing Factors to Gangsterism on the Cape Flats." *Scriptura* 95: 278-289.

Myers, Bryant L. 2011. *Walking with the Poor: Principles and Practices of Transformational Development.* Maryknoll: Orbis

Mummenday, Amilie, Thomas Kessler, Andreas Klink, and Rosemarie Mielke. 1999. "Strategies to cope with negative social identity: predictions by Social Identity Theory and Relative Deprivation Theory." *Journal of Personality and Social Psychology* 76 (2): 229-245

Naude, Piet J. 2013. " 'Am I my brother's keeper?' An African Reflection on Humanisation." *Nederduitse Gereformeerde Teologiese Tydskrif* 54 (3-4): 241-253

Petrus, Theodore. 2013. "Social (re) organisation and identity in the coloured street gangs of South Africa." *Southern African Journal of Criminology* 26 (1): 71-84

Petrus, Theodore and Wendy Isaacs-Martin. 2012. "The Multiple Meanings of Coloured Identity in South Africa." *Africa Insight* 42 (1): 87-102

Rubin, Mark and Miles Hewstone. 1998. "Social Identity Theory's Self Esteem Hypothesis: Av Review and Some suggestions for Clarification." *Personality and Social Psychology Review* 2 (1): 40-62.

Ruiters, Michelle. 2009. "Collaboration, Assimilation and Contestation: Emerging Constructions of Coloured Identity in Post-apartheid South Africa." In *Burdened by Race: Coloured Identities in Southern Africa,* edited by Mohammad Adhikari, 104-133. Lansdowne: UCT Press

Sands, Paul. 2010. "The Imago Dei as Vocation." *Evangelical Quarterly.* 82 (1): 28-41

Stets, Jan. E. and Peter I. Burke. 2000. "Identity Theory and Social Identity Theory." *Social Psychology Quarterly* 63 (3): 224-237

Thielicke, Helmut. 1966. "Theological Ethics." In *Volume 1: Foundations,* edited by William H. Lazareth, 151-180. Philadelphia: Fortress Press

Trotter, Henry. 2009. "Trauma and Memory: the Impact of apartheid Era Forced Removals on Coloured Identity in Cape Town." In *Burdened by Race: Coloured Identities in Southern Africa,* edited by Mohammad Adhikari, 49-78. Lansdowne: UCT Press

Webber, Craig. 2007. "Revaluating Relative Deprivation Theory." *Theoretical Criminology* 11 (1): 97-120

Ubuntu or *into*?
South African perspectives on preaching

Johan Cilliers

Abstract

Recognizing the complexity of a pluralistic South African society, and taking our frag-mented history into account, this chapter attempts to identify some ethical movements in preaching in South Africa. A sermon by Dr Koot Vorster (a former moderator of the Dutch Reformed Church) preached in 1971, is presented as an example of an ethics of ex-clusion, and in effect, degrading of human dignity – which could be described by means of the notion of *into*. Furthermore, cognisance is taken of a historical sermon by Arch-bishop Desmond Tutu, preached three days before the first democratic elections in South Africa (27 April 1994), as representative of the ideal of *ubuntu*, with ethics of inclusion, and the fostering of human dignity. The paper concludes with a discussion of two South African artworks, created respectively by the well-known protest artist, Willie Bester, as well as by an unknown, so-called "pavement" artist.

Ubuntu into *into* ?

The concept of *ubuntu*, although somewhat elusive, has become well-known all over the world as being typical of African, and more specifically, South African culture (cf. Punt 2004, 88). Welile Mazamisa claims that *ubuntu* "defies all man-ner of definition because it is the very essence of being-in-the-world" (Mazamisa 1995, 18). It is impossible to do justice to the richness of the concept of *ubuntu* within the limitations of this paper (cf. Cilliers 2010, 77-78). It has been described as a way of life, a universal truth, an expression of human dignity, an underpin-ning of the concept of an open society, African humanism, trust, helpfulness, re-spect, sharing, caring, community, and unselfishness. In short, it means *humanity*, or*humanness*. It stems from the belief that one is a human being through others – "I am because you are" (cf. Ramose 1999, 49-50; Shutte 1993, 46; Van Binsbergen 2003, 428). Etymologically speaking, the term *ubuntu* comes from the Zulu and Sotho versions of a traditional African aphorism, often translated as "A person is a person through other persons:" *Umuntu ngumuntu ngabantu. Motho ke motho ka batho. Ubuntu* is a combination of *ubu* and *ntu* – the latter being a common root in most Sub-Saharan African languages, resulting in variations such as *shintu, muntu, Bantu, wuntu, kantu, buntu,* etc. *Ntu* as such simply means "human."

Our relatively peaceful political transition in 1994, viewed by many as a miracle, could be ascribed *inter alia* to the African sense of *ubuntu*. This brought an end to the times when people were stripped of their dignity and had to use *ubulwane* (animal-like behavior) to uphold the laws of apartheid (cf. Cilliers 2015, 216). According to Maphisa "The transformation of an apartheid South Africa into a democracy is a rediscovery of *Ubuntu*" (Maphisa 1994, 8). The spirit of *ubuntu* has undoubtedly helped us, specifically in the sphere of *reconciliation*. In short: without *ubuntu*, there would probably be no "new South Africa." However, on the other hand, it is also well-known, that the notion of *ubuntu* has drawn its fair share of reservations, and even outright criticism (cf. Mdluli 1986, 60-77). *Ubuntu* could also be, and has often been, romanticised or used to promote political and exclusivist positions that function as a sort of ostracising and populist ideology (cf. Van Binsbergen 2003, 450). It could serve as a useful, but premature, pacifier. Worst of all: it may be distorted, specifically in the South African context, to legitimise a new form of "apartheid" or ethnocracy or pigmentocracy, in which culture or race or ethnicity draws new, or redraws old, boundaries between the diversity of people that constitute our society.

In this chapter I will not endeavour to describe the characteristics or shortcomings of *ubuntu* – this has been done adequately by countless scholars – but rather indicate how it has been articulated and embodied in a historic sermon by Archbishop Desmond Tutu. Before doing so, however, I venture to add a few comments on the notion of *into* – a notion that is perhaps not that well-known, but which could be seen as the direct opposite of *ubuntu. Into* literally means "a thing." Some African initiation rituals act out the metamorphosis from being an "it" (not yet a person) into being a member of society, of being a person within humanity. In the African context the reality of becoming a person through other persons is constituted through these ceremonies and specifically initiation rituals: "Before being incorporated into the body of persons through this route, one is regarded merely as an 'it', i.e. not yet a person. Not all human beings are therefore persons" (Louw 2002, 8). The opposite is also true: once you become severed from the community, or distance yourself from the community, you no longer belong to humanity, and in a sense become a thing without humanness. Then you have a movement from *ntu* (the root word for human) into *into*.

I want to argue that South Africa is once again going through such a movement from *Ubu-ntu* into *Into*, in which people often treat one another not as human beings, but as things – knowing quite well that such an argument could be contentious and indeed one-sided. It could even be construed as a typically Western construct or projection. A stark reminder of at least our capability of practicing *into*, rather than *ubuntu*, is the widespread xenophobic attacks that recently took place in South Africa. Already in 2008, and again in 2015, South Africa has been plagued by unprecedented and widespread incidents of xenophobia. It seems as though, at least under certain circumstances, people are no longer viewed as *people*, but as commodities, as irritating and threatening objects, as *things*. These and other incidents seem to suggest that *ubuntu* is being shattered and fragmented by, and into, *into*. Certain social phenomena in present-day South Africa could indeed be viewed from this perspective: the alarming crime statistics, with some accounts of unspeakable brutality, and literally thousands of people being murdered per annum; the stigmatisation flowing from HIV and AIDS; the reality of poverty, in which poor, homeless people are often still treated as less than human.

How should we understand these perversities taking place in our society, renowned for its spirit of *ubuntu*? Perhaps we have underestimated the devastating impact of apartheid on this society, even up to now. Perhaps we did not bury racism deep enough – and now we see resurrections of it everywhere. Three hundred years of racism cannot be obliterated within the very short time span of twenty or thirty years. Perhaps we have even misused the notion of *ubuntu*, also pursued by the Truth and Reconciliation Commission, as a premature pacifier, which has had the ultimate effect of creating a spirit of denial among us, as Van Binsbergen (2003, 451) claims.

This phenomenon of treating fellow human beings as *into* is nothing new: under apartheid different forms of *dehumanising-into-into* were practiced and indeed officially legitimised. *Ubulwane* (animal-like behavior) was ingrained into our DNA. Perhaps this is why it is still with us, and very much alive. In a recent survey, conducted in Gauteng, the economical heartland of South Africa, it was found that the level of trust between black people and white people in South Africa is diminishing year after year. The GCRO – a partnership between the University of Johannesburg, the University of the Witwatersrand, the Gauteng government, and the SA Local Government Association – conducted this study with over 25 000 people to gauge satisfaction levels with governance in Gauteng province. Other surveys seem to confirm these sentiments (cf. Lefko-Everett et al. 2011).

Obviously many reasons why we are still battling against the syndrome of *into* could be listed. However, the question that I would like to pose here is, to what extent can the tendency towards *into* be traced back to certain forms of "apartheid preaching" that not only perpetuated the ideology of apartheid, but in fact also created the syndrome of *into*? In short, to what extent was *into* created and perpetuated from Christian pulpits?

Preaching *into*

I restrict myself to one rather blatant example of preaching from the apartheid era in this regard. In a sense, this sermon by Dr J.D. (Koot) Vorster on Psalm 62:6 – published in *Die Kerkbode*[1] on the 26th of May 1971 – speaks for itself. Some quotes from the closing paragraphs of the sermon follow:

In these hours of crisis in their existence, the nation of South Africa must expect much from God. We must not have our view obstructed by powerful enemies, but must focus on the Almighty. We must have great expectations of God and must be alive in faith.

And, on the road of South Africa, there are beacons of light as symbols of glorious victory, because our people expected everything of God.

In an alien, wild country, at the beginning of the people's settlement, Jan van Riebeeck brought a dark Africa before God in prayer, and Africa opened up for the Gospel and civilisation.

Farmers moved into a cruel and wild country where predators and barbarians were a dangerous threat, but, in lonely farmhouses, the Word of the Lord saved a nation from being frightened away.

In very dark moments – Vegkop, Marico, Blood River – a small nation just trusted in God, and, for God, a small minority was a majority.

In their struggle for freedom, a courageous nation lost, but, in their defeat, they became silent before God and placed their expectation only on Him. A free, united nation grew from the remaining stump.

And now again, the people of South Africa must expect much from God. Our Father never gives his children a stone when they ask for bread. 'Seek the kingdom of God and his justice and all these things will also be given to you.'

In prayer and witnessing about the Lord, expect a renewal of his church.

Pray that the Word of God will be proclaimed with power and that our people will act righteously, will consider love and walk humbly with God.

Then the Lord will be our shield and fortress in the struggle.

Then a beautiful future will be our destiny and our people will also be able to provide leadership in the world.

We must expect also this from the Lord – that when the hour comes for our nation to provide leadership – and it will come; that we will then provide leadership according to the guidance of the great Leader who leads all things to a triumphant end.

The God of heaven will make us happy, and we, his servants, will prepare and build.

Just be quiet before God, my soul, because my expectation is on Him –

Amen.

---

[1]   Official Journal of the Dutch Reformed Church in South Africa (trans. Cilliers 2006, 35ff).

The first paragraph begins with an exclusive claim, namely, that there is no other "nation of South Africa" except the Afrikaner nation (later on called "the people of South Africa"), followed by the imperative flowing from the national history, emphasised by "must" no less than five times in this short paragraph. For this, the "beacons of light" on "the road of South Africa" offer encouragement. Even more important: the nation's historical performances become the most profound basis and reason for the glorious victories in South Africa: because this "small nation just trusted in God." The nation's history itself becomes the *source* of the revelation ("beacons of light"), becomes revelatory history; it operates as the *norma normata* according to which the South African history, and eventually also the future, is to be judged.

The point of departure is this: previously, the whole nation was for God (trusting "just" and "only" in God, without exception), therefore God was for the whole nation. The people's religious standards of performance ensured their triumph. This is spelled out with the assistance of four reminders of the forefathers' performance, and described in such legendary and idyllic terms, that the fathers become people without shadows, a great crowd of national witnesses, as it were, who must inspire the present generation.

First, Jan van Riebeeck breaks open a "dark Africa" with his prayer "for the Gospel and civilisation." His pious prayer in fact acts as the conduit that brings light (salvation, civilisation) into the darkness of Africa – a light which was presumably previously not there.

Second, the farmers move into "a cruel and wild country," peacefully residing "in lonely farm houses," contemplating "the Word of the Lord." These pious actions stand in strong contrast to the threat by the combination (!) of "predators and barbarians." In effect, the indigenous people ("barbarians") are seen as less than human, as being on the same level as the wild animals ("predators"). Posed as an opposite to this, the preacher speaks about "the beginning of the people's settlement" taking place "in an alien and wild country…" One could indeed ask whether there were no "people" there before the "settlement?"

Third, dark moments of the national history ("Vegkop, Marico, Blood River") are lined up and the national idyll repeated: not only did the nation expect "everything" of God, but also "trusted only in God." "Everything" and "only" means their dedication was complete.

Fourth, as a consequence of this unblemished devotion they therefore had the ability to again place their expectation "only" on God after their defeat in the freedom struggle against the British. This expectation caused their so impressive growth that the preacher can validate it with a prophetic word: "A free, united nation grew from the remaining stump" (cf. Isa 11:1).

The preacher then uses these historical "beacons of light" as the basis for the imperative of the national legend, and states: "And now again, the people of South Africa must expect much from God." Again, we hear what "we" "must" do.

For instance, as an ethnic body, the people must, "In prayer and witnessing about the Lord, expect a renewal of his church;" the people's prayer and witness must allow the church to relive. This is possible because the people are "children" of "our Father." The people's prayer acts as the condition for the Lord to ensure the future, so that He will be the "shield and fortress in the struggle" – against other nations (with emphasis: "Then...then..."). This is also the condition for the nation to "provide leadership in the world." Here the idyll reaches its apex; it becomes a fantasy of omnipotence: the nation definitely will be the world leader ("and it will come"). For this, he needs a triumphant example, that the preacher does not name ("the great Leader"), but infers Christ. Christ becomes the example for the nation on the basis of the pious performance of the nation and with the view to the consolidation and stabilisation of this piety.

If I understood it correctly, this sermon does not so much interpret the Bible text (Ps 62:6) and respectively proclaim the Gospel to the congregation, but proclaims the national history as legend and idyll to the people. This forms the actual text, and actual gospel of the sermon. In the process, all that fall outside of this legend are dehumanised, in fact changed into *into*. Those that do not form part of "the people of South Africa," are stereotyped as "barbarians" (in the past) or as enemies against which one must "struggle" (the present and future). There is obviously a *struggle* going on here, for which the legend of the "people" forms the basis, and also provides a (pious) imperative.

Retrospectively we could say that one of the driving forces behind sermons like these was the experience of threat, resulting in fear. As a psychological phenomenon, fear is not as evident as, for example, the explicit articulation of threat in the sermons, and yet, without doubt, it plays a decisive role. In a certain sense, it can even be regarded as the *heuristic principle*, as the factor that opens the mouths of preachers and forces the nation to listen with new attention. This determines the sermons' foundational structure in the sense that everything possible is done to counteract this fear. The one pole in the sermons is the detailed description of the threat; the other is the "solutions" that are presented. This takes place within the field of fear and tension.

One of the characteristics of fear is that it can cause a variety of reactions. For example, in situations of fear, *defensives* can be built up aimed to protect one's own existence. This can stretch from primitive reactions to nuanced mechanisms. A common phenomenon is that fear about guilt, or better: the fear about the consequences of own guilt is replaced by fear about the impact of something external and threatening (Cilliers 2006, 75). Guilt fear becomes fate fear. This applies not only to individual behavioral patterns, but also to society. *Collective* guilt is suppressed by finding a communal external cause for the very circumstances in which those who are involved and responsible or co-responsible find themselves. With the assistance of social behavioral patterns, guilt is worked away and removed from the system (Mitscherlich 1967, 21). However, in this way, fear may be replaced, but it is not removed. It continues to influence, no matter how strenuous the attempts to eliminate it.

Admitted, superficially, fear seems like a significant factor. For example, it can be a powerful social manipulator that can be applied to keep masses in check or to induce them to move, especially if it deals with primeval anxiety for extinction. *Yet, in my opinion, fear is dangerous, perhaps even more dangerous than hatred.* On the basis of fear, appeals bring about little true change, and rather create sensitivity for new fears. Ethical action manipulated through fear, does not last long. On the contrary, it forms a destructive cycle that is extremely difficult to break through. The fear that should have been stilled becomes intensified. The longer the fear is kept alive, the more active it becomes, and the more it dims the view on reality and the possibility to co-operate in the transformation of this reality.

Preaching *ubuntu*

The opposite of *into* is *ubuntu*. Although *ubuntu* as an African cultural expression could strictly speaking not be called "theology," there are many prominent theologians who interpret this concept in theological terms. Desmond Tutu, for instance, has developed and practiced what could be called a "theology of *ubuntu*." In fact, Tutu's theology must be viewed through the lens of *ubuntu*, because according to him we can be human only in community, in *koinonia*, in peace (Battle 1997, 5). Tutu's theology is probably one of the most representative expressions of African *ubuntu*. For Tutu, *ubuntu* has a profound theological meaning, because God has created us to need each other. We are made to be part of a "delicate network of interdependence" (Tutu 1994, 261).

We see something of this spirit of *ubuntu* in a moving and historical sermon by Archbishop Desmond Tutu, preached three days before the first democratic elections in South Africa (27 April 1994). He takes his cue from Psalm 77:14 ("You are a God that works wonders"), and speaks about "The God of surprises, the God who lets miracles unfold before our eyes" (Tutu 1994, 261). In this sermon, fear is substituted by joy, by amazement – Tutu starts his sermon, characteristically, with a *Wow!* And ends of with a *Hey!* Amongst other things, he states:

The Cross is God's mark of the depth of his love for us, for you, for me… You are very special to God. You are of infinite worth to God… Each one of us is of infinite worth because God loves each one of us, black and white, with his infinite, everlasting love…

There is life after April 28. We are all wounded people, traumatised, all of us, by the evil of apartheid. We all need healing and we, the Church of God, must pour balm on the wounds inflicted by this evil system. Let us be channels of love, of peace, of justice, of reconciliation. Let us declare that we have been made for togetherness, we have been made for family, that, yes, now we are free, all of us, black and white together, we, the Rainbow People of God! (Tutu 1994, 261-262)

Could one find a starker contrast than between the apartheid sermon quoted above, and this utterance of Tutu? The former separates; the latter celebrates. The one fights against the exposure to the so-called "enemy;" the other stands in awe of our diversity. The one divides; the other is amazed. It is on these grounds – the all-inclusive pathos of God for all human beings, irrespective of whom they are, or where, particularly in the South African context – that Tutu says "must" as an ethical appeal to the church to "pour balm on the wounds inflicted by this evil system." It is from this basis – the inter-dependence of human beings, as envisioned by his *ubuntu*-theology – that Tutu calls for a new "struggle," not against a stereotyped "enemy," but to heal the wounded.

This represents an ethics not of fear for the enemy, or a heuristic syndrome of anxiety, but rather acceptance, but even stronger than that, *an ethics of celebration* of the so-called "other." Fear indeed does not transform anybody, at least not fundamentally, and not in the long run; awe and celebration invite one into a world that is not threatening. This mode of ethics is no whip, chasing people into an enclosure; it rather is a hand, beckoning. It indicates a world, an alternative, of which one could voluntarily say: this is where I want to be; in this space I long to live.

Tutu ends his sermon with the following paragraph:

And let us make a success of this democracy. And we are going to make it. For we have a tremendous country, with tremendous people. Our God, who makes all things new, will make us a new people, a new united people in a new South Africa. And when we make it – not if but when we make it – it will be because God wants us to succeed, for we will be a paradigm for the rest of the world, showing them how to solve similar problems. Hey, if God be for us who can be against us! (Tutu 1994, 262-263)

This is truly remarkable. Both Dr Koot Vorster and Archbishop Desmond Tutu envisage that South Africa will become a leader in the world, a paradigm worthwhile following. As a matter of fact, both stress that it is *inevitable* that it will happen. Compare these utterances:

Then a beautiful future will be our destiny and our people will also be able to provide *leadership in the world*...We must expect also this from the Lord–that when the hour comes for our nation to provide leadership – *and it will come*; that we will then provide leadership according to the guidance of the great Leader who leads all things to a triumphant end (Vorster; emphasis added).

And when we make it – *not if but when we make it* – it will be because God wants us to succeed, for we will be *a paradigm for the rest of the world*, showing them how to solve similar problems (Tutu; emphasis added)

Vorster grounds his claims on exclusivity; Tutu argues from the basis of inclusivity. Vorster separates the pious "people" inside the nation's circle from the "less-than-people" – the "barbarians" – outside this circle; Tutu includes those outside and those inside the circle in the reciprocity of embracement, and declares that "... we have been made for family, that, yes, now we are free, all of us, black and white together, we, the Rainbow People of God!"

In 1971 Koot Vorster told us that the "people" will provide leadership in the world; in 1994 Desmond Tutu was of firm conviction that the "Rainbow People" will be a paradigm for the rest of the world. The lingering question in 2015 is: what type of "leader" will we in fact be, if any? What 'paradigm' will we embody, as the future unfolds...? Will we fall from *ubuntu* into *into*; or will *into* be conquered by *ubuntu*? I do not know.

I leave you with two art works by South African artists – art works that depict both these possibilities in an aesthetically moving manner.

The first is a chilling expression of our capability towards *into* in an art installation by Willie Bester, one of South Africa's most prominent protest artists. In this work, created in 2001 and entitled *Who Let The Dogs Out,* he depicts an incident during which a police dog unit (six policemen) "used" three illegal immigrants for the purposes of dog training: the dogs were simply let loose on the unprotected immigrants in a space from which they could not escape (Bester 2001). Dare I say: the "predators" were incited to attack the "barbarians?" Even more appalling: one of the policemen took a video-clip of the whole incident, showing in explicit detail the mauling and wounding of the men. Bester incorporated this voyeuristic element into his artwork. One could say: the policemen turned their faces away from (the humanness) of the other, and the effect was the face that can be seen in Bester's depiction, the face of a human being that is being mauled by a dog – a human being who has been degraded into a *thing*.

The notion of *ubuntu* is sensitively depicted in an "African crucifixion" scene by an unknown African artist, sold on a pavement in Cape Town (Louw 2014, 42). A community surrounds the dying Christ; He is encircled by people. As a matter of fact, this composition is all about circles. Even the circle of the clock above Christ's head indicates a different, communal understanding of time. The circular light, shining from behind the head of the Crucified, nullifies all notions of a "dark Africa." On the contrary, life – that which the dying Christ offers – is emphasised by communality, by the embracement of encircling, by *ubuntu*.

Figure 1

Figure 2

I repeat: will we fall from *ubuntu* into *into*; or will *into* be conquered by *ubuntu*?

Ubuntu or *into*? I do not know.

References

Battle, Michael. 1997. *Reconciliation: The Ubuntu Theology of Desmond Tutu*. Cleveland: Pilgrim.

Bester, Willie. 2001. *Who let the dogs out?* Metal sculpture. Goodman Gallery, South Africa.

Cilliers, Johan. 2006. *God for us? An Analysis and Assessment of Dutch Reformed Preaching During the apartheid Years*. Stellenbosch: Sun Press.

Cilliers, Johan. 2010. "In Search of Meaning Between Ubuntu and Into: Perspectives on Preaching in Post-apartheid South Africa." In *Preaching: Does It Make a Difference? Studia Homiletica 7*, edited by Mogens Lindhardt and Henning Thomsen, 77-78. Frederiksberg: Aros Vorlag.

Cilliers, Johan. 2015. "The Role of the Eucharist in Human Dignity: a South African Story." In *Religion and Human Rights. Global Challenges from Intercultural Perspectives*, edited by Wilhelm Gräb and Lars Charbonnier, 201-220. Berlin: De Gruyter.

Lefko-Everett, Kate, Ayanda Nyoka and Lucia Tiscornia, eds. 2011. *The South African Reconciliation Barometer Survey: 2011 Report*. Cape Town: Institute for Justice and Reconciliation.

Louw, Daniël J. 2002. *Ubuntu: And The Challenge of Multiculturalism in Post-apartheid South Africa*. Utrecht: Zuidam and Uithof.

Louw, Daniël J. 2014. *Icons. Imaging the Unseen. On Beauty and Healing of Life, Body and Soul*. Stellenbosch: Sun Press.

Maphisa, Sisho. 1994. *Man in Constant Search of Ubuntu: A Dramatist's Obsession*. Pietermaritzburg: University of Natal, AIDSA.

Mazamisa, Welile. 1995. "Re-reading the Bible in the Black Church: Towards a Hermeneutic of Orality and Literacy," *Journal of Black Theology in South Africa* 9 (2): 1-22.

Mdluli, Praisley. 1986. "Ubuntu-Botho: Inkatha's 'People Education.' " *Transformation*. 5: 60–77.

Mitscherlich, Alexander and Margarete Mitscherlich, 1967. *Die Unfähigkeit zu trauern. Grundlagen kollektiven Verhaltens*. München: Piper Verlag.

Punt, Jeremy. 2004. "Value of Ubuntu for Reading the Bible in Africa." In *Text and Context in New Testament Hermeneutics*, edited by Jesse Ndwiga Kanyua Mugambi and Johannes A. Smit, 88-107. Nairobi: Acton.

Ramose, Mogobe B. 1999. *African Philosophy through Ubuntu*. Harare: Mond Books.

Shutte, Augustine. 1993. *Philosophy for Africa*. Rondebosch, South Africa: UCT Press.

Tutu, Desmond. 1994. *The Rainbow People of God: The Making of a Peaceful Revolution*. Edited by John Allen. New York: Doubleday.

Tutu, Desmond. 2011. *God is not a Christian. Speaking Truth in Times of Crisis*. London: Rider.

Van Binsbergen, Wim M. J. 2003. *Intercultural Encounters, African and Anthropological Lessons Towards a Philosophy of Interculturality*. Münster: Lit Verlag.

Ubuntu and interconnected personhood: A practical-theological reflection

Fritz de Wet

Abstract

In the post-apartheid landscape, much was expected from *"ubuntu"* as a concept that could potentially be embraced by all South Africans to realise the dream of a "rainbow nation." However, an analysis of the different notions South Africans have of the role of *ubuntu* has revealed a complex tension that indicates that the ideal of interconnected life and a dignified space for all, seems to be more elusive than was anticipated. The aim of the chapter is to contribute, from a practical-theological perspective, to an understanding of these underlying complexities. A large percentage of South Africans are Christians. The chapter aims to open up possibilities of interconnected personhood from the vantage point of all being members of the body of Christ. It traces the progression from "I think, therefore I am" to "I participate, therefore I am" to "in Christ I give myself to others, therefore I am."

Introduction

In the post-apartheid landscape much was expected of *ubuntu* as an expression of a dignified life, an interconnected personhood, in which all could share and that could unify South Africans to truly becoming a "rainbow nation" (Tshawane 2009). Because practical theology is interested in understanding the heart of human actions, and *ubuntu* expresses the very soul of Africa, the differences in how this key concept of personhood and interconnectedness is understood, its unifying potential and possible religious undertones will be explored. Though *ubuntu* is virtually universal to the African context, it meaning and function are not understood the same by all. The popularity of *ubuntu* has resulted in it becoming "anything to anyone who so wishes to deploy it" (Matolino 2013, 197-205). South Africans tend to deploy either in an inclusive or in an exclusive way. For South Africans of European descent, the question is whether they, who have their roots in the highly structured categories of Western thinking and individualism, can truly grasp the soul of *ubuntu*. Can *ubuntu* be taken as point of departure when their aim is critical correlative and integrative communication with fellow South-Africans from different backgrounds?

The richness of *ubuntu* is first explored for its potential to create a sense of interconnectedness. The process of developing personhood takes place in the context of an increasingly unequal and polarised South African society. This reflection is followed by a brief analysis of the different notions of *ubuntu* and their role in defining the interconnectedness of life. Contrasting notions of *ubuntu* contribute to creating a chasm between those who hold inclusive and those who hold exclusive views. Both the reflection and the analysis provide insight. Thirdly, we will explore the contribution of practical theology with its theological vantage point on the depth level of human actions, towards better understanding and possibly changing the disintegrative dynamics of this concept. The article concludes with a theological exploration of the role of Christian communities who understand and put into practice what it means to be members of the body of Christ. In this way they can imagine a kind of *ubuntu* that transcends the disintegrative and exclusivist forces in contemporary South African society.

Ubuntu, belonging and rootedness

The term *ubuntu*, traditionally used throughout Sub-Saharan Africa, defines people's behavior and interaction. Togetherness is central. People see themselves as members of an interconnected community. In post-apartheid South Africa, *ubuntu* has gained prominence due to its use by Desmond Tutu (1999), as well as the role envisioned for it by business leaders, academics and the South African Constitutional Court. This role entails the creation of a sense of committed participation and belonging in the reconciliatory and restorative actions that are so vital to the construction of a post-segregation society (Taylor 2014, 331-345). A deep sense of interconnectedness lies at the heart of *ubuntu*. The ancient Zulu people believed that persons and their environment were inseparable. *Ulutho* (the nameless substance in which reality is rooted), *uluntu* (the vital force that emanates from the environment), *umuntu* (the person), *isintu* (humanity) and *ubuntu* (the art of being human) are all derived from the root word *ntu* meaning "inseparably interconnected" (Bhengu 1996). The element of connectedness with the living environment implies a perpetual fellowship with the whole lineage of humanity. This includes fellowship with the living, the dead (ancestors) and those yet to be born. To an "African mind", humans are who they are because of their attitude to the mysterious depths of life, symbolised by birth and death, harvest and famine, ancestors and the unborn (Makumba 2007).

This interconnected worldview is deeply rooted in religious experience. African religion functions as a way of interpreting the world and understanding existence. To be human, is to belong to a community and participate in its beliefs, rituals and religious festivals. To many if not most in the Western, the Nguni phrase *umuntu ngumuntu ngabantu* ("a person is a person through other persons") does not have obvious religious connotations. At face value it seems no more than an African form of humanism: to treat others with dignity. However, these words transcend the here and now in African traditions. "A person is a person through other persons" ultimately has to do with achieving the stature of an ancestor beyond this earthly dimension. Dying is a homecoming, finding a permanent residence and a revered dignity, being permanently connected to life in its reciprocal beauty (see Louw 2001, 15-36). The question is to what extent *ubuntu*, with its deep reverence for interconnected life, can play an integrative role in a polarised society with its ever increasing gap between rich and poor, and its divisions caused by disillusionment, distrust and the threat of violence.

Conceptualisations of *ubuntu*

Different conceptualisations of *ubuntu* lead to different expectations with regard to how interconnected life among South Africans of different backgrounds can develop. When such conceptualisations become polarised, a disintegrative tension results. Reflection on the dynamics of this tension requires a discussion of both inclusive and exclusive views of *ubuntu*.

Inclusive views

An inclusive view of *ubuntu* could imply that all South Africans, irrespective of their past or roots, are part of the interconnectedness of human society and therefore have the potential to share in and act according to the spirit of *ubuntu*. apartheid as a political system deliberately prevented social cohesion. The post-apartheid democratic dispensation is based on the constitutional value of non-discrimination. Policies are intended to foster reconciliation and uphold the rights and dignity of all citizens.

Ubuntu can play a critical role in South Africans achieving a common understanding *vis-à-vis* constitutional values (Letseka 2012, 48). To understand *ubuntu* as interconnected life, personhood validated in harmonious and respectful relationships, and a shared identity based on goodwill (see Metz 2007, 331-335), has unifying potential. The growth and well-being of people depends upon relations with others. In this sense, *ubuntu* becomes a matter of life and death. It resonates with the very essence of being human. Participation in the spirit of *ubuntu* brings people in touch with the essence of their humanity. Then they can say: "I am human because I belong" (Tutu 1999, 34).

However, such an inclusive view of *ubuntu* is challenged by some. The ideal of a harmonious society has not been realised in the twenty years since the dream of the rainbow nation was born. The question is whether South Africans anchored in patterns of Western thinking are able to connect with *ubuntu* at the depth level of interrelations. Do South Africans of European descent simply see *ubuntu* as an easy way of benefiting from the goodwill of fellow South Africans without truly sharing their own lives and resources with their fellow humans under the African sun. The attempt to transpose an African notion such as *ubuntu* to a Western mindset often means taking something concrete and make it into something abstract. This is not entirely viable (Letseka 2012, 51; cf. Tutu 1999, 34). With regard to the development of personhood, Western thought patterns determine the interpretation of interconnected life, relationships and the collective. Rooted in the Greek idea of human beings as rational animals, Western thinking tends to see human beings as transcending the rest of the world and therefore entitled to exercise creative power over it. When humans intentionally choose to do something they deem worthwhile, they are self-determining, free from outside influence. Of course social forces do play a role, but not a decisive one (Shutte 1993, 11).

In Cartesian thinking, individual human beings exist prior to and independent of the community or society. Community is composed of individual members. This is the exact opposite of an African view of the relationships between individuals and the community (Louw 2001, 24). *Ubuntu*, rooted in an African way of thinking, unites the self and the world in a web of reciprocal relations. The subject and object become indistinguishable. The Western idea of "I think, therefore I am" is well translated in Africa as "I participate, therefore I am." The one emphasises individuals through whom communities are formed. The other emphasises communities through which individuals exist (Shutte 1993).

From Western perspectives there is no easy entry into *ubuntu*-thinking. The possibility of a paradigm-switch by means of interactive dialogue in the dynamic field of intercultural hermeneutics (see Louw 2011, 173-192) may be more difficult to achieve than was initially anticipated. Moving from autonomous individuality emphasising self-culture to interconnectedness where freedom-based independence and community-based dependence are not seen as irreconcilable opposites (see Hankela 2014) is a difficult divide to cross.

Exclusive views

An exclusive view is that only some *homo sapiens* become persons in the *ubuntu*-sense of the word. In traditional African thinking, *homo sapiens* are not persons at birth, but become a person. In order to become a person, a human individual goes through various stages as prescribed by the community. They take part in ceremonies and rituals. Only on completion of all of this, do they acquire the status of persons. Prior to these ceremonies and rituals, individuals are regarded as nonentities. They are not yet incorporated into the body of persons. Personhood can, therefore, be described as an acquired state (Ramose 1999). *Ubuntu* is the self-realisation of persons when they manifest as human beings. People can achieve *ubuntu* when they exhibit humane and respectful behavior, or lose it if they do not. Those who exhibit inhumane behavior are seen as less than human (Hankela 2014, 52). People who have not achieved *ubuntu* are regarded as outsiders. Non-Xhosa speakers, for example, are called *Intlanga* (persons of another nation) or *Makwerekwere* (outsiders or barbarians). Strangers are not accorded full humanity, since they do not fulfill the normative criteria of that specific ethnic community (see Eze 2010). An exclusive mindset brings with it the danger that outsiders can be treated as non-humans. Generally, however, *ubuntu* is accommodating. Those who genuinely want to be part of a community, should not be rejected. They should then be ready to accept the privileges as well as the responsibilities of being part of a family or a community (Hankela 2014, 59).

It is understandable that an exclusive view can develop when people are disillusioned because of the repeated exploitative and dehumanising behaviour of colonial powers and the apartheid regime. The reason why white people are sometimes labeled "not human" (*makgoa ga se batho*) and therefore cannot participate in *ubuntu*, comes from a history of prolonged racial oppression. The oppressed people cannot believe that human beings are capable of treating others like that.

However, the question is whether those who see others as unworthy of participating in *ubuntu* have the right to treat them as non-persons. Would that not be inhumane behavior that would render the people themselves inhuman? When faced with a plurality of cultures and the unhappy history that resulted from the contact between them, people often resort to an absolutism in their assessment of the other. By definition, absolutism is a violation of the self-understanding of others. It manifests itself in a colonising hegemony. One example of this is when Western norms were forced onto "undeveloped" African minds. Another example is tribal conformity to group loyalty that brushes off all external critique of nepotism, for instance, as the arrogant and unfounded remarks of nonpersons who do not understand the idea of a living community (cf. Louw 2001, 16). An exclusive view of *ubuntu* is confined to the in-group. It distinguishes between "those who are part of us and those who are not." In a post-apartheid context, that could set in motion another vicious cycle of nationalistic exclusivity. A qualification that prevents those who are not members of a particular group to be part of the inner circle, has proved to be corruptive and destructive in the contemporary African socio-political imagination. It can be used as the justification for corruption and ethnic-based dictatorships in some post-colonial systems. In its worst form, it can lead to ethnic cleansing, as evidenced in Burundi and Rwanda (Eze 2010, 255; cf. Hankela 2014, 59).

A practical-theological contribution

To what extent can practical theology, as a discipline that purposefully engages with the depth level of the tension fields in human interaction, contribute to an understanding of and engagement with the complexities in this tension field? It is the nature of practical theology to problematise a particular religious community's understanding of the prevalent dynamics and of its involvement in particular situations. Understanding moves beyond surface meanings to uncover the depth level of social dynamics that may unwittingly be the cause of dehumanising behaviours which lead to estrangement, disillusionment, oppression, discord and disconnectedness. At the same time, a religious community's understanding of its own intended role and impact on its surrounding social space can be protected from oversimplification (Osmer 2014, 61-78). By acquiring sensitivity for the social dynamics in a particular society and its history, a religious community can refrain from repeating the colonialising and dehumanising patterns of the past. Through a process of critical reflection, practical theologians seek ways to faithful practice and authentic human living.

The focus of practical theology is not limited to intra-human and inter-human behaviour. It is particularly concerned with the religious dimensions of lived life. Purposeful life, beautiful life, ethical life, dignified life, graceful life and connected life are anchored in the relationship with the Divine. Contours of lived human experiences are viewed in relation to theological issues that play a role in faithful practices and authentic human living. These include questions regarding the transcendence and immanence of God, the problem of evil and suffering, the relationship between divine grace and human responsibility, power structures, transformation and the eschatological dimension (cf. Cahalan and Mikoski 2014, 5). Practical theology is deployed at the interface between God's self-revelation in Christ and the actions of the faith community, which is constantly in need of deepening its faithful participation in God's redemptive practices in and for the world (Swinton and Mowat 2006). Through a process of critical reflection on situations and the action fields embedded in these situations, practical theologians seek to point towards faithful practices and authentic human living in the light of God, the source of and criterion for faithfulness and authenticity.

True to the gospel of Jesus Christ, practical theology can play a "servant role", in that tension that exists among the different conceptualisations of *ubuntu*. It aims to function as a catalyst for a faithful and authentic communal life in which all South Africans can find the deepest roots of their interconnected personhood as human beings. Where the Spirit of Jesus Christ is present, one opinion preferred by a certain group that marginalises or dominates others, will not prevail. Where the Word of Christ, Mediator of the New Covenant, is ministered, all members of that community will potentially be united. It is about being what they are destined to be, rather than being forcefully shaped into something they are not, something that is foreign to their identity and beliefs, both of which are rooted in a specific environment. An attitude of servanthood under the guidance of the Spirit of Christ will keep what Osmer calls the normative task of practical theology from becoming an alternative kind of colonialism. Such a form of colonialism could, for example, result in African theologians and church leaders thinking that their insights are inferior and that they should adopt Western categories and methods in order to ensure credibility (see Lartey 2013).

The body of Christ and interconnected personhood

The question is to what extent Christian communities as the body of Christ can contribute to some measure of consensus on what connected humanity and its wholesome effect on the quality of life could mean. Rather than insisting on one's own preferred interpretation of *ubuntu* with the focus on self-preservation (e.g., committing to *ubuntu* only in as far as it can enrich myself or bring stability to my life), Christian communities as the body of Christ should adopt the selfless attitude of Christ. Such a mindset could lead to a different idea of what *ubuntu* is meant to be.

Before this is explored further, the problem of how an atomistic, Western interpretation of the body of Christ was imposed on people with an African mindset, should be considered. When African people were first introduced to the idea of the body of Christ it was interpreted by Western Christian missionaries. Missionary activity coincided with the advent of colonialism, which engendered conformity. Against this background the idea of the body of Christ was received as a *Fremdkörper* in the African world. Can this idea contribute in a meaningful way to rethinking the meaning and implementation of *ubuntu* today?

In a survey on how African scholars deployed the metaphor of the church as the body of Christ in the context of HIV and AIDS (see Van Klinken 2008, 319-336), two predominant conceptualisations and a third less pronounced notion were found. The first is about the *likeness to Christ*. A church that claims to be the body of Christ should demonstrate the care and compassion of Christ, especially toward the marginalised of society. By doing so, they continue the work of Christ. The second is about the church as a manifestation of *the presence of Christ*. Here the emphasis shifts from the church imitating Jesus Christ to Christ manifesting himself through the church. The healing church becomes a concrete manifestation of the healing presence and deeds of Christ in a time of crisis. A third notion does not equate the body of Christ primarily with the actual institutional church. Rather, the body of Christ is understood in a way that is critical of the institutional church. From the metaphor "body of Christ" and the parable in Matthew 25:31-46, it is argued that the church of Christ is found where Christ is encountered, namely *in the least ones*, in the faces of the poor, the hungry, the sick and in those who live with HIV and AIDS. The "poor" cannot be reduced to the object of the church's compassion. Any dichotomy between the poor and the church is false and invalid. The poor are the church.

For African theologians the metaphor of the church as the body of Christ provides a strong case for an open, inclusive and compassionate attitude of churches in the midst of the HIV and AIDS crisis. This metaphor is valuable in the quest for solidarity when both the church and society face a crisis such as the HIV and AIDS pandemic (Van Klinken 2008, 37). To live in the likeness and presence of Christ does not entail a forced conformity that isolates the communal expression of life from the heartbeat of Africa. Conceptualisations of the body of Christ should not be framed in a subject-object dichotomy which introduces an element of un-African distance from interconnected life.

All members of Christian faith communities, whatever their roots and background – whether of African or European descent, rich or poor, female or male, healthy or ill – should be free to commit themselves to a mutual, non-predisposed interpretation of how the body of Christ metaphor can become an authentic expression of what the Creator intended for interconnected life in which there is a place for all. In this way the disintegration of the fabric of society can be overcome (Nessan 2012, 43-52)[1]. The church as body of Christ is compromised when stigma, exclusivity and judgmental attitudes characterise the relationships of its members (Ackermann 2006, 221-242). The unity of the body of Christ should be so strong that if one member suffers, all the members suffer. If one member is honoured, all the members rejoice together (cf. 1 Cor. 12). St. Paul called his communities to give honour to all. This was not the honour of social status, but the honour of receiving God's radical love and justice. In Paul's community all were

---

[1] As Nessan (2012, 43-52) points out, the normative tradition of the Bible immerses the body of Christ in a narrative of deep respect for others and the defence of human dignity. The indispensable foundation for affirming human dignity and solidarity with those who suffer is contained in the seminal description of the nature of human beings as created in God's image (Gen. 1:27). The work of Jesus Christ, as the image of the invisible God, the Firstborn of Creation (Col. 1:15), is interpreted as restoring the image of God after the fall into sin (cf. 2 Cor. 4:4). Through Christ, the image of God is restored to fullness in humanity according to the image of its Creator (Col. 3:10).

called to be equal partners in the church of God (Kim 2013, 20-29). This expression of interconnected life and mutuality is not merely a self-actualising imitation of Christ, but is an act of being led by the Spirit of Christ. In a world formed by the ideas of human beings, relationships often contribute more to isolation than connectedness. Christ, on the other hand, transforms human beings in his image. This transformation occurs when people are drawn into the form of Jesus Christ and conform to the unique form of the one who became human, who was crucified and is risen (see Bonhoeffer 2005). Members of Christian communities should be willingly guided by the Spirit of Christ. They should trust Christ in faith to do his work through them. An authentic, interconnected life is only possible when people are drawn into a living and maturing unity with Christ. This interconnected life gives them a strong sense of belonging. They find their worth and value as connected human beings in a life of service. For the church to be true to its Spirit-endowed identity as body of Christ, its existence should reflect that of the humble Christ. The body of Christ should reflect the mind of Christ.

Conclusion

The article explored whether a communal expression of Christian life guided by the Spirit of Christ, could contribute to a unifying understanding of *ubuntu* and avoid regression to prescriptive, colonialising conceptualisations. A pneumatological approach, anchored in the communal action of willingly placing one's mind under the guidance of the Spirit of Christ, can enable Christian communities to: 1) anchor their conceptualisation of interconnected personhood in their being a member of the body of Christ; 2) reach maturity in faith, no longer prone to self-interest, greed and superficial conceptualisations of interconnected life, but able to form meaningful relationships also with estranged, marginalised and uprooted human beings; 3) grow beyond dichotomies and reject what is foreign to the essence of interconnected life, such as distance, isolation, conforming to pressure of the majority, hegemony and individualism; 4) transform to the selfless mind of Christ and conceptualise an interconnected personhood in which dignity and deeply rooted belonging are possible for all.

Such Christian communities can provide a new perspective on *ubuntu* and what it could become if the transition can be made from "I think, therefore I am" and "I participate, therefore I am" to "in Christ I give myself to others, therefore I am."

References

Ackermann, Denise. 2006. "From Mere Existence to Tenacious Endurance: Stigma, HIV/AIDS and a Feminist Theology of Praxis." In *African Women, Religion, and*

Health. Essays in Honor of Mercy Amba Ewudziwa Oduyoye, edited by Isabel Phiri and Sarojini Nadar, 221–242. Maryknoll, NY: Orbis Books.

Barnett, Paul. 2011. *1 Corinthians: Holiness and Hope of a Rescued People.* Fearn: Christian Focus Publications.

Bhengu, Mfuniselwa. 1996. *Ubuntu: The Essence of Democracy.* Cape Town: Novalis.

Bonhoeffer, Dietrich. 2005. *Ethics.* Edited by Clifford Green, translated by Reinhard Krauss, Charles West, and Douglas Stott. Minneapolis, MN: Augsburg Fortress.

Cahalan, Kathleen, and Gordon Mikoski, eds. 2014. *Opening the Field of Practical Theology: An Introduction.* Lanham, MD: Rowman & Littlefield.

Eze, Michael. 2010. *Intellectual History in Contemporary South Africa.* New York: Palgrave Macmillan.

Hankela, Elina. 2014. *Ubuntu, Migration and Ministry: Being Human in a Johannesburg Church.* Leiden: Brill.

Kim, Yung. 2013. "Reclaiming Christ's Body (*soma christou*): Embodiment of God's Gospel in Paul's Letters." *Journal of Bible and Theology* 67 (1): 20–29.

Lartey, Emmanuel. 2013. *Post-colonializing God: New Perspectives on Pastoral and Practical Theology.* London: SCM Press.

Letseka, Moeketsi. 2012. "In Defence of Ubuntu." *Studies in Philosophy and Education* 31 (1): 47-60.

Louw, Daniël. 2011. "Noetics and the Notion of *Ubuntu*-Thinking within an Intercultural Hermeneutics and Philosophical Approach to Theory Formation in Practical Theology." *International Journal for Practical Theology* 15: 173–192.

Louw, Dirk. 2001. "Ubuntu and the Challenges of Multiculturalism in Post-apartheid South Africa." *Quest* XV (1-2): 15-36.

Makumba, Maurice. 2007. *Introduction to African Philosophy.* Nairobi: Paulines Publications Africa.

Matolino, Bernard, and Wenceslaus Kwindingwi. 2013. "The End of Ubuntu." *South African Journal of Philosophy* 32 (2): 197–205.

Nessan, Craig. 2012. "What If the Church Really is the Body of Christ" *Dialogue: A Journal of Theology* 51 (1): 43–52.

Osmer, Richard. 2014. "Empirical Practical Theology." In *Opening the Field of Practical Theology: An Introduction,* edited by Kathleen Cahalan and Gordon Mikoski, 61-78. Lanham, MD: Rowman & Littlefield.

Ramose, Mogobe B. 1999. *African Philosophy Through* Ubuntu. Harare: Mond Books.

Shutte, Augustine. 1993. *Philosophy for Africa.* Rondebosch: UCT Press.

Swinton, John and Harriet Mowat. 2006. *Practical Theology and Qualitative Research.* London: SCM Press.

Taylor, Douglas. 2014. "Defining *Ubuntu* for Business Ethics: A Deontological Approach." *South African Journal of Philosophy* 33 (3): 331–345.

Tshawane, Nwamilorho. 2009. "The Rainbow Nation: A Critical Analysis of the Notions of Community in the Thinking of Desmond Tutu." Ph.D. dissertation, University of Pretoria.

Tutu, Desmond. 1999. *No Future Without Forgiveness.* New York: Random House.

Van Klinken, Adriaan. 2008. "The Body of Christ has AIDS: A Study on the Notion of the Body of Christ in African Theologies Responding to HIV and AIDS." *Missionalia* 36 (2/3): 319–336.

The *ubuntu*-theology of Desmond Tutu: A theological interplay between religious pluralism and the universal validity of human rights

Wilhelm Gräb

Abstract

The author emphasises that the development of human rights has not been achieved by one or more concrete religions but by a universal religion of humanity; this is illustrated with a South-African example, Desmond Tutu. Human Rights are not the result of a religion, or of Christian faith, but the fundamental basis of religion; it is a religious consciousness that was given initially to human beings. The emergence of human rights shows that people from all cultures all over the world can agree to humanistic beliefs like an inherent dignity to which every human being is entitled. This contribution attempts the mediation of the universality of human rights with the particularity of religious traditions.

The particularity of religious traditions and the universality of human rights

The *Universal Declaration of Human Rights* (1948) did not emerge from any concrete religion, not even from Christianity and its churches. Its starting point was the experience of pain and harm, the experience of brutal non-recognition, "barbarous acts" (*Universal Declaration of Human Rights* 1948, Preamble). The cries of those deprived of their right to live by the totalitarian regimes of National Socialism and Stalinism, of those tormented, tortured, and killed because of racial, national, political or religious reasons or because of their sexuality, can still be heard in the declaration. Even today, it is the violations of human rights that provide the appeal to keep and enforce them. Yet, this is only possible because such rights have a global status as a universally valid norm under international law and were turned into enforceable rights in the constitutions of many countries. If a blatant violation becomes public anywhere in the world, one will immediately appeal to human rights.

For this reason, the defense and enforcement of human rights is often sus-pected of acting in a cultural-imperialistic way. Furthermore, when wars are de-clared under the pretext that they contribute to supporting human rights – although in reality the main interest is more mundane, e.g., rights to oil production – these suspicions are clearly supported. Hence, human rights are often understood as a continuation of western colonialism. Nevertheless, it must be said that only through an intervention in the affairs of a state that either threats the security of its citizens or is not able to ensure it, legitimated by international law, is it possible to prevent further violations.

The question is whether international interventions for the enforcement of hu-man rights – especially if they induce a military conflict that creates additional more harm – have cultural-imperialistic features, even if the intention for such is good. This question opens a quite difficult issue because the intention behind such interventions to enforce the human rights is the claim of a universal validity. A theological concept of Desmond Tutu offers a good example how to deal theolog-ically with the tension between the universal validity of the human rights and the particularity of religious traditions. Tutu shows us that the African concept of an *ubuntu*-theology provides a special possibility to convey an African understand-ing of being human with the Christian concept of human dignity and the universal normativity of the declaration of human rights as well.

The *ubuntu*-theology of Desmond Tutu addressing the human right debate

Desmond Tutu's book *God is not a Christian* is a collection of sermons, speeches and statements from the former Anglican bishop of Cape Town. In a sermon de-livered in the church of St. Martin in The Fields near Trafalgar-Square in London, after the fall of the Berlin Wall and at the end of apartheid in South Africa, Tutu insisted "God is clearly not a Christian. His concern is for all his children" (Tutu 2012, 12).

For Tutu, there is no conflict between human rights' universal validity and the obligation of Christians to speak up for human rights out of their Christian belief. This is not because Christianity might have invented human rights and their worldwide distribution would be more successful under the Christian prefix. Such a cultural imperialistic interpretation of the relationship between human rights and Christianity was far from what Tutu had in mind. It was rather his deep concern to win over all religions in the universal enforcement of human rights, something that marked his global speaking and preaching since the 1980's.

Tutu confesses his Christian faith in strong terms. He often underlines that it is essential for him to take his own faith seriously. Yet, taking his own religion seriously does not mean devaluing other religions or refusing to believe in the idea of a natural universal religion that is inherent in the very nature of human beings from the beginning. Religions are different; the Gods in whom they believe are different. Despite all that they have something in common: they reveal a transcendent element in humanity.

"God is clearly not a Christian. His concern is for all his children." Christians do not have an exclusive relationship to God, and God has no exclusive relationship to Christians. He is the God of all human beings and they have their different relations to him. This also is important to Tutu: religions are not identical; "the" God can be understood in many different ways. As God is never without the individual relation, "we must hold to our particular and peculiar beliefs tenaciously" (Tutu 2012, 6). Tutu combines these confessions with a religious individuality through the opinion that God generally could only be thought of and believed in through the different relationships people have with Him. God is only God in the plurality of individual religious perspectives about Him. For relations among religions, Tutu stresses, this means that "we must be ready to learn from another, not claiming that we alone possess all truth and that somehow we have a corner on God" (Tutu 2012, 6).

By acting in this way we will discover many things we have in common. What we actually have in common depends on what that for which we search. For Tutu the direction is clear. For him all religions have a transcendent referent that is compassionate and concerned; all see human beings as "creatures of this supreme, supra-mundane reality, with a high destiny that hopes for an everlasting life lived in close association with the divine" (Tutu 2012, 7). This distinction of human beings as "creatures" of a higher reality in "close association with the divine" is what Tutu hopes to find as the common ground of the different religions. Each human being is holy; thus, it would be a taboo to hurt her or him.

Tutu is delighted that he finds this holiness of human beings in the Christian tradition as well. "Surely, it is good to know that God (in the Christian tradition) created us all (not just Christians) in his image, thus investing us all with infinite worth" (Tutu 2012, 7). It is equally important for Tutu to emphasise that just like Christianity other religious traditions regard human beings with holiness as well:

Surely we can rejoice that the eternal word, the Logos of God, enlightens everyone – not just Christians, but everyone who comes into the world; that what we call the Spirit of God is not a Christian preserve, for the Spirit of God existed long before there were Christians, inspiring and nurturing women and men in the ways of holiness, bringing them to fruition, bringing them to fruition what was best in all. We do scant justice and honour to our God if we want, for instance, to deny that Mahatma Gandhi was a truly great soul, a holy man who walks closely with God. Our God would be too small if he was not also the God of Gandhi (Tutu 2012, 7).

Christianity is neither allowed to claim to be the religion that discovered the holiness of human beings (which would also be historically inaccurate), nor is it allowed to claim that Christianity alone is the best and only vehicle for the promotion of humanity's holiness. The access to the "holy sanctuary" of humanity and work towards the preservation of this sanctuary can be found in other religious teachings as well.

Tutu is obviously illustrating that religion – and the relation between humanity and the transcendent – are expressed in various ways within different religions. Each religion has its own specific way to express this relation. Today many religions are even respectful of people who have abandoned their original religious affiliation or who do not believe in God.

Religion provocatively insists that one has dignity simply because one is a human being, regardless of one's characteristics or affiliations, independent from one's deeds or misdeeds. Religion shifts one's being into an unconditioned horizon. One's right to exist derives from conditions that are independent of oneself. A human being is not able to and does not have to earn this right. One's right to exist is derived from something that is beyond oneself, it derives from God. In Christian discourse this means that a person is God's creature, his beloved child, and a justified sinner. But Tutu only speaks rarely and cautiously in this biblical language. Tutu counts on a transversal theology to which all humans with good will are responding. This transversal theology articulates the truly religious matter in all religions, i.e., religion sees the individual human being from the perspective of a self-transcended humanity founded in the Unconditioned. Religion is a transcendent determination of human existence that, then in a twist, revokes itself and gives humanity back to itself.

Tutu's theology used such common religious language, compelling even for secular people, in referring to the "essential humanity of the perpetrator of even the most gruesome atrocity" (Tutu 2012, 42) in his plead for a path of reconciliation. He could have spoken about the public-political force of Christian belief in reconciliation. Instead he makes recourse to the "essential humanity" even of "the perpetrator." He notes that no one could deny the human dignity of a person, however heinous his deed. This is a reformulation of a religious interpretation of human rights discourse from Tutu's Christian orientation. Tutu emphasises that the evidences of what religion generally contributes to human life and society show religion indispensable in the realisation of humanity.

In this way the path of restorative justice should become passable for people who come from other non-Christian, religious worldviews too. Tutu specifically points towards the African worldview of the *ubuntu*. *Ubuntu* is a Xhosa-word that expresses the essential individual's affiliation to a community. *Ubuntu* also stands for the transcending of each individual human being in a larger, infinite reaching reality. For the community of *ubuntu*, the being of an individual is not only linked to the visible tribal community but also to the ancestors. The African worldview of *ubuntu*, together with the idea that human beings are made in God's image found in the Hebrew Bible, and the Christian understanding of the unconditioned justification of the sinner, together represent for Tutu an integral expression of a natural theology grounding the universal validity of the human rights (cf. Tutu 2012, 21-24).

Everyone of God's human creatures has the capacity to know something about God from the evidence God leaves in his handiworks (Romans 1:18-20); this is the basis for natural theology and natural law. Immanuel Kant spoke about categorical imperative. All human creatures have a sense that some things ought to be done just as others not to be done. This is a universal phenomenon – what varies is the content of natural law. [...] In his speech before the Areopagus, Paul speaks about how God created all human beings from one stock and given everyone the urge, the hunger, for divine things so that all will seek after God and perhaps find him, adding that God is not far from us since all (not just Christians) live and move and have their being in him (Act. 17: 22-31). Talking to pagans, Paul declares that all are God's offspring (Tutu 2012, 10).

In Tutu's theology the "universal phenomenon" is the phenomenon of a religious consciousness that was given initially to each human being. This religious consciousness becomes concrete in openness to transcendence: searching for and questioning something that is beyond oneself. Particular religions build themselves up on this natural religion. But they also presuppose this natural religion as the universal resonance chamber that outlives their own history. Natural religion exists in the particular religions but not exclusively. There is one universal faith in all concrete religions that acts through and beyond them, a faith that we should by all means call: the faith in human rights.

Although Tutu has not articulated it in such an explicit way, it seems implied by his argumentation in the way he describes the particular, concrete religions – and not only Christianity – by interrogating their contribution to the enforcement of human rights. Doing this he tries to see the best in each of them as something that serves the humanity of human beings.

We must not make the mistake of judging other faiths by their least attractive features and adherents: It is possible to demolish the case for Christianity by, for instance, quoting the Crusades, or the atrocities of the Holocaust, or the excess of apartheid. But we know that that would be unfair in the extreme, since we claim them to be aberrations, distortions and deviations. What about Francis of Assisi, Mother Teresa, Albert Schweitzer, and all the wonderful and beautiful people and things that belong to Christianity? We should want to deal with other faiths and their best and highest, as they define themselves, and not shoot down the caricatures that we want to put up (Tutu 2012, 16).

A cultural transformation and adaption is in fact what happened at the beginning and merged in the process of placing the *Universal Declaration of Human Rights* in different cultural and religious traditions. The process is not at all completed and is, with regard to religion, often controversial because the role of religion in human rights discourse often becomes closely related to specific religions. Then one often sees oneself quickly involved in a very ambivalent history. One has to confess that Christian churches accepted the idea of human rights quite late and even today are often accused of not advocating for human rights very strongly. Religions have their own legal orders that can lead to conflicts with national law and even with human rights, especially in cases where human rights have entered into state legal systems. Yet a theology like the transversal natural theology of Desmond Tutu enables us to make explicit that a religious faith constitutively belongs to human beings. The transversal natural theology of Tutu is his *ubuntu*-theology. In the context of this *ubuntu*-theology it is possible to register the faith based implications of the declarations of human rights from their beginning, i.e., we can call the *Universal Declaration of Human Rights* the confessional base of a universal belief on Human Rights. Tutu's concept of an *ubuntu*-theology combines elements of an African ethics of humanity with a non-exclusive understanding of the Christian implications of human rights.

The mediation of the universal validity of human rights with the particularity of religious traditions

It must be generally accepted that, on the one hand, human rights require self-determined values and on the other they support certain values that are not equally appreciated and practiced in all cultures and religions around the world. Next to the universal claim of the validity of the human rights, cultural and religious differences will also continue to exist. Religious ties supply these values with a strong potential of motivation for daily living. All religious cultures are different in what they consider law and rights and in how they appreciate individual choice with regard to sexual orientation and the choice of partnership, profession and residence. One can find many different cultural opinions about the relation between the individual and the community, about the idea of physical integrity, about who takes precedence in the relation of individual and community and in the hierarchy of individual and community (e.g., family, clan, and nation). They might all be different but at the same time, they all have a religious foundation. Likewise, one will find different but always religiously founded opinions about the idea of equality of men and women, about religious tolerance or about the estimation of democratic participation.

During the drafting phase of the *Universal Declaration of Human Rights*, the UN-Commission already knew that there was great tension between a universal normativity of human rights and the pluralism of all the different religious cultures. In his book on human rights' genealogy, sociologist Hans Joas offers a helpful insight into the work of the UN-Commission, comprised of delegates from 18 nations (cf. Joas 2012, 251-281, 273f). He especially focuses on two particular delegates, i.e., the Lebanese representative Charles Malik and the Chinese representative Peng-Chun Chang. Charles Malik, speaker for the Arabian world, was an orthodox Christian whereas Pen-Chun Chang, according to Joas, often referred to his Confucian background during the drafting process. Yet Pen-Chun Chang was also the person who warned on the one hand against a foundation for the human rights that is limited to reason and on the other against a special emphasis of one single religious tradition. He was interested in a synthesis of all the different religious traditions of vindication into one common value system. This is consistent with the fact that there is no reference to a universal *ratio* of humans but to a universal "faith" in a human religious' conviction, i.e., "the faith in fundamental human rights, in the dignity and worth of the human person" (*Universal Declaration of Human Rights* 1948, Preamble).[1] As Hannah Arendt[2] interpreted the *Universal Declaration of Human Rights'* fundamental claim, it proclaims the human rights movement as something like a religious movement, as a movement that is based on a confession of faith, faith in the possibility of creating conditions around the world that gives every human being access to the right, to have basic rights as a human being, especially to be acknowledged as a human being.

The *Universal Declaration of Human Rights* was the work of people from different contexts, cultures, religions and parts of the world. What becomes evident is that this declaration never would have gained such popularity if it was not to a large extent compatible with the different value systems that are practiced in the different religions, cultures and contexts in so many different ways. Still, what remains important is the question of who will take charge when the concrete religions and cultural traditions merge to be mediated through the normative moral claims of the *Universal Declaration of Human Right*. Will it be the normative universality of human rights with its attempt to find recognition as official rights? Or will it be the particular religious traditions who only want to assign human rights

---

[1] Jan Smuts was responsible for the drafting of the United-Nations Charter's preamble and penned these words. Smuts was head of the South-African government several times in the 1930s and the early 1940s although he was not responsible directly for the policy of racial apartheid, enacted in the same year of the *Universal Declaration of Human Rights* (1948).

[2] Cf. Hannah Arendt, Es gibt nur ein einziges Menschenrecht. In *Die Wandlung* 4, Dezember 1949.

to own fellow believers as they think them to be maintained according to their own norms of faith this way?

There is no doubt, that the validity of universal human rights has to be transmitted in accordance with the self-understanding of particular and regional religious cultures and contexts. To a certain extent, to establish a motivational basis for action, human rights have to incarnate in the minds and hearts of people in the different contexts, cultures and religions. Therefore, one speaks of a necessary cultural-contextual synthesis and value generalisation in human rights discourse. Yet, in this process of synthesis and generalisation it has to be ensured that human rights remain intact and inviolable and that states and societies follow their requirements. Cultural-contextual synthesis and value generalisation will only be helpful if they support the enforcement of human rights within historical religions, and if the human rights find recognition in the particular religions and in the cultures and contexts that are merged with them. This will have practical consequences for religious as well as for judicial practice in the countries in which human rights claim validity.

First of all, this means that religious cultures have to legitimise themselves according to the standards of human rights and not vice versa. Religions, their practices and legal interpretations have to prove themselves to be compatible with human rights. Secondly, one has to insist on the validity of human rights, in particular on the right to self-determination, even if they are opposed to religious ideas of morality. When the human right for self-determination, for justice and security is valid in a state, these rights have to be valid for all people, independent of their religious denomination or ethnicity, even if this right might contradict the norms of a religious community, for instance freedom of sexual expression and self-identification.

The universal validity of human rights can hardly be enforced without conflicts with religious and political powers. Hence this religion will be all the more vigorous the more states implement human rights into their constitutions and the more people are committed to human rights. People might come from concrete religions, they might stay in contact with them or just pass them by, but they are all connected in a worldwide community with the same spirit of something like a universal confession of human rights. It is also clear that faith in the holiness of every human being, confessed by the global movement of human rights, will gradually change the different religions. It is a faith in the holiness of the human being – not a human being formed and acting in thus and such a way, but of each human being just the way she or he already exists. This faith alone will change the world. It changes the world through the way that justice in the sense of love, mercy and forgiveness are practiced, that there will be help where people are victimised by violence and state terror, where hungry people suffer from starvation and have to escape from their home countries.

Many things need to be done from this perspective. Without the implementation of human rights into the constitutions of states and the enforcement of their validity under international law, much less would have been achieved towards a more human world. Yet, all this effort is based on a faith in the holiness of the human being. It is this faith that encourages people to fight for adherence to and enforcement of human rights, whether they are members of a religious community or not.

However, it should be underscored that people with religious backgrounds and motivations, just like Desmond Tutu, do fight for human rights worldwide – and so do with theological reasons. Tutu's *ubuntu*-theology realises an integration of different religious traditions by itself. Doing so this theological concept establishes a theological base upon which the universal validity of human dignity is religiously grounded.

In conclusion, the possible impact of an *ubuntu*-theology on the practice of churches and Christian communities could become obvious. At the end the *ubuntu*-theology of Desmond Tutu gives the format of a theological base for an active collaboration of Christian communities with NGO's on human rights issues. It also stimulates churches and Christian communities to offer room and financial help to human right groups.

References

Arendt, Hannah. *"Es gibt nur ein einziges Menschenrecht."* In: Praktische Philosophie/Ethik, Reader zum Funk-Kolleg, Frankfurt am Main, 1981, 152-167. (originally published as Essay, in: Die Wandlung, 4, 1949, 754-770)

Joas, Hans. *Die Sakralität der Person: Eine neue Genealogie der Menschenrechte.* Berlin: Suhrkamp, 2012; English translation, *The Sacredness of the Person: A New Genealogy of Human Rights.* Georgetown: Georgetown University Press, 2013.

Tutu, Desmond Mpilo. *God is not a Christian*, edited by John Allen. New York: Harper One, 2012.

Universal Declaration of Human Rights, Preamble: 1948. http://www.ohchr.org/EN/UDHR/Documents/UDHR_Translations/eng.pdf[3]

---

[3] The person, who was responsible for the drafting of the United-Nations Charter's preamble, was Jan Smuts. He wrote the impressive words of "the faith in fundamental human rights, in the dignity and worth of the human person" that I just quoted (Preamble, *Universal Declaration of Human Rights*). Smuts was head of the South-African government several times in the 1930s and the early 1940s although he was not responsible directly for the policy of racial apartheid, enacted in 1948, the same year the *Universal Declaration of Human Rights* was enacted.

The dynamic interplay between African spiritualities (*ubuntu*- and *ũtugi*-thinking) and *xenophilia* (*sapientia*-thinking): On becoming a "caring community" within the public space of civil society

Daniël J. Louw

Abstract

Instead of xenophobia (the fear for the stranger), it is argued that a kind of xenophilia (a hospitable space for the stranger) is most needed in processes of radical change, transformation and democratisation. In this regard, African spiritualities (for example, *ubuntu*- and *utugi*-thinking) should be merged with the Christian spiritual position/habitus of kenotic love in order to address the paranoia of fear for the stranger (xenophobia) and many obstacles in the establishment of a free and just civil society (processes of democratisation). Within a practical, theological approach to effective participation in the public space of life, a pastoral mode of advocacy is proposed, (*fides quaerens actum*). The concept of paraclesis could be rendered as an appropriate pastoral category for the establishment of a caring community: *hospitium publicum*.

Introduction

The basic thesis of the chapter is: constructive change in civil society, due to radical, political transformation, needs paradigmatic frameworks – philosophical schemata of interpretation – that can serve as indicators for sustainable processes of democratisation (patterns of thinking that safeguard an ethos of human dignity, mutual trust and caring sensitivity). The South African, civil and political scene desperately need a moral sense of destiny and a taxonomy of spiritual values in order to establish a just and more compassionate society. Thus, the focus on three paradigmatic frameworks: *ubuntu*-, *ũtugi*- and *sapientia*-thinking.

Furthermore, the core argument will deal with the following theological questions: How should communities of faith respond to the challenge of caring, helping and healing within the paranoiac turmoil of xenophobia? What are the implications for a practical-theological engagement (performative solidarity) and ministerial structures of ecclesial involvement in public, civil matters (operative ecclesiology)?

Practical theology as 'life science'

The emphasis on public issues in an operative ecclesiology[1] implies a radical shift from the 'pomp and glory of the cathedral' to the 'public of the market place'; public settings as *locus theologicus* (Kessler 2014). With such a point of departure the society as a whole should become the object of theological and practical reflection (Ferreira 2009, 4; Leiner and Palme 2014, 10).

Public issues concerning the quality of life in civil society are becoming focal areas in practical-theological reflection. Thus, the argument that practical theology should move away from religious meaning 'beyond the everyday' to religious meaning in the mundane' (Miller-McLemore 2012, 7). Most scholars nowadays agree that practical theology at its best functions "as a kind of public theology sensitive to the individual but directed toward the wider social area" (Miller-McLemore 2012, 14). Clerical needs and hierarchical issues (Reader 2008) often dominated the practical-theological discourse. Gradually there is a shift to normative construction (Osmer 2008, 4) and practical engagement (action orientation).

According to Grethlein (2012, 143-192), practical theology should be transformed as the theory of communicating the gospel within the realm of existential life issues (*cura vitae*) (Louw 2008). In this regard, the concept 'life' (Lauster 2007, 142-143) is emerging more and more as a theme in practical-theological reflection.

Martina Kumlehn (2011, 4) advocates for practical theology as a kind of life science (*Lebenswisssenschaft Praktische Theologie*). Together with religious experiences and spiritual awareness or transcendent experiences (Grethlein 2012, 177), the interplay between life, civil society, local communities, meaning-formation and spirituality[2] have become focal points in practical-theological reflection.

---

[1]   "Operative ecclesiology" here means: practical-theological reflection on ecclesial matters not merely from the viewpoint of denominational traditions and dogmatic confessions, but within communal life systems. Ecclesiology may be studied inductively and can thus draw support from various other disciplines, such as political science, history and sociology (see Bergson 2015). Practical-theological reflection should start with social contexts, for example the current refugee crisis, as *locus theologicus* (Polak 2014, 1-2).

[2]   "Spirituality is an essential element of humanity. It encompasses individuals' search for meaning and purpose; it includes connectedness to others, self, nature, and the significant sacred; and its embraces secular and philosophical, as well as religious and cultural, beliefs and practices" (Puchalski, Blatt and Butler 2014, 10).

Archbishop Desmond Tutu offered the following challenge to communities of faith: "We were involved in the struggle because we believed we would evolve a new kind of society. A caring compassionate society. At the moment many, too many, of our people live in gruelling demeaning, dehumanising poverty. We are sitting on a powder keg. We really must work like mad to eradicate poverty" (Tutu 2004, 33).

With reference to current signs of intolerance, violence and xenophobia in the South African civil society, the question is whether a dynamic interplay between African spiritualties and the Christian tradition of wisdom (*sapientia*) can contribute to the shaping of a more democratic, caring and compassionate, civil society.

Democratisation under the pressure of global paranoia: terrorism and the fear of the stranger (xenophobia)

The Turkish President, Tayyip Erdogan, sums up the global paranoia as follows: "We are confronted with collective terrorism activity around the world as terrorism does not recognise any religion, any race, any nation or any country" (Reuters 2015, 11). This is the reason why president Barack Obama is convinced that the terrible attacks and the killing of innocent people based on a twisted ideology is an attack not just on France or Turkey, but it is an attack on the civilised world (Reuters 2015, 11) and the citizens of the "global village" (McLuhan 2015); it is a global threat to the meaning and significance of our being human.

Democracy is currently under huge pressure due to the refugee and migrant crisis. Instead of a politics of democratic integration, it seems as if European nations, under the threat of violence, move into the paranoia of exclusive nationalism rather than trans-nationalism (Vick 2015, 32). The attack on innocent civilians in France on 13 November 2015, left human beings all over the globe speechless. Paris has become the epitome of a global network of fear and unqualified anxiety. The discovery of a possible attack on vulnerable human beings (tourists) at Checkpoint Charlie in Berlin (February 2016) evokes many negative reactions.

According to Von Stephan-Andreas Casdorff, these kinds of events question the current "*Willkommenskultur*" (a culture of sincere hospitality) in Germany and fuel radical reactions and aggressive attitudes (Casdorff 2016, 1). Chancellor Angela Merkel of Germany captured the dilemma of welcoming the stranger or defending one's own territory, by saying: "Our free life is stronger than terror" (Faulconbridge and Young 2015, 1). Poland's European affairs minister designate said after the attacks in Paris, Warsaw would not be able to accept refugees despite the fact that in September of that year, Poland backed an EU plan to accept 120,000 refugees across the 28-nation bloc (Faulconbridge and Young 2015, 1).

The refugee crisis has become a crisis of spiritual intoxication, i.e. a crisis of negative perceptions and dehumanising prejudice (Kizilhan 2016, 15).

Very surprisingly Klaus Schwab, the founder of the World Economic Forum, said that we need a spiritual revolution to solve problems in the global village. Life in the global village demands a different, and more human, kind of leadership. "If you think what a human being is, we exist because of brains, soul, heart. What we can replicate in a robot is the brain. But you never will replicate the heart, which is passion, compassion. And the soul, which enables us to believe. The robot will never have the ability to believe in something. So perhaps we will have at the end of this revolution – possibly, possibly – a basis for a new human renaissance" (Schwab in Duffy 2016, 12).

One can further argue that the African continent, especially South Africa, desperately needs "a basis for a new human renaissance" in order to establish what Desmond Tutu called a "compassionate society." If we need to explore anew the human soul, "which enables us to believe" (Schwab in Duffy 2016, 12), the following question surfaces: Do we have the spiritual capacity and paradigmatic framework in practical-theological reflection to overcome the spreading of a global paranoia that is, in fact, derailing processes of democratisation, not only in Europe, but also on the African continent?

Public theology: the turn to civil engagement and community care

In the words of sociologist Peter Berger, we urgently need "signals of transcendence" (Berger 1992, 121) in order to establish a more humane society. The consequent challenge for communities of faith is to attend less to internal denominational issues and to focus more on issues concerning the quality of life in our civil society. "In the public arena where discourse of tolerance and mutual respect is the key to social and political relationships, the Constitutional guarantee of freedom of religious belief, expression and practice without governmental regulation, requires great understanding and discipline form amongst the faith communities" (SACC 2006, 8).

Consequently, communities of faith should attend to a kind of community care and to different modes of public concern and participation. The challenge for theologising and the values and tenets of the Christian faith, is the creation of a just society. "The aim of our advocacy is to raise a Christian 'voice' to policymakers on those social, political and economic policies that affect our lives and communities" (SACC 2006, 16). Public policy advocacy, as the influencing of the environment, become a challenge to caregiving in civil societal matters.

The idea of civil society

The concept of civil society is difficult to define because it deals with issues and processes within different social realities and community structures. "*The* civil society" does not exist as a kind of natural and factual phenomenon. It is in fact a political concept emanating from many social, economic theories and ideas (philosophies) regarding the structural shaping of daily life.

Seligman, in his research on *The Idea of Civil Society* (1992, 200-204), differentiate between three basic descriptive functions, namely political, socio-scientific and philosophical prescriptive functions. Due to the influence of economic forces on social and cultural processes, another function surfaced, namely the mobilisation of forces and social energy outside the sphere of organised political powers and the connection to state and governmental structures. " 'Civil society' entails more than merely the mobilisation of the private sector. 'Civil society' becomes a collective for local and grassroots energy to be mobilised in order to act on behalf of minorities, oppressed groups, the voiceless, the outsider, marginalised and stigmatised people/citizens. In this regard, the 'healing of society' in terms of common goods and general well-being, become connected to the fact that the concept 'civil society' is not value free and indeed have a moral function" (Seligman 1992).

J. Keane (2003, 8) refers to the fact that the construct "civil society" is not a static *fait accompli*. "It is an unfinished project that consists of sometimes thick, sometimes thinly stretched networks, pyramids and the hub-and-spoke clusters of socio-economic institutions and actors who organise themselves across borders, with the deliberate aim of drawing the world together in new ways."

"Civil society" should thus be rendered as an inclusive concept referring to the quality of human life within political, economic, judicial and social structures as established by local government and central exponents of the state in the light of prevailing polity and ideology (spiritual realm of guiding ideas about the administration and regulation of daily life).

Towards civil engagement: taxonomy of performative actions

Civil engagement needs metaphors for the instigation of sustainable, performative actions. The following taxonomy of actions (civil actions) could serve as paradigmatic framework for the praxis of a practical-theological engagement in societal matters (*fides quaerens actum*):

a) *Disputing* the paradigmatic framework that directs acts of practising faith in the public arena. In this regard, the connection between the constitution of

South Africa and the interpretation of processes of democratisation should be revisited critically.

b) *Mobilising* local spiritual energy and goodwill amongst ordinary people/citizens outside governmental structures in order to organise themselves within local communities around social issues of common interest or need.

c) *Voicing* the needs and concerns of ordinary citizens and protecting basic human rights.

d) *Addressing* the quest for human dignity within the context of processes of democratisation and transformation (caring for the well-being of humans in societal realities).

e) *Shaping* and *empowering* human capital in order to maximise social efficiency within local communities.

f) *Reaching out* to basic community needs with actions of diaconic service.

g) *Advocating* (SACC 2006, 6) on behalf of the voiceless in order to create more structure and order within societal disorder.

With reference to the previous praxis engagements, the following question surfaces: but what about sustainability and motivation? What could be possible driving factors for mobilisation of spiritual energy? What are possible paradigmatic frameworks for meaningful societal change and the establishment of a humane, civil society?

With reference to the paradigmatic framework for meaningful change, two philosophical positions in African thinking (schemata of interpretation) have been selected, namely *ubuntu*-philosophy (communality and the care for the other), and *ũtugi*-philosophy (sharing and freedom of the guest). The reason for the selection is that both reflect "signals of transcendence" (Berger) and deal with the question of humanizing the society. They are deeply embedded in African culture and spiritual thinking, but at the same time set a moral and spiritual framework for performative actions. Due to possible links with wisdom thinking (*sapientia*) in Christian spirituality (the ethos of kenotic love), the paradigms of these three modes of spiritualties are explored in order to see how the notion of spirituality in wisdom thinking can contribute to a taxonomy of shared values, a hermeneutics of democratisation and the possible healing of civil society.

The spirituality of *ubuntu*-philosophy

It was the former president of Zambia, Kenneth Kaunda, who wrote a book in the 1960s: entitled *A Humanist in Africa.* He advocated for a humanist approach to life (*Christian humanism*) because of the communal spirit within different African spiritualities. For Africa the aesthetic rhythm of life, the singing and dancing, was more fundamental than the awareness of evil forces that determine the value of human relationships. Hence, the following challenging remark by Kenneth Kaunda: "Let the West have its Technology and Asia its Mysticism! Africa's gift to world culture must be in the realm of Human Relationships" (Kaunda 1967[2], 22).

The spirit of *ubuntu* – that profound African sense that we are human only through the humanity of other human beings – is not a parochial phenomenon, but has added globally to our common search for a better world (Mandela 2005, 82); to improve the world is intrinsically an aesthetic endeavour, not merely a moral issue.

In an African approach to anthropology, *ubuntu*-thinking and the notion of *homo aestheticus* (the human being as the enjoyer of life) are more fundamental than the aggressive approach of *homo faber* (the human being as the maker of things). What is envisaged in an African spirituality is harmony (the beautification of life) within interpersonal relationships: *Umuntu ungumuntu ngabantu/motho ke motho ka batho* – approximately translated as: "A person is a person through other people" (Mtetwa 1996, 24).

One of the most remarkable and tangible dimensions of African spirituality relates to the unique notion of communality and collective solidarity that African societies exhibit in all spheres of life. There is a profound sense of interdependence, from the extended family to the entire community. Actually, everybody is interrelated; this includes relations between the living and those who have departed. African spirituality is structured, not along the lines of a pyramid, but of a circle – community and communality as the centre of religious life (Bosch 1974, 40; Kretzschmar 1996, 63-75).

Spirituality thus reflects ultimate and aesthetic values within cultures; spirituality is concerned with life as a whole. "It is not a pious behaviour but rather a commitment and involvement in a manner that gives meaning to life. Spirituality means that unseen dimension which influences a person to live in a mode that is truly fulfilling" (Skhakhane 1995, 106). To live is to celebrate life within the rhythm of daily events. In addition, life fulfilment is to experience, despite the overwhelming awareness of the transience of life, that life can indeed be beautiful.

The spirituality of *ūtugi*-philosophy

In the Agĩkũyũ-tradition in Kenya, being human is closely related to the notion of *ūtigi* (a hospitable sense of treating the outsider not as enemy, but as insider through communal sharing).

Josiah Murage (2011), in his research on *The Concept of Ūtugi within the HIV & AIDS Pandemic*, advocates for the connection between pastoral caregiving and the Christian tradition of hospitality within the cultural context of Kenya. The concept of *ūtigi* is related to the language of the Agĩkũyũ community in Kenya.

It can be translated as hospitality and refer to what one can call the freedom of the guest (Murage 2011, 82). "It means the creation of a free space where the vulnerable people in the society are welcomed, not only as guests, but also as part of that community" (Murage 2011, 82). *Ūtugi* is an exposition of the cultural custom in African spirituality, namely to share love and affection to others and to put the idea of sharing into practice. The saying in Kenya-culture and Agĩkũyũ-tradition is that to live with others is to share and to have mercy on one another since only witchdoctors are allowed to live and eat alone (Murage 2011, 82).

According to Mutugi (2001, 4), "African hospitality is expressed in a loving way ... when a visitor comes, you welcome him or her by ushering him or her to a seat, and then you give him or her something to eat or drink. Then you share or socialise, seek to know, politely the problems or issues or news that brought him or her."

The Agĩkũyũ community refers to a hospitable person as *mũtugi*, which simply means a hospitable person who is also a gracious person (Muragi 2011, 84). The opposite of *ũtigi* (hospitality) is *ũkarĩ* (selfishness). Cares, charity, hospitality, communal sharing, all of them help to shape caregiving within the Agĩkũyũ-culture.

Respect is another important feature that is highly emphasised in the practice of *ũtigi* in the Agĩkũyũ-tradition (Murage 2011, 87). This is in line with the Swahili saying, *Heshima si utumwa*, which means, respect is not slavery, nor is it a burden, it is simply a costly undertaking. Respect presupposes honesty and integrity. "Due to the emphasis on sincerity and honesty, the hungry visitor or stranger would obey the above principle of *Ũtigi*, for failure to do so would not only affect his or her conscience and annoy the living, but it would also annoy the ancestors, who, are believed to be exemplary beings, hence are sincere and honest" (Murage 2011, 87). *Ũtugi* thus operates even as a religious principle. "Among the ancient Agĩkũyũ the people perceived *Ngai* (God) as unique and *Ũtugi* was extended to this *Ngai* and *Ngoma*, i.e. spirits (cf. *theoxenic* hospitality)" (Murage 2011, 93). This is affirmed by Kenyatta (1938, 259) "In the Agĩkũyũ custom of 'give and take' (*Ũtugi*) ... when *Mwene-Nyaga* (God) has given the rain to people ... he is entitled to be rewarded by a gift of the first crops of season. For it is said that without his aid the people could not have any crops. Thus for a man (sic) to fail to pay tributes to his benefactor would be contrary to the established custom and would be regarded as shameful and greedy."

As in the Kenyan culture, the *ũtugi*-principle of the Agĩkũyũ-tradition demonstrates how an existing social structure can become a vehicle of meaning-giving and signal of transcendence.

In both *ubuntu*- and *ũtugi*-thinking the sense of belonging (Mbiti 1969, 108) expresses the following communal principle: "I am, because we are; and since we are, therefore I am." This is an illustration of how the principle of communality, as connected to the notion of hospitality, can be viewed as the cornerstone for appropriate actions of civil engagement. *Ubuntu*-philosophy and *ũtigi*-hospitality can indeed be rendered as spiritual pointers for constituting a more human society.

Within a constructive interplay between *ubuntu*-thinking, *ũtigi*-thinking and the ethos of sacrificial outreach (Christian spirituality) what is the unique contribution of Christian, wisdom-thinking (*sapientia*) in the overcoming of paranoiac perceptions?

The hospice metaphor (*hospitium*): *diakonia* (charity) as social and cosmic healing (*tikkun odam*)

Due to the existential locus of God language, two metaphors are extremely relevant for the design of practical-theological actions (*fides quaerens actum*): (a) the hospice metaphor of *xenophilia*, and (b) the paracletic metaphor of non-discriminatory advocacy (*paraclesis*).

Hospitality and how one deals with the stranger or outsider, could be viewed as one of the cornerstones of a praxis of love and hope in the Old Testament. The basis for hospitality is the conviction in Israel that the encounter between God and his people is based on the principle of God's hospitality (Vosloo 2006, 64). It is closely connected to what Fitchett and Grossoehme (2012, 388) calls the tenet of *tikkun odam* (to repair the world) in Judaism. "Efforts to repair the world are *mitzvot* acts of human kindness rooted in commandments" (Fitchett and Grossoehme 2012, 388).

In order to differentiate from African spiritualities (in this case *ubuntu* spirituality and *ũtigi* spirituality), the spirituality of *tikkun odam* is framed by devotion to the law, the principle of the holiness of God, and the sanctification of everyday life. For example, land and life will be repaired (cosmic healing) if one becomes "holy" in acts of harvesting: "Do not go over your vineyard a second time or pick up the grapes that have fallen. Leave them for the poor and the alien. I am the Lord your God" (Lev. 19:10). (Healing as obedience to the commandments.)

The Pentateuch contains specific commands for the Israelite to care for life and for the stranger as themselves (Lev. 19:33-34; Deut. 10:19-19); to look after the welfare of the other (Deut. 24:17-22). The practice of hospitality was extended to every sojourner, even a runaway slave (Deut. 23:16-17) or one's archenemy (Deut. 24:17-22) (Butler 1991, 670).

In the Old Testament Abraham is depicted as the prototype of the good host in Jewish culture (Wright 1996, 431) even though he was actually considered a sojourner in the land (Gen. 23:4). Hebrews 13:3 summons one not to forget to entertain strangers, for by doing so some has unwittingly entertained angels. Pohl

(1999, 24) pointed out that Abraham's kindness to the strangers connects hospitality to the presence of God (Bratcher (2002, 2); hospitality exhibits the blessings and promises of God. Therefore, possessions and land were not possessions (Brueggemann 1977, 23), but merely gifts to be shared with the poor and the less fortunate in the society (Davies 1989, 351). Therefore, to be hospitable is to represent God within a space wherein even the enemy becomes a guest.[3]

Hospitality establishes an inclusive communality; a *banquet community* (*koinonia*) based on the principle of *agápē*-love, and thus embodies a non-discriminatory, destigmatised praxis of hope.

Spiritual networking: toward an inclusive and supplementary approach

Henry Nouwen in his book *Reaching Out* (1998), identified the shift from hostility to hospitality as one of the most important shifts or spiritual movements of the human soul in order to foster wholeness, healing and growth. Hospitality exceeds the threat of *xenophobia* (the fear of strangers) and racial or cultural discrimination; it represents unqualified *xenophilia*. Derrida (2001, 16-17) asserts: "Hospitality is culture itself and not simply one ethic among others."

Hospitality introduces true friendship. To abuse strangers or for strangers to take advantage of the host was interpreted as an improper act that totally breached the treaty of guest friendship (Matthews 1991, 523). That was even the case in ancient Greek and Roman culture (Koenig 1985, 5) wherein hospitality became a public virtue: *hospitium publicum* (Matthews 1991, 523).

With reference to the three spiritual traditions discussed in the previous outline, one can say that the metaphor of hospitality within different cultural settings, include the following positive, vital elements (Muragi 2011, 150-151): openness in the encounter between the host and the guest (the stranger); obliging invitation; embracement and whole-hearted welcoming; the principle of sharing; the giving of protection; the opening of a new future and promising future and altruistic generosity.

What becomes clear, is that a kind of inclusive approach in terms of mutual sharing, a sense of belongingness and hospitable outreach to the stranger, are com-

---

[3] Bretherton (2006, 129) links the whole understanding of Christian hospitality to all the stories of hospitality in the Old Testament as linked to the notion of the reconciling work of God to his covenantal people and to creation. The early Christians offered hospitality to the sick, the injured, widows, orphans, sojourners, strangers, the aged, slaves, prisoners and the hungry (Oden 2001, 20). "To be moral is to be hospitable to the stranger" (Ogletree 1985, 1).

munal features between the spirituality implied by *ubuntu, tikkun odam, ūtigi* and *xenophilia*.

The unique contribution of Christian spirituality to foster a spirit of democracy and hope resides in the *paraklesis* metaphor (compassionate advocacy).

In the LXX *parakaleo* is mainly used for the Hebrew *naham* which denotes sympathy and comfort. It was the prophet's task also to comfort the people. "Comfort, comfort my people, says your God" (Is 40:1). When *parakaleo* is used to translate *naham* specifically, it expresses compassion, sympathy and caring (Ps 135:14). When *parakaleo* is used for other Hebrew equivalents, it denotes encouragement, strengthening and guidance (Braumann 1978, 570). *Parakaleo* is also linked to the term *parakletos* which can be translated into helper, advocate, counsellor, comforter, and persuader/convincer.

One can conclude and say that practical theology (*fides quaerens actum*) as life care should represent the following caring activities in civil society: (a) sensitivity and compassion (*pathos*); (b) identification (woundedness); (c) insight and understanding in terms of paradoxes (wise fool); (d) hospitable outreach to the stranger, the outcast and the outsider, (e) compassionate advocacy (*paraclesis*) and empowerment of the stranger. For the practising of faith in the public arena, the concepts "God as friend," "God as our soul companion" or "host;" "God as our partner for life" (God's friendship in terms of his covenantal and compassionate faithfulness) should play an important role in a practical-theological engagement in civil society.

Conclusion

The metaphor of the host communicates sharing, welcoming, embracement, inclusive communality (*koinonia* as the *hospitium* of God). In this regard *ubuntu,* as the humanising factor in relationships, *ūtigi* as the liberating act of making outsiders, insiders, and the kenotic love of a sacrificial ethos (unconditional inclusivity), should supplement and enrich one another in the attempt to introduce justice and reconciliation. Democratisation needs hospitable paradigms ("*Willkommenskultur*") in order to establish sustainable change (an integrative spiritual factor for the healing of life). Civil society needs public forums and "ideas" (philosophies of *ubuntu* and *ūtigi*) that can steer citizens into the formation of a "compassionate society." *Paraclesis* advocates on behalf of the other; *xenophilia* heals and can overcome *xenophobia*.

A compassionate community is about the challenge to provide "hospitals" (*xenodochia*), safe havens (monasteries of hope, places of refuge) where threatened people can become whole again. Hospitality is actually about a public virtue:

hospitium publicum; one's calling in civil life is to make hope a home (*Heimat*) for homeless people by means of *diakonia* and *koinonia* (operative ecclesiology).

References

Berger, Peter. L. 1992. *A Far Glory: The Quest for Faith in an Age of Credulity*. New York: The Free Press.

Bergson, Eric. 2015. *Catholicity Challenging Ethnicity. An Ecclesiological Study of Churches in Post-apartheid South Africa*. Uppsala: Uppsala University.

Bosch, David. J. 1974. *Het evangelie in Afrikaans gewaad*. Kampen: Kok.

Braumann, George. 1978a. "Advocate, Paraclete, Helper." In *Dictionary of New Testament Theology*, edited by C. Brown, 1: 569-573. Exeter: Paternoster Press.

Braumann, George. 1978b. "Parakaleo." In *Dictionary of New Testament Theology*, edited by C. Brown, 1, 88-91. Exeter: Paternoster Press.

Bretherton, Luke. 2006. *Hospitality as Holiness: Christian Witness amid Moral Diversity*. London: Ashgate.

Brueggemann, Walter. 1977. *The Land. Place as Gift, Promise and Challenge in Biblical Faith*. Philadelphia: Fortress Press.

Butler, Trent. C. 1991. *Holman Bible Dictionary*. Tennessee: Holman Bible.

Casdorff, Von Stephan-Andreas. 2016. "Gefährdete Demokratie. Rational gegen radikal." *In Der Tagesspiegel*, Februar 5: 1.

Davies, Eryl W. 1989. "Land. It's Rights and Privileges." In *The World of Ancient Israel*, edited by R. E. Clements, Cambridge: Cambridge University Press: 349-369.

Derrida, Jacques. 2001. *On Cosmopolitanism and Forgiveness*. London: Routledge.

Duffy, Matt. 2016. "Klaus Schwab on the Digital revolution." *Time* 187 (2): 12.

Faulconbridge, Guy, and Sarah Young. 2015. "World unites on Paris, Beirut." *Cape Times*, November 16: 1.

Ferreira, Naas. 2009. Wolf en Rooikappie. *By (Burger)*, May 9: 4.

Fitchett, George., and Daniel Grossoehme. 2012. "Health Care Chaplaincy as a Research-Informed Profession." In *A Practical Clergy and Chaplain's Handbook*, edited by Stephan B. Roberts, 387-406. Woodstock: Skylight Paths.

Grethlein, Christian. 2012. *Praktische Theologie*. Berlin & Boston: De Gruyter.

Kaunda, Kenneth. 1967. *A Humanist in Africa. Letters to Colin Morris*. London: Longman.

Keane, John. *Global Civil Society?* Cambridge: Cambridge University Press.

Kenyatta, Jomo. 1938. *Facing Mount Kenya*. London: Heinemann.

Kessler, Tobias. 2014. *Migration als Ort der Theologie*. Regensburg: Verlag Friedrich Pustet.

Kizilhan, Jan. I. 2016. "Vorurteile gegenüber 'dem Fremden' lassen sich nur schwer ändern." *Der Tagesspiegel*, Februar 14: 5.

Koenig, John. 1985. *New Testament Hospitality. Partnership with Strangers as Promise and Mission Overtures to Biblical Theology*. Philadelphia: Fortress Press.

Kretzschmar, Louise. 1996. "A Holistic Spirituality. A Prerequisite for the Reconstruction of South." *Journal of Theology for Southern Africa* 95: 63-75.

Kumlehn, Martina. 2011. "Einleitung: Praktische Theologie als Lebenswissenschaft?!" In *Lebenswissenschaft Praktische Theologie?!*, edited by Thomas Klie, Martina Kumlehn, Ralph Kunz, and Thomas Schlag, *Praktische Theologie im Wissenschaftsdiskurs*, Band 9, 1-8. Berlin & New York: De Gruyter.

Lauster, Jörg. 2007. "Leben. Genetischer Code/Lebensphilosophie/inneres Leben/ewiges Leben." In *Handbuch Praktische Theologie*, edited by Wilhelm Gräb and Birgit Weyel, 137-148. Gütersloh: Gütersloher Verlagshaus.

Leiner, Martin., and Maria. Palme. 2014. "Introduction to the Present Volume." In *Societies in Transformation. Sub-Saharan Africa between Conflict and Reconciliation*, edited by Martin. Leiner, Maria. Palme, and Peggy Stöckner, 1-12. Göttingen: Vandenhoeck & Ruprecht.

Louw, Daniël. J. 2008. *Cura Vitae. Illness and the Healing of Life*. Wellington: Lux Verbi.

Mandela, Nelson. 2005. *In the Words of Nelson Mandela*. London: Penguin Books.

Matthews, Victor, and Don C. Benjamin. 1991. *Old Testament Parallels. Law and Stories from the Ancient Near East*. New York: Paulist Press.

Mbiti, John. S. 1969. *African Religions and Philosophy*. London: Heinemann.

Miller-McLemore, Bonnie J. 2012. "Introduction. The Contributions of Practical Theology." In *The Wiley-Blackwell Companion to Practical Theology*, edited by Bonnie J. Miller- McLemore, 1-20. Malden, Oxford & Chichester: John Wiley & Sons.

Mtetwa, S. 1996. "African Spirituality in the Context of Modernity." *Bulletin for Contextual Theology in Southern Africa and Africa* 3: 21-25.

Murage, Josiah. K. 2011. *The Concept of Ũtugi within the HIV and AIDS Pandemic: A Pastoral Assessment of the Ecclesial Praxis of the Anglican Church of Kenya*, Unpublished D.Th. dissertation. Stellenbosch: University of Stellenbosch.

Mutugi, Julius G. 2001. *The Truth about African Hospitality: Is there Hope for Africa?* Mombasa: The Salt Productions.

Nouwen, Henry. J. M. 1998. *Reaching Out*. London: Fount Paperbacks.

Oden, Amy. G. 2001. *And You Welcomed Me. A Sourcebook on Hospitality in Early Christianity*. Nashville: Abingdon.

Ogletree, Thomas W. 1985. *Hospitality to the Strangers. Dimension of Moral Understanding*. Philadelphia: Fortress Press.

Osmer, Rick R. 2008. *Practical Theology. An Introduction*. Grand Rapids: Eerdmans.

Pohl, C. D.1999. *Making Room: Recovering Hospitality as a Christian Tradition*. Grand Rapids: Eerdmans.

Polak, Regina 2014. "Migration als Ort der Theologie." In *Migration als Ort der Theologie*, edited by T. Kessler, 1-20. Regensburg: Verlag Friedrich Pustet.

Puchalski, Christina M., Benjamin Blatt, Mikhail Kogan and Amy Butler. 2014. "Spirituality and Health: The Development of a Field." *Academic Medicine* 89 (1): 10-16.

Reader, John 2008. *Reconstructing Practical Theology. The Impact of Globalisation*. Aldershot: Ashgate.

Reuters, 2015. "Paris Killings an Attack on the Civilised World, says Obama." *Cape Argus*, November 16: 11.Rizzuto, Anna-Maria. 1979. *The Birth of the Living God. A Psychoanalytic Study*. Chicago, IL: University of Chicago Press.

SACC, Vermeulen, Keith and Scot Lovaas. 2006. *Practising Faith in the Public Arena:*

Advocacy and Public Policy. Marshalltown & Johannesburg: South African Council of Churches Parliamentary Office.

Seligman, Adam, B. 1992. *The Idea of Civil Society*. New York: Free Press.

Skhakhane, Jerome. 1995. "African Spirituality." In *The church and African culture*, edited by Mohlomi Makobane, 101-113. Germiston: Lumko.

Tutu, Desmond. 2004. "Nelson Mandela annual Lecture." http://nelsonmandela.org/uplo ads/files/NMF_Lecture_Book_small.pdf.

Vick, Karl. 2015. "The Great Migration." In *Time. Special Report. Exodus. The Epic Migration to Europe & What Lies Ahead*, October 19: 26-34.

Vosloo, Robert. 2006. *Engele as gaste. Oor gasvryheid teenoor die ander*. Wellington: Lux Verbi.

Wright, Christopher. J. H. 1983. *Living as the People of God. The Relevance of Old Testament Ethics*. Leicester: Inter-Varsity Press.

Ubuntu in flames – injustice and disillusionment in post-colonial Africa: A practical theology for new "liminal *ubuntu*" and personhood

Vhumani Magezi

Abstract

The dawn of democracy at the end of colonial rule brought much hope and promise to Africans. With *ubuntu* as a distinctive African feature, hopes for collective good and life improvement were expected. However, these hopes are being increasingly dashed by corruption, oppression and schemes that put the individual first at the expense of others. These developments are in stark contrast to the principles of *ubuntu*. Colossal injustice and rampant corruption are causing disillusionment in post-colonial Africa. What options exist for a new path that upholds and instils people's personhood and dignity? What positive contribution can practical theology make to the situation? In response to these questions, a practical theology that reforms traditional African *ubuntu* to a new *ubuntu* informed by Christian values provides a constructive approach to humanness and personhood. Such a practical-theological approach should have as its starting point an appreciation of the concept of *ubuntu*.

Introduction and background

The dawn of democracy across the African continent brought hope and promise to many people, but their hopes are being increasingly crushed by corruption, oppression and schemes that put the individual first at the expense of others. Transparency International's Corruption Perception Index measures the perceived levels of public sector corruption worldwide, where 100 is very clean and 0 is highly corrupt. Every African country scores less than 50 points, except Botswana with 63, which is ranked 31 in the world. The global average score is 43, while for Sub-Saharan Africa it is 33 (Ernst and Young 2014, 9). It is worrying that 92% of Sub-Saharan African countries scored below 50 points. Nussbaum observed that African political leaders have betrayed their fundamental humanness (*ubuntu*) values (Nussbaum 2003, 1).

Macheka rightly points out that African leaders have tended to embrace corruption and have departed from the cherished values and ideals aspired for in post-colonial Africa (Macheka 2014, 1). Masango echoes the same concerns. He states that African leadership is plagued by corruption, dictatorship and many other bad governance practices (Masango 2002, 707). Jones explains that corruption undermines democracy and good governance, violates human rights, distorts markets, erodes the quality of life and destroys people (Jones 2015, 6). Corrupt leadership dispenses with moral principles and the norms of social justice, which creates disillusionment. Madamombe notes that people feel betrayed and their lives are filled with uncertainty and fear (Madamombe 2008, 1). Igué aptly states that this situation highlights "a troubled African leadership" (Igué 2010, 2).

Ubuntu is a distinctive African quality that values collective good, humaneness and respect for the community. Colossal injustice and rampant corruption are in stark contrast to ubuntu. People's hopes for collective good and improvement of life are fading away, and they have become disillusioned. What positive contribution can practical theology make to the situation? A practical-theological approach that reforms traditional African *ubuntu* to a new *ubuntu* informed by Christian values would provide a constructive approach to humanness and personhood.

Ubuntu and its challenges

Bhengu describes *ubuntu* as the art of being human (Bhengu 1996, 10). Broodryk adds that *ubuntu* is rooted in African values that include humanness, caring, sharing, respect and facilitation of the quality of community life (Broodryk 2002, 56). *Ubuntu* is practiced in most parts of Africa (Nabudere 2008, 1). It gives African people a sense of identity, self-respect and achievement. Van Niekerk states that *ubuntu* is a fluid concept that is difficult to pin down (Van Niekerk 2013, ix). Tutu explains the challenge of defining *ubuntu*:

Ubuntu is very difficult to render into a Western language. It speaks to the very essence of being human. When we want to give high praise to someone we say. "Yu, u nobuntu"; "Hey, he or she has ubuntu." This means they are generous, hospitable, friendly, caring, and compassionate. They share what they have. It also means my humanity is caught up, is inextricably bound up, in theirs ... A person with Ubuntu is open and available to others, affirming of others, does not feel threatened that others are able and good; for he or she has the proper self- assurance that comes from knowing that he or she belongs in a greater whole, and is diminished when others are humiliated or diminished, when others are tortured or oppressed, or treated as if they were less than who they are. (Tutu 1999, 31-32)

The difficulty in rendering *ubuntu* is compounded by the many diverse voices on the subject. This diversity is characteristic of African philosophy, under which *ubuntu* discussion usually falls under. Van Niekerk calls African philosophy a broad church that is vague (Van Niekerk 2013, ix). This comment certainly applies to *ubuntu*, which is a central African philosophical concept.

Notwithstanding the fluidity of the concept of *ubuntu*, there are core features that characterise it. *Ubuntu* refers to a constellation of value claims and the morally normative requirements they entail, drawn from Africa's folk psychology. The concept of *ubuntu* was popularised in post-apartheid South Africa through the Truth and Reconciliation Commission (TRC) chaired by Bishop Desmond Tutu. The core value claim constituting *ubuntu* is humanness (Bennett 2011, 30-31; Sigger, Polak and Pennink 2010). Metz describes *ubuntu* under the following principles: first, an action is right when it respects a person's dignity and wrong if it degrades humanity. Second, an action is right when it promotes the well-being of others and wrong if it fails to enhance the welfare of one's fellows. Third, an action is right when it promotes the well-being of others without violating their rights and wrong if it either violates or fails to enhance the welfare of one's fellows. Fourth, an action is right when it positively relates to others and thereby realises oneself and wrong if it does not perfect one's nature as a social being (Metz 2009, 2013).

Nussbaum states that *ubuntu*'s underlying values seek to honour the dignity of everyone and are concerned with the development and maintenance of mutually affirming and enhancing relationships (Nussbaum 2003, 1-2). *Ubuntu* expresses compassion, reciprocity and humanity in the interests of building and maintaining a just and mutually caring community. The inconsistency between the *ubuntu* values and the reality of rampant corruption and injustice prompts the question of whether *ubuntu* exists (Louw 1998, 3).

Eliastam notes that there are scholars who argue that *ubuntu* offers significant possibilities while others argue that it is vague, full of contradictions and subject to manipulation (Eliastam 2015, 2). Matolino and Kwindingwi argue that people use the notion of *ubuntu* whichever way they like. They maintain that *ubuntu* is an outdated notion that does not change people's ethics to curb corruption and injustice (Matolino and Kwindingwi 2013, 200). Ngwenya dismisses *ubuntu* as a cliché and is merely Africa's search for distinctiveness from the West (Ngwenya 2012, 2). However, these views do not meaningfully address the issues causing disillusionment. In fact, despite the *ubuntu* rhetoric in South Africa, political leaders and the general population are clearly disrespecting humanness. People are treating one another in many cases as things ("*into*") (Cilliers 2008, 7). This is evident from inhumane acts of xenophobia and disregard of the poor and marginalised.

One other major concern raised against the current view of *ubuntu* is its ex-clusiveness. *Ubuntu*'s definition of community narrowly refers to people bound geographically and relationally. *Ubuntu* tends to exclude people who do not come from the same geographical area (ethnicity) or not filially related. Eliastam notes that this narrow approach to *ubuntu* leads to corruption and nepotism (Eliastam 2015, 5).

While the positive contributions of *ubuntu* are apparent, the negatives are equally notable (Masango 2006, 938; Metz 2011, 1). Prinsloo views *ubuntu* as having the potential to provide a framework for responding to practices that sus-tain corruption and unjust practices (Prinsloo 2013, 2). Chaplain believes that *ubuntu* is an ideal that people should strive towards (Chaplain 1996, 1). However, to what extent are the *ubuntu* values of compassion, reciprocity, dignity, harmony and humanity being lived in the interests of building and maintaining a community with justice and mutual caring? Moreover, how can *ubuntu* shift from a narrow fil-ial and geographical view of community and humanity to one that embraces all humanity?

From traditional *ubuntu* to new liminal *ubuntu*

Nabudere (2008, 1), Tutu (1999, 31-13), Nussbaum (2003, 1) and many other African scholars view *ubuntu* as uniquely African. *Ubuntu* arises from an African cultural context whose concepts are significantly distinct from Western concepts. However, Van Niekerk notes that when *ubuntu* was used in nation building in South Africa, it was cast as a variant of universal concepts cross-shared in post-apartheid South Africa (Van Niekerk 2013, 10). This indicates that *ubuntu* should have a much broader perspective than the current narrow view.

Sigger, Polak and Pennink ask the following searching question: since the *ubuntu* philosophy focuses on values such as respect, solidarity and compassion, are these values uniquely African or are they are values that should be universal (Sigger, Polak and Pennink 2010, 1)? From their extensive empirical study, they observed that at the core of *ubuntu* is the idea of humanness. Thus if *ubuntu* is applicable to all of humanity, the concept cannot be uniquely African. This view of *ubuntu* challenges African people to explore possibilities of meaningfully shar-ing *ubuntu* with the world. This should cause theologians to reflect on how it can be integrated in Africa beyond filial and geographical links. Nabudere points out that during the TRC in South Africa, while Bishop Tutu was guided by the constitution, it is clear that he firmly believed that the *ubuntu* philosophy could exist alongside Christianity and could play a role in reconciling the people of South Africa (Nabudere 2008, 1). Therefore, *ubuntu* is a philosophical concept of African culture that shifts to one that functions at the intersection of public space. This shift entails transitioning *ubuntu* from a traditional concept to *ubuntu* in transition, i.e., liminality (Eliastam 2015, 8).

Liminality was first described by Van Gennep (1960) and later developed by Turner (1967, 1969). Turner observed three phases in transition experiences: separation – losing an old world; margin (liminality) – entering an unknown world; and re-aggregation – re-emerging into a new world. For Turner the liminal function is the period of transition from "one type of stable or recurrent condition that is culturally recognised" to another (Turner 1967, 94). Gade noted that *ubuntu* as a concept has not been static but has changed. He describes stage one of *ubuntu* as a period in which *ubuntu* was defined as a human quality; stage two as a period in which *ubuntu* was defined as something either connected or identical to a philosophy or an ethic; and stage three as a period in which *ubuntu* was defined as African humanism. Stage four is the period in which *ubuntu* was defined as a world view, and stage five is the period in which *ubuntu* was defined as something connected to the proverb "*umuntu ngumuntu ngabantu*." He further notes that the designation of the stages of development of *ubuntu* is problematic as they cannot be strictly differentiated since they exist together. *Ubuntu* as a concept bears all the different dimensions (Gade 2011, 315-316). Thanks to Gade, it is now recognised that the concept of *ubuntu* is changing. This change therefore makes *ubuntu* to be understood in terms of liminality.

Liminality presents opportunities and risks. The shift to a liminal *ubuntu* prompts questions about the nature of this new *ubuntu*. The traditional African *ubuntu* with its narrow, limited idea of community needs to be extended to universal *ubuntu*. This extrapolation calls for the integration of reformulated and moderated traditional values. Practical theology needs to explore an approach that harnesses the concept and optimises its utility for quality life and development.

Towards a practical theology and shift of *ubuntu* to liminality

Practical theology should provide an alternative perspective that shifts and in some cases shakes off the localisation and narrow African view of *ubuntu* to encompass broader humanity. Such a fresh perspective would contribute to disentangling the notion of traditional *ubuntu* – arguably a "zombie" category – to a fluid and adaptive concept that responds to pressing African contextual challenges. Practical theologians Reader and Louw describe zombie categories as concepts that no longer do justice to the world we experience and yet are difficult to abandon because of tradition and also because they are not yet totally redundant. Zombie categories are therefore described as the "living dead;" the tried and familiar frameworks of interpretation that have served us well for many years and continue to haunt our thoughts, even though they are embedded in a world that is passing away before our eyes (Reader 2008, 4; Louw 2011, 1). Kumlehn considers practical theology as a science that should give attention to promoting a kind of religion of life (Kumlehn 2011, 40). The notion of zombie *ubuntu* should be reconsidered within the perspective of life's experiences in order to transition and transform it into a contemporary mode that addresses real-life issues (life science). By doing so, practical theology will contribute to changing a docile (zombie) notion of *ubuntu* to liminal *ubuntu* that actively engages with contemporary challenges.

To overcome the pitfalls of zombie categories and optimise opportunities ushered in by new *ubuntu* liminality, practical theology should envisage new ways of viewing *ubuntu*. To shift from traditional *ubuntu* to new liminal *ubuntu*, the following illustration may be used. Broodryk stated that according to *ubuntu* (traditional approach), my neighbour and I have the same origins, the same life experiences and common destiny. However, the neighbour described by Broodryk is a relationally and geographically bound neighbour (Broodryk 2006, 5). To shift to new liminal *ubuntu*, theological *ubuntu* should transform its notion of neighbour from a filially and geographically bound to one of broader community and humanity. This will have positive results for the public, particularly public office bearers who are trapped in nepotism and the cult of greed that results in short-changing the public (structural engagement). A neighbour should be a person whom we serve rather than a relative or political affiliate (tyranny of nepotism, "buddyism" and "friendism").[1] Jesus redefined neighbours (Luke 10) to include people outside our circles.

Ubuntu revolutionised by Christian values reshapes people's destiny and life. Such an approach to *ubuntu* will include a transcendent dimension rather than benevolence judged by peers and family members who share in one's booty whether corruptly obtained or not. Christian values of *ubuntu* (liminality) are universally bonded by Christ. Thus to develop such a model of *ubuntu*, practical theology is challenged to develop a public dimension that engages and influences life by drawing on traditional African practices such as *ubuntu*. This way Christian ministry and service assume more of an incarnational dimension than a foreign and irrelevant religion within life spaces. Chaplain's summation of *ubuntu* clearly indicates that it is an ideal to which people should aspire (Chaplain 1996, 1).

---

[1]   By "buddyism" and "friendism" I mean the general tendency of public office bearers and individuals in decision-making positions to parcel out deals and business contracts to friends and people closely related or connected to them.

Towards a practical theology of shifting traditional *ubuntu* to liminal *ubuntu*

A practical theology that seeks to shift *ubuntu* from its current state to broad humanity (liminality) needs to explore an alternative approach to *ubuntu*. Such an approach should view *ubuntu* not as a "frozen and static" concept (zombie) but as a description of an ideal (*telos*) that people should strive towards (energising power for better humane-ness). To explain the shift that should be made, a visual model provides insight into the dynamics of the required movement/shift.

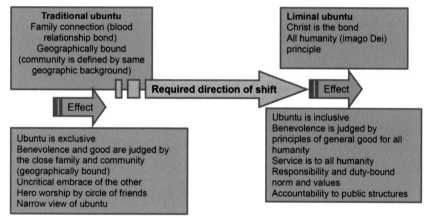

Figure 1: Directional shift from traditional ubuntu to liminal ubuntu

In the traditional *ubuntu* framework an individual feels bound and obligated to respond to the needs of people related to them. They are also inclined to assist people who come from the same geographical area. This is evident in political and employment circles. When a new president is elected there is generally a tendency to appoint someone from the same geographical area. Similarly, it is not uncommon that when someone is appointed to a senior government position s/he recruits family and community members. While this is viewed as nepotism, to the community the appointed person is practicing *ubuntu*. Thus traditional *ubuntu* in its current practice is exclusive to "your people." Benevolence and acts of good and bad are determined by the family and community. The Nigerian philosopher Turaki (2015) commented in an unpublished lecture given at North-West University that working in government or public office is like hunting. You kill a gazelle and share it with your relatives and community. This practice dates back to wars between villages where the warrior defeats another village and plunders their livestock. His entire village welcomes him as a hero. Therefore, some government officials take plunder back to their villages. These people would be viewed as practicing true *ubuntu*, where *ubuntu* is narrowly limited to friends, relatives and the close geographical community. No one accuses the individual of corruption, but rather praises him or her for "thinking of his/her people back home in the village" (Turaki 2015:1).

Africa has moved away from the traditional practices of *ubuntu*. African states are democratically and constitutionally governed. This calls for a change in the view and practice of *ubuntu*. Bowers notes that African theology has been engaged in the discourse of cultural contextualisation and its theological implications but has neglected emerging contemporary issues. It differs from the theological reflections in Europe and North America, which concern prevailing intellectual trends. This has resulted in intellectual issues such as a renewed approach to *ubuntu* remaining unexplored in Africa. African theology is still preoccupied with establishing Africa's identity distinct from the West which has resulted in a one-sided view where the West is criticised while African traditional culture is romanticised (Bowers 2009, 102). Gifford observes that this situation has caused a deficiency in African theology on issues such as corruption and bad governance (Gifford 2008, 25-27). Bowers notes that there is a critical deficiency in African theological reflection, which is increasingly being acknowledged by African theological scholars (Bowers 2009, 101).

My proposal for a liminal *ubuntu* is an attempt to address the above a gap. Practical theology as a life science should explore creative ways of engaging contemporary challenges. A shift from traditional *ubuntu* to liminal *ubuntu* implies that people are bound by a "Christ bond" and the *imago Dei* principle that all people are created in the image of God. Jesus radically transformed our view of neighbour (Luke 10) and family (Luke 9), and redefined family (Luke 8; Matthew 12) as people who carry out the will of God. The proposed focus is not to dwell on a tainted image but rather to view all humanity as people bearing the image of God who must be treated with dignity and personhood. The redefinition of neighbour and family implies a spirit driven person (Louw 2014). An *ubuntu* person alive in the spirit views humanity as bonded by Christ and his/her actions are informed by the positive principle of *imago Dei*.

A shift from traditional to liminal *ubuntu* suggests a radical shift in the way we approach other human beings. All people deserve to be treated with *ubuntu*. The principles and values used to judge the worth of actions are not subjective community values but standards that apply across all of humanity. We have to account to public structures upon which *ubuntu* should be evaluated as the concept is extrapolated to the public space. Benevolence is, therefore, a public matter where universal good is cherished rather than a few related individuals.

As African people are communal and bound by strong family ties, the inevitable question is the place of family in one's life. The role of the individual in the family should be understood when shifting to liminal *ubuntu*. This approach is aptly captured in U.S. President Obama's tribute to Nelson Mandela when he thanked South Africa for sharing Nelson Mandela with the rest of the world (*Mail and Guardian* 2013). In this approach, family and friends are not disregarded, but the relationships are put in perspective. In liminal *ubuntu* you do not take from one hand to give to another hand. Human beings are equal and deserve equal treatment whether they are family members or not. Only when one is bound by a sense of duty to all humanity is the preference for some people at the expense of others overcome.

Towards liminal *ubuntu* realism

A key question that emerges from the foregoing discussion and proposal is whether or not this is merely utopian thinking, and giving the limitations, even depravity of humanity. The response to this scepticism is an emphatic no! Liminal *ubuntu* is possible from both historical and process reasons.

The Center for the Study of Global Christianity estimates that the number of Christians is expected to grow as a proportion of Africa's population from 143 million in 1970 (38.7% of the continent's population) to 630 million by 2020 (49.3%). In a number of African countries, the Christian population in 2014 was already over 70%, e.g., Democratic Republic of Congo and Zambia 80%, Angola 75%, Gabon 73%, South Africa and Zimbabwe 70% (The Center for the Study of Global Christianity 2013). If these numbers reflect true Christianity it is realistic to view liminal *ubuntu* as possible. The role played by Christians in influencing social and community change cannot be underestimated. Truth in History records the following effects of the Welsh Revival in 1904-1905:

Whole communities were turned upside down, and were radically changed from depravity to glorious goodness. The crime rate dropped, often to nothing. The police force reported that they had little more to do than supervise the coming and going of the people to the chapel prayer meetings, while magistrates turned up at courts to discover no cases to try. The alcohol trade was decimated, as people were caught up in more by what happened in the local chapels than the local public houses and bars. Families experienced amazing renewal, where the money-earning husband and father, the bread winner, had wasted away the income and sowed discord, but now under the moving power of the Holy Spirit, following the conversion to be a follower of Jesus Christ, he not only provided correctly for family needs, but was now with the family, rather than wasting his time, and wages, in the public houses of the village or town. (Truth in History 2015, 1)

The above example suggests that where genuine and authentic Christianity is present, change will occur.

Secondly, achieving liminal *ubuntu* is a process. Louw calls the shifting of mind-sets to adopt a new ethos and attitude a habitus (Louw 2008, 21). Theologically life can be considered a pilgrimage of pressing on to higher ideals in Christ (Philippians 3:13). A theology of shifting to liminal *ubuntu* reminds Christians that they are on a journey of growth that should progress daily. Practical theology as a science of life should contribute to develop tools and progress markers to assess and diagnose people's growth. Without overplaying the notion of "what cannot be measured cannot be improved," a mantra of empirical science, there is value for practical theology to assess progress. The assumption is that effective spiritual transformation will result in some kind of quantifiable or observable changes in people's lives.

Conclusion

This article discussed the problem of corruption and injustice in post-colonial Africa and proposed a practical theology that reforms traditional African *ubuntu* to a new *ubuntu* informed by Christian values as a constructive approach to humanness and personhood. It argued that true *ubuntu* is achieved by pneumatological empowerment. It is only when efforts to live according to true *ubuntu* are viewed pneumatologically that *ubuntu* becomes a reality within liminal opportunities. It ceases to be a utopian view of humanness and becomes more than a philosophy, but a practical life ideal by which people allow themselves to be shaped (Nussbaum 2003, 10).

References

Bennett, Thomas, W. 2011. "Ubuntu: An African Equity." *PER: Potchefstroomse Elektroniese Regsblad* 14 (4): 29-61.

Bhengu, Mfuniselwa, J. 1996. *Ubuntu: The Essence of Democracy*. Cape Town: Novalis Press.

Bowers, Paul. 2009. "Christian Intellectual Responsibilities in Modern Africa." *Africa Journal of Evangelical Theology* 28: 91-114.

Broodryk, Johann. 2002. "Ubuntu: Life lessons from Africa." http://books.google.co.za/books/about/Ubuntu.html?id=5iV7AAAAMAAJ.

Broodryk, Johann 2006. "Ubuntu: African Life Coping Skills." http://www.topkinisis.com/conference/CCEAM/.

Center for the Study of Global Christianity. 2013. "Christianity in its Global Context, 1970-2020. Society, Religion, and Mission." http://www.globalchristianity.org.

Chaplin, Kevin. 1996. "The Ubuntu Spirit in African Communities." https://www.scribd.com/document/211612962/Ubuntu-Spirit.

Cilliers, Johan. "In Search of Meaning between *Ubuntu* and *Into*: Perspectives on Preaching in Post-apartheid South Africa." Paper delivered at the Eighth International Conference of *Societas Homiletica*. http://www.researchgate.net/publication/237526176.

Eliastam, John. L.B. 2015. "Exploring Ubuntu Discourse in South Africa: Loss, Liminality and Hope." *Verbum et Ecclesia* 36 (2). doi: 10.4102/ve.v36i2.1427.

Ernst and Young. 2014. "Transparency International. Corruption Perceptions Index." http://www.transparency.org.

Gade, Christian. B.N. 2011. "The Historical Development of the Written Discourses on Ubuntu." *South African Journal of Philosophy* 30 (3): 303-329.

Gifford, Paul. 2008. "Africa's Inculturation Theology: Observations of an Outsider." *Hekima Review* 38: 18-34.

Igué, John O. 2010. "A New Generation of Leaders in Africa: What Issues Do They Face?" *International Development Policy* 1. Doi: 10.4000/poldev.139.

Jones, Edmund G. 2015. "The Vicious Cycle of Corruption. Accountable Leadership and Sustainability in Africa." 2015. Conference on Religion, Democracy and Civil Society, UNISA, April 21-24. http://www.unisa.ac.za/contents/faculties/theology/docs/Sessionbreakdownb.pdf.

Kumlehn, Martina. 2011. "Einleitung: Praktische Theologie als Lebenswissenschaft?" In *Lebenswissenchaft Praktische Theologie?! Praktische Theologie im Wissenschaftsdiskurs,* edited by Thomas Klie, Martina Kumlehn, Ralph Kunz and Thomas Schlag, 1-8. Berlin & New York: De Gruyter.

Louw, Daniël J. 1998. "Ubuntu: An African Assessment of the Religious Other." The Paideia Archive. http://www.bu.edu/wcp/Papers/Afri/AfriLouw.htm.

Louw, Daniël J. 2008. *Cura Vitae. Illness and the Healing of Life.* Wellington: Lux Verbi.

Louw, Daniël J. 2011. "Ta splanchna: A theopaschitic approach to a hermeneutics of God's praxis: From zombie categories to passion categories in theory formation for a practical theology of the intestines." *HTS Theological Studies/Teologiese Studies* 67 (3): 65-77. http://dx.doi.org/10.4102/hts.v67i3.1087.

Louw, Daniël J. 2014. *Wholeness in Hope Care.* Zurich: Lit Verlag.

Macheka, Mavis Thokozile. 2014. "An Evaluation of Post-Colonial African leadership: A Study of Ayi Kwei Armah's The Beautiful Ones Are Not Yet Born, and Chinua Achebe's A Man of the People." *International Journal of English and Literature* 5 (1): 14-18.

Madamombe, Esrina Pedziseni. 2008. "Hope and Disillusionment: A Postcolonial Critique of Selected South African and Zimbabwean Short Stories." Ph.D. dissertation, University of Fort Hare.

Masango, Maake J.S. 2002. "Leadership in the African Context: Words on Leadership." *Verbum et Ecclesia* 23 (3): 707-718.

Masango, Maake J.S. 2006. "African Spirituality that Shapes the Concept of Ubuntu." *Verbum et Ecclesia* JRG 27 (3): 933-934. http://dx.doi.org/10.4102/ve.v27i3.195.

Matolino, Bernard and Wanceslaus Kwindingwi. 2013. "The End of Ubuntu." *South African Journal of Philosophy* 32 (2): 197-205.

Metz, Thaddeus. 2009. "African Moral Theory and Public Governance: Nepotism, Preferential Hiring, and Other Partiality." In *African Ethics: An Anthology of Comparative and Applied Ethics,* edited by Munyaradzi Felix Murove, 335-336. Pietermaritzburg: University of KwaZulu-Natal Press.

Metz, Thaddeus. 2011. "Ubuntu as a Moral Theory and Human Rights in South Africa." *African Human Rights Law Journal* 11 (2): 532-559.

Metz, Thaddeus. 2013. "African Ethics." In *The International Encyclopedia of Ethics,* edited by Hugh LaFollette, 129-138. Malden, MA: Wiley-Blackwell.

Nabudere, Dani W. 2008. "Ubuntu Philosophy: Memory and Reconciliation." https://repo sitories.lib.utexas.edu/handle/2152/4521.

Ngwenya, Amanda. 2012. "Ubuntu, a Cliché not a Philosophy." http://thoughtleader.co. za/amandangwenya/2012/01/27/ubuntu-a-cliche-not-a-philosophy/.

Nussbaum, Barbara. 2003. "African Culture and Ubuntu." *Perspectives* 17 (1): 1-12.

Obama, Barack. 2013. "Obama's tribute to Mandela. The Full Speech." http://mg.co.za/ article/2013-12-10-obamas-tribute-to-mandela-the-full-speech.

Prinsloo, Aidan Vivian. 2014. "Prolegomena to Ubuntu and Any Other Future South African Philosophy." M.A. thesis, Rhodes University.

Reader, John. 2008. *Reconstructing Practical Theology: The Impact of Globalisation.* Aldershot: Ashgate.

Religious Population. 2014. "Africa Religious Population in 2014." http://www.religiouspopulation.com/africa.

Sigger, Dominique S., Polak Barbra J., and Pennink, Bartjan J W. 2010. " 'Ubuntu' or 'humanness' as a management concept." CDS Research Report No. 29. https://www. rug.nl/research/.

Truth in History. 2015. "The Welsh Revival of 1904-1905." http://truthinhistory.org/the -welsh-revival-of-1904-1905.

Turaki, Yusufu. 2015. "Colonialism, Slavery and Islam." Lecture, North-West University, Vaal Triangle, May 14.

Turner, Victor W. 1967. *The Forest of Symbols.* New York: Ithaca.

Turner, Victor W. 1969. *The Ritual Process: Structure and Anti-Structure.* Chicago: Aldine Publishing.

Tutu, Desmond. 1999. *No Future without Forgiveness.* New York: Random House.

Van Gennep, A. 1960. *The Rites of Passage.* London: Routledge.

Van Niekerk, Jason. 2013. "Ubuntu and moral value." Ph.D. dissertation, University of the Witwatersrand.

Practicing *Ubuntu*[1] *beyond*, *against* or *with* Christian texts

Johann Meylahn

Abstract

The chapter responds to two challenges. The first challenge is to think *Ubuntu beyond, against* or *with* the Christian text. Theories of *Ubuntu* are developed from oral traditions of African practices but developed in European languages, and therefore the terms used to describe *ubuntu* are informed and shaped by the Western heritage. The dominant role of the Christian text in this heritage cannot be denied. The consequence of this is that *ubuntu* is interpreted in Christian language and it becomes very difficult to differentiate *Ubuntu* from certain interpretations of Christianity. Is it possible to think *Ubuntu* beyond or against Christianity or should one accept that it will be thought with the Christian text as long as it is thought within a world that has been carried out to a large extent by the predominance of Christian texts? The second challenge is to then think personhood and human dignity, both terms that are part of the carried-out world of the Christian-Western texts, and the possible injustice of that, as well as the alternatives that *ubuntu* might offer even if it is thought *with* the Christian Texts.

The challenge to talk on *Ubuntu*

It is an intimidating challenge to present a chapter on *Ubuntu* taking the colour of my skin into consideration, as one cannot separate discourses on *Ubuntu* from the politics of race. Who am I, a white South African, to talk on *Ubuntu*? A politics of African or black difference haunts any discourse on *Ubuntu*. Discourses are haunted by the ghosts of the mothers and fathers of the various political-philosophical traditions from which or within which one is working. One can only face these ghosts, respond to them with the necessary respect due to them, as one would respect and honour the living dead – the living dead who haunt discourses, more specifically the living dead of my philosophical and theological traditions, who haunt my theology and philosophy. Are the intimidating ghosts who haunt this article not true of any discourse, as discourses are, one speaking of the other,

---

[1] I follow Leonhard Praeg (2014a; 2014b) with the capitalisation of *Ubuntu* as worldview, philosophy or ethic to differentiate it from *ubuntu* as a human quality.

for the other, naming the other, speaking in the name of the other, that is the *arché*, the original violence of language. So what makes these racial differences different to difference as such? I believe these questions map the context in which most discourses on *Ubuntu* unfold. Who is authorised to speak of or for whom and who is this who, that speaks? It is about naming the other as African (Black) by the colonial powers, and then subsequently the post- or de-colonial response to that Western naming of Black difference, which creates the context of most discourses on *Ubuntu* and/or African humanism.

Discourses on *Ubuntu*

Gade traces the historic development of texts on *Ubuntu* from the earliest known recording of the term in 1846 (Gade 2011, 306; cf. 2012) till the present day New South Africa. There is a development in the use of the term *ubuntu*, from referring to a human quality (Gade 2011, 307) or ethnic morality (see Prozesky 2009, 5) to referring to an African worldview (Gade 2011, 309), philosophy or an ethics as a way of life.

Gade's mapping of the development of *ubuntu* into discourses of *Ubuntu*, indicates that it is only after 1995 that there was an exponential growth in texts mentioning and reflecting on *ubuntu* (Gade 2011, 315-316). The texts published on *ubuntu* during the 2000s, "either quote the proverb or refer to the idea of the proverb that people are interconnected" (Gade 2011, 318). Such a map indicates that something changed with regard to the understanding and the use of the term, *Ubuntu*, and it seems as if the change took place in the context of political transition, from the Old to the New South Africa.

Praeg refers to this transformation as a translation or codification of the *work of ubuntu* into a *discourse on Ubuntu* (Praeg 2008, 373). Throughout Africa, as African states liberated themselves from colonial rule and sought to establish a post- or de-colonial states, there was a need to re-think what it means to be African. It is in such contexts of transformation that African humanism, Negritude, Ujamaa, African socialism and *Ubuntu* can be interpreted. The work of *ubuntu*, as a human quality, had to be fleshed out in the post-colonial context, as part of the de-colonialisation, with the question, what makes one African. Colonial powers had classified and named the African as the other to the European. In the post-colonial period Africa needed to decide what to do with these colonial names, characterisations and definitions of what being African means. The first task was to re-discover what it means to be African and then the question, how that relates to the rest of humanity.

Ubuntu is generally understood as a way of *being, as belonging* in Africa. The African community was held together by the work of *ubuntu*, made up of various stories, fables, poetry, practices and rituals that facilitated *being as belonging*. This is then translated or codified into a discourse on *Ubuntu*. Praeg also speaks of the praxis of *ubuntu*, "what one could also call the living ubuntu, *that unification of being as belonging, which will always precede and remain irreducible to any translation or codification of ubuntu as Ubuntu*" (Praeg 2014b, 77). The work of *ubuntu, the unification of being as belonging,* is translated and codified into discourses on *Ubuntu*, for example as *political economy of obligation* (Chabal 2009), *African gnosis* (Mudimbe 1988, 9), the *African Soul* (Nussbaum 2003), or *interconnectedness-towards-wholeness* (Krog 2008a; 2008b). The work of *ubuntu* translated into discourses on *Ubuntu* can be seen as being part of the identity politics of post-colonial Africa. Discourses, which developed on African Humanism, African Socialism, were attempts to construct an African "we" in the context of the "Black" or "African" as constructed by the colonisers. As part of this construction of an African "We," select elements of the past (pre-colonial) Africa were remembered and translated for the future of post-colonial Africa (Jewsiewicki and Mudimbe 1993, 10).

It is not a matter of randomly selecting a few memories and identifying certain practices. It is a very selective process guided by the plot of a political narrative, which enables the work of *ubuntu* to be translated into a discourse on *Ubuntu*. The plot guides what is remembered and what is forgotten as well as how certain practices and rituals are interpreted in the construction of a discourse on *Ubuntu*. It is constructed on the basis of a specific plot, which in turn is determined by the particular politics of the context of construction, so that one could speak of politics as first philosophy (see Praeg 2014b, 12). Mudimbe suggests that one should always ask: "Who's speaking, and from which intellectual background, and in order to produce what and communicate a knowledge to whom?" (Mudimbe 2003, 205).

Discourses on *Ubuntu* are academic constructs (Van Binsbergen 2001, 62) and one could argue that they are ideological constructs in that they serve a particular political narrative within a particular context. Wilson, for example, argues that *Ubuntu* is the ideological or political "wrapping" to legitimate a new government (Wilson 2001, 403). Verdoolaege argues that *ubuntu* is part of an "ideological master narrative," part of a "nation building project" (Verdoolaege 2007, 403).

If one accepts this narrative that discourses on *Ubuntu* emerged in the political context of transition, then it might also be understood as something that was and is necessary in the constitution of a post-colonial state or the constitution of a New South Africa, in a similar way that Negritude was needed or African Socialism was needed to constitute a "we" of post-colonial Africa. This idea that the New South Africa needs *ubuntu* becomes clear from a conversation between then President Mbeki and Shutte on the eve of the launch of the *Ubuntu* Project

(Gade 2011, 321-322). Discourses on *Ubuntu* are needed to develop an Ethic for the New South Africa; therefore, the work of *ubuntu* needs to be translated and codified into a Spirit of *Ubuntu*, as Shutte (2001) argues. This need for *Ubuntu* was also expressed in the epilogue of the Interim Constitution of South Africa, which called for work to be done on *Ubuntu* (Constitution of the Republic of South Africa, Act 200 of 1993, Epilogue after Section 251).

The different narratives of return (Gade 2011, 304) or ethno-philosophies (Hountondji 1983, 39), all made a call for Africanisation (Gade 2011, 304), and although there are differences, they seem to be in search of that which could constitute the African *we* over and against the European I (Individualism). For example, consider how *ujamaa* (Nyerere 1966, 169-170) is described in comparison and in contrast to European socialism.

For Metz it is not so much about the past, narratives of return, but about the future (Metz 2011, 535). Cornell and Van Marle argue that it is about both the past and the future (Cornell and Van Marle 2005), just as the archive and constitution are about remembering the past as well as creating the space for the constituting of a New South Africa in the future. In other words, an element of ethno-philosophy is necessary to constitute a New South Africa.

In this context of an expressed need for discourses on *Ubuntu*, the discourses increased tremendously. Today there is such a variety of discourses that many people dismiss *Ubuntu* as being too vague, or see it as a term that can be used for anything, an empty signifier that can be filled at will.

In an attempt to understand the vast variety of discourses on *Ubuntu*, Metz identifies the following groups: traditionalist, revisionists, those who reject *Ubuntu* as an ethic or way of life, and those who "explore *what talk about* ubuntu *currently means for society*" (Metz 2014, 448).

Ubuntu as glocal phenomena and its Christianisation

Ubuntu with a capital U is the translation or codification of the work of *ubuntu*, the living *ubuntu*, into a discourse on *Ubuntu* within a specific historical-political context. To understand this historical-political context, Praeg argues that *Ubuntu* is a glocal phenomenon that should be interpreted within the context of four *a prioris*, two local and two global (Praeg 2014a, 96-120; 2014b, 48-64). What is selected from the work of *ubuntu* to construct a discourse on *Ubuntu* is determined by a political narrative. Each political narrative creates different personae; Praeg identifies five such personae: "Prophet (with a subdivision into the Revolutionary and the Saviour), the Archivist, the Conformist, the Cosmopolitan and the Text Worker or Construction Worker" (Praeg 2014b, 100). I do not want to engage in the debate on the meaning of the work of *ubuntu* nor argue for a specific discourse on *Ubuntu*. I want to understand these discourses as glocal phenomena embedded in particular political narratives. Discourses on *Ubuntu*, as glocal phenomena, are translations of the work of *ubuntu* into Western language, making use of Western terms, philosophical paradigms and figurations. These cannot deny their Christian heritage. Terms such as communitarianism, human rights, human dignity, and interconnectedness are not unrelated to the Christian texts, which have shaped and formed Western philosophy, thought and culture.

The human subject, subjectification, personhood, and liberated personhood are themes deeply embedded in the monotheistic traditions that have shaped Western thought. The monotheistic traditions, specifically Judaism as a passional, post-signifying sign regime – as Deleuze and Guattari interpret it – offer powerful resources on identity formation, group formation, liberated from the dominant despotic Gods of the signifying sign-regime (Deleuze and Guattari 2011, 121f). Deleuze and Guattari argue that the post-signifying sign regime united with the imperial signifying sign regime in Christianity, and formed the Abstract Machine of the West. They argue that the Face-of-Christ is the Abstract Machine of the West, a combination of the post-signifying, passional sign regime with the imperial signifying sign regime (Deleuze and Guattari 2011, 176-183, and 125). Therefore, any discourse in Western languages will be constructed by the Abstract Machine of the West or the Face-of-Christ. Nancy echoes this when he argues that all thought (Western influenced) is Christian (Nancy 2008, 142).

This is where the conversation with *ubuntu*, or the conversation with Africa, becomes interesting if we take that journey to the ultimate extremity of Christianity and, thereby, to the ultimate extremity of the West. Is it possible or necessary to deconstruct Christianity and thereby deconstruct the Face of Christ, which is the White-Man's-Face, so as to create a space to think beyond this Face, what is other to this face? What is beyond this "text" that dominates Western thought? "To deconstruct Christianity is to accompany the West to that limit, to that *pass at which* the West cannot do otherwise than let go of itself in order to continue being the West, or still be something of itself beyond itself" (Nancy 2008, 143).

The work of *ubuntu*, as constructed by some, is such an attempt, to surpass the West, that limit. The challenge is to think the West against the West, and thereby contribute something to the West, as for example Mudimbe's (1991, 13) retro-diction. If one takes the arguments of Deleuze and Guattari into consideration, discourses on *Ubuntu* are Christianised. There are those who have consciously tried to think Christianity and *Ubuntu* (Tutu) together, but also those who have consciously tried to construct *Ubuntu* against Christianity (Krog). Yet it seems unavoidable that any discourse on *Ubuntu* is Christian or a construct of the Face-of-Christ.

Against the Christian text

Krog is an example of reading the translation of *ubuntu* into *Ubuntu* against the Christian text (Krog 2008a; 2008b). There is a political narrative at play here, a narrative of decolonisation, and of liberating people and their thoughts from the spiritual colonialism of Christian missionaries. Yet, such an attempt is a reduction of Christianity to what Nancy calls, in reference to Nietzsche, a pious Christianity (Nancy 2008, 142), and does not fully appreciate the dominant role the Christian texts have played in shaping Western thought and culture, even those thoughts that stand in opposition to pious Christianity, such as secularisation, Marxism, etcetera.

Before the Christian text, or at the limit of the Christian text

Ramose separates *ubu-* from *-ntu*, where *ubu-* can be understood as enfolding be-ing and *-ntu* as concrete beings (Ramose 1999, 50). This can be compared to Heidegger's *Austrag* or dif-ference (Meylahn 2010, 3). Ramose's *Ubuntu* is a glo-cal phenomenon, constructed within a particular political narrative and responding to global and local demands (*a prioris*) (Ramose 1999; see Praeg 2014b, 48-58). In his construction of a discourse on *Ubuntu* he situates *Ubu-ntu* as the *arché* of human being as belonging, as the universal music to which all who hear the music are invited to join the dance (Ramose 1999, 59).

Maybe it is good discourse to start to think about *ubuntu* before it is embedded in particular political narratives, before it engages particular Western interpretations on humanness, human dignity, personhood and justice, maybe even before the violence of the construction of a we and a you on the basis of cultural or racial difference. Maybe Ramose's *Ubuntu* leads us to a "dif-ference" prior to the construction of differences, prior to the division of the world into European and African, prior to the Christianisation of *Ubuntu*.

Prior is used here, not in the sense of linear time – as I am not referring to pre-colonial times – but prior, in the sense of prior to hi*story* and the various discourses on history; prior, as the speaking of language is prior to the various spoken languages. The *Austrag* (see Heidegger 1971, 206) creates (carries out) the worlds, as the habitat of differing we's (beings); each *Austrag* of a particular world is carried by its own particular political narrative, thereby creating a particular world with its particular understanding of who the beings of that world are in which they belong. In this way *Ubu-ntu* avoids the conflict of the different personae in Praeg's sense, as it avoids the conflict of the different worlds by avoiding the battle between the differing identity politics. It avoids these battles by being the *arché* of these differences, or being that which is prior, whilst being the insufficient cause of the question, how things (concrete beings) are enfolded differently according to different political narratives.

In that sense *Ubu-ntu* would be prior to all these different political discourses, but not separate from them, as there always is a political narrative that determines the *Austrag* of a particular world. This carrying out could may be understood as the work of *ubuntu*. The discourses on *Ubuntu* start once the politics of identity, human dignity and personhood become relevant. The different political narratives of *Ubuntu* interpret this differently. Some argue that personhood and human dignity are universal, another that only Africans can have *ubuntu*, humanness, personhood; yet others argue that only Africans who show particular qualities, have learnt to belong or have been initiated into personhood have *ubuntu* (see Gade 2012, 494f). This is a dangerous politics in the context of liberal constitutionalism. It could easily be translated into violence against those who do not belong, those not deemed persons because they do not have *ubuntu*. Individuals, who do not fit the norms of a particular community, for example gays, or foreigners, people of other faiths or with other cultural practices, do not have being as they do not belong and therefore become non-persons, without personhood. In his speech, *I am an African,* Mbeki tried to be as inclusive as possible in his understanding of *Ubuntu*, a discourse on *Ubuntu* that would include all into the community of the New South Africa. He not only includes the mountains and the valleys, oceans and rivers, but all the different people of South Africa (Mbeki 2001, 9-10).

In each discourse there is a specific sovereign, or sovereign principle, that holds that discourse together in an attempt to create a *polis* on the basis of some understanding of what the *politeia* is or should be. With every creation of a *polis* (a place of belonging) there is always injustice, as belonging and being thought together will inevitably divide concrete beings into those who belong and those who do not on the basis of some norm. Some will be classified as non-beings and thereby excluded. The South African constitution seeks to be as inclusive as possible. That is maybe the beauty of the first fathers' dreams for the new democracy. Yet a person's dignity becomes conditional to the extent they are integrated (belong) or to the extent that they have been initiated into the *politeia*, integrated, included and interconnected in a community and, therefore, have been initiated into personhood. There will be those who would argue for a universal community (universal belonging) to which everyone belongs because they are human. Yet you only belong to this universal community if you subscribe to the ideology of universal human rights. If not, you are classified a rogue or terrorist and thus become a non-person, a beast to be hunted down in the deserts of this world.

These different discourses, and therefore worlds are at times in conflict with each other, but if one thinks *Ubuntu* in the abstract (as does Ramose), and even more abstract as the speaking of language, then it is prior to all these political conflicts. It is more *arché*, although there is never a beginning, as one is always already in the midst of things responding to the dance, or the *Geläut* of the peal of stillness (the speaking of language). It is a call that is maybe more sovereign than these different sovereign political principles and interpretations, a *Walten der Differenz* as Derrida once referred to Heidegger's *Austrag* (Derrida 2011, 207). It is maybe a *Walten der Differenz*, which is prior to the particular *Walten* of the different *logoi* (political narratives) which constitute the different spaces of belonging (worlds) and thereby constitute different kinds of beings.

Language is the house of being where each house is carried out on the strength of the speech of a certain *logos*, a politics that binds that world together. Yet there are different *logoi*, depending on your politics, depending on the calling of a particular context. Celan's beautiful poem, *Grosse, Glühende Wölbung* ends with the verse, *Die Welt is fort, ich muss dich tragen* ("The world is gone, I must carry you"). The world as such is gone, the human being as such is gone, *ubuntu* as such is gone, *ich muss dich tragen*, I must carry you. You and I must carry each other and carry out a world where we both can live. Maybe that is the work of *ubuntu*.

All these different *logoi*, or political narratives, carry out different worlds, with different personae. The result is a relativity of worlds, all equally carried out. *Die Welt* as such is *fort*; therefore, all the different carried-out-worlds are equally justified, equally violent, equally just and equally unjust. Such relativity would make life unbearable. It is ironic that the bearing of each other and together the bearing of the worlds, becomes unbearable in different senses. It is unbearable because of the relativity, or unbearable because of the weight of responsibility. Maybe the unbearableness would be a good place to start to move beyond such unbearableness.

Maybe unbearable because of responsibility and unbearable because of the relativity can be overcome when turning to those in each world who are *weltlos* (world-less) or *weltarm* (world-poor) (Derrida 2011, 6), because they have no voice, no language, no discourse on *Ubuntu* which would ensure them a right to belong, but who are the victims of somebody else's discourse on *Ubuntu*. They are those in each of these political worlds, who do not have the power to co-create the *polis*, because they do not belong, and because they do not belong they have no being: the non-beings, the world-less and world-poor. Twenty-five years into the South African democracy that tried to be as inclusive as possible, we are maybe beginning to see the *Weltlosen*, *Weltarmen* of the New South Africa: those without a future, those without hope, those who are not connected, those who have not enjoyed the fruits of transformation, those who have not yet tasted economic freedom. The world-less and world-poor are not interconnected but disconnected, not initiated but excluded and marginalised. In these discourses there are victims, marginalised, the world-less and world-poor. At times victims might be perpetrators in a different discourse. Is there a way beyond such relativity and would it require an absolute sovereign beyond the sovereignty of the various political narratives that carry out the particular worlds? Heidegger argues for the *Walten der Differenz* (see Derrida 2011, 207). Is this a new absolute sovereign, beyond the sovereigns of the various worlds of being as belonging? Would the *Walten der Differenz* not just be another *logos* that gathers together a world of different worlds by carrying out a worlding-space? Or is it really something different, something sovereign beyond the sovereignty of the different carried out worlds defined and determined by their particular sovereign principles or discourses on *Ubuntu*?

Walten der Differenz cannot be equated with the various sovereign *logoi*. "*Walten* would be too sovereign still to be sovereign, in a sense, within the limits of the theologico-political. And the excess of sovereignty would nullify the meaning of sovereignty" (Derrida 2011, 279).

Die Welt ist fort, ich muss dich tragen – thinking *Ubuntu* with the Christian text

Die Welt ist fort, ich muss dich tragen, ich muss dich Austragen, ich muss dich ertragen (see Derrida 2011, 268)! The world is gone and I must take responsibility for you and for it. I must carry it, carry it out, take the burden of it upon myself, take the responsibility for you and for it upon myself. The world is gone, the world must be carried-out (*Austragen*). This opens the way for an *ethos* of responsibility for the other, whoever or whatever the other is.

If one reads the discourses on *Ubuntu* not against nor before, but *with* the Christian texts, one could narrate the story of Christ as the generic story of the creator Father becoming flesh, son in human history. The world-creating and world forming *Logos* became flesh (John 1:14). The logos entered into the world-creation, and in that history was accused of blaspheming the onto-theological gods, blaspheming the sovereigns and, thus, crucified. The world-creating *logos* was crucified and thus the world is gone with the crucified *logos, die Welt ist fort*. We are all like stones, *weltlos oder weltverlorene* – unchained from the sun, the *logos*-light which creates the world is dead. The world has been unchained from its sun (Nietzsche 1974, 181-182). It is unchained from the sovereign *logos,* which had the power to *Walt* over the world. That leaves one as a child, the last *Verwandelung* (Nietzsche 2000), without a world, besides the world that one has co-created. Nietzsche's last *Verwandelung* into a child, is a child who needs to be carried, both carried to be born and carried until it can stand on its own feet: *ich muss dich tragen*.

Die Welt ist fort, ich muss dich tragen. Who is authorised to say these words and to whom are they said? Who carries whom in this *weltverlorene, weltlose Welt* of the child without a sovereign Father or Mother? We could carry each other and each other's worlds by respecting each other's worlds. All the different worlds would stand next to, equal to each other, yet without a universal *Logos,* universal discourse on *Ubuntu,* by which to compare, judge or evaluate the different worlds. This would be absolute relativism and the result would be a total breakdown of communication in the global village. Are all these worlds equal? They are equally created and haunted by différance, or what they exclude. Maybe the *ethos* that I am proposing is not an ethic of *Streit* and *Krieg* on the basis of some arbitrating principle, but rather an *ethos* of listening to the haunting cries of those who are *weltarm* or even *weltlos* in these various worlds. The stones who are *weltarm* and *weltlos* will cry out (Luke 19:40) to prepare the way for a king, a sovereign who is dif-ferent. It is an *ethos* of listening to those who carry the burden of their particular worlds. They, who are *weltarm* or even *weltlos* carry the burden of the *weltbildenden* sovereigns or sovereign politics. Listen to their stories, not because their stories are truer or better, but because only they can tell us the weight of the world they carry.

It is not the Western world with its sovereignty that can judge Africa, nor the discourses on *Ubuntu,* which are better. Both are world-creations. Often these world-creations are embedded in different global-political or geo-political world-creations as glocal phenomena. All these worlds are equally *weltbildend* and, therefore, *weltlos* as such. From no point of view would one have a better view, except maybe from the view of those who suffer the weight of these worlds. An *ethos* is offered of listening to the cries of the destroyed lives that haunt these world-creations. The cries of those who are truly *weltlos,* because they are either dead or treated like the dead, the living dead, offer a perspective (hauntology) by which to weigh the weight of these worlds, thereby offering these crying-out-stones and restless souls, a place in a world where they can be at home, no longer *weltlos,* as they pray to the sovereign of the world still to come. It is not a Western world nor an African traditional world, but a world to come, a world of the child, beast and stone: where the wolf shall dwell with the lamb, and the leopard shall lie down with the kid; and the calf and the young lion and the fatling together; and a little child shall lead (carry) them (Is 11:6).

So I end where I began, with the haunting of the ghosts, the haunting of the *Weltlosen* and *Weltarmen.* Is that not where many discourses on *Ubuntu* began, as an attempt to give voice to those whose voices had been silenced by the sovereign power of European colonialism? Yet, the work of *Ubuntu* is not complete and never will be, as there are always stones who cry out. South Africa is crying in so many places, die *Welt is fort, ich muss dich tragen.* It is time to carry each other out into a truly new South Africa.

References

Caputo, John D. 1993. *Demythologizing Heidegger.* Indianapolis, IN: Indiana University Press.

Chabal, Patrick. 2009. *Africa: The Politics of Suffering and Smiling.* London: Zed Books.

Cornell, Drucilla and Karin van Marle. 2005. "Exploring Ubuntu: Tentative Reflections." *African Human Rights Law Journal* 5: 195-219.

Derrida, Jacques. 2009. *The Beast & the Sovereign,* Vol. 1. Translated by Geoffrey Bennington. Chicago, IL: University of Chicago Press.

Derrida, Jacques. 2011. *The Beast & the Sovereign,* Vol. II. Translated by Geoffrey Bennington. Chicago, IL: University of Chicago Press.

Gade, Christian. 2011. "The Historical Development of the Written Discourses on Ubuntu." *South African Journal of Philosophy* 30 (3): 303-329.

Gade, Christian. 2012. "What is *Ubuntu*? Different interpretations among South Africans of African Descent." *South African Journal of Philosophy* 31 (3): 484-503.

Heidegger, Martin. 1957. *Identität und Differenz.* Pfullingen: Verlag Günther Neske.

Heidegger, Martin. 1971. *Poetry, language and thought.* Translated by Albert Hofstadter. New York: Harper & Row.

Heidegger, Martin. 1983. *Die Grundbegriffe der Metaphysik: Welt – Endlichkeit – Einsamkeit, Freiburger Vorlesung Wintersemester 1999/30.* Translated by Friedrich-Wilhelm von Herrmann. Frankfurt am Main: Vitorio Klosterman.

Hountondji, Paulin. 1983. *African Philosophy: Myth and Reality.* London: Hutchinson University Library for Africa.

Jewsiewicki, Bogumil, and Valentin-Yves Mudimbe. 1993. "African's Memories and Contemporary History of Africa." *History and Theory* 32 (4):1-11.

Krog, Antjie. 2008a. " This thing called reconciliation': Forgiveness as part of an interconnectedness-towards-wholeness." *South African Journal of Philosophy* 27 (4): 353-366.

Krog, Antjie. 2008b. " 'If it means he gets his humanity back': The Worldview Underpinning the South African Truth and Reconciliation Commission." *Journal of Multicultural Discourses* 3 (3): 204-220.

Mbeki, Thabo. 2001. "I am an African." *Quest: African Renaissance and Ubuntu Philosophy,* Special Issue 15 (1/2): 9-14.

Metz, Thaddeus. 2011. "Ubuntu as a Moral Theory and Human Rights in South Africa." *African Human Rights Law Journal* 11: 532-559.

Metz, Thaddeus. 2014. "A Report on Ubuntu." Review of *Ubuntu: Curating the Archive,* ed. Leonhard Praeg and Siphokazi Magala. *Philosophical papers* 43 (3): 447-453.

Meylahn, Johann-Albrecht. 2010. "Poetically Africa dwells: A dialogue between Heidegger's Understanding of Language as the House of Being and African Being-with (ubuntu) as a possible Paradigm for Postfoundational Practical Theology in Africa." *Verbum et Ecclesia* 31 (1). doi:10.4102/ve.v31i1.381.

Mudimbe, Valentin-Yves. 1988. *The Invention of Africa: Gnosis, Philosophy, and the Order of Knowledge*. Indiana, IN: Indiana University Press.

Mudimbe, Valentin-Yves. 1991. *Parables and Fables: Exegesis, Textuality and Politics in Central Africa*. Madison, WI: University of Wisconsin Press.

Mudimbe, Valentin-Yves. 2003. "Globalisation and African Identity," *CR: The New Centennial Review* 3 (2): 205-218.

Nancy, Jean-Luc. 2008. *Dis-Enclosure: The Deconstruction of Christianity*. Translated by Bettina Bergo, Gabriel Malenfant, and Michael.B. Smith. New York: Fordham University Press.

Nietzsche, Friedrich. 1974. *The Gay Science*. Translated and edited by Walter Kaufmann. New York: W. Vintage.

Nietzsche, Friedrich. 2000. *Also sprach Zarathustra*. E-book, Projekt Gutenberg. www.gutenberg2000.de/nietzsche/zara.also.htm.

Nussbaum, Bruce. 2003. "Ubuntu: Reflections of a South African on Our Common Humanity." *Reflections* 4 (4): 21-26.

Nyerere, Julius. 1966. *Freedom and Unity*. Dar es Salaam: Oxford University Press.

Praeg, Leonhard. 2008. "An Answer to the Question: What is [ubuntu]." *South African Journal of Philosophy* 27 (4): 367-385.

Praeg, Leonhard. 2014a. "From ubuntu to Ubuntu: Four Historic a prioris." In *Ubuntu: Curating the Archive*, edited L. Praeg, and S. Magdala, 96-120. Pietermaritzburg: University of KwaZulu-Natal Press.

Praeg, Leonhard. 2014b. *Report on Ubuntu*. Pietermaritzburg: University of KwaZulu-Natal Press.

Prozesky, Martin. 2009. "Cinderella, Survivor and Saviour: African Ethics and the Quest for a Global Ethic." In *African Ethics: An Anthology of Comparative and Applied Ethics*, edited by M.F Murove, 3-14. Pietermaritzburg: University of KwaZulu Natal Press.

Ramose, Mogobe. 1999. *African Philosophy through Ubuntu*. Harare: Bond Books.

Shutte, Augustine. 2001. *Ubuntu: An Ethic for a New South Africa*. Pietermaritzburg: Cluster Publications.

Van Binsbergen, Wim. 2001. "Ubuntu and the globalisation of South African thought and society." *Quest: An African Journal of Philosophy, African Renaissance and Ubuntu Philosophy* 15 (1/2): 53-90.

Verdoolaege, Annelies. 2007. *Reconciliation discourse: The case of the Truth and Reconciliation Commission*. Amsterdam: John Benjamins.

Wilson, Richard. 2001. *The Politics of Truth and Reconciliation in South Africa: Legitimizing the Post-apartheid State*. Cambridge: Cambridge University Press.

The long road to practicing *Ubuntu*[1]-leadership: Practical-theological perspectives from a Malawian case study

Ian A Nell

Abstract

In discourses on leadership within the African context one regularly finds a contrast between a Western approach to leadership, characterised by a preference for individualism with rational thinking as a central feature, and an African approach to leadership, linked to notions of an African value system characterised by the concept of *Ubuntu*. This paper first illustrates that this dualistic approach to leadership underwrites considerable contestation over the notion of *Ubuntu* leadership and can easily contribute to gender discrimination. Second, this problematic situation is illustrated with a case study on the absence of women from leadership positions within a specific denomination in Malawi. Lastly, the paper voices the trust that a more nuanced approach to leadership from an *Ubuntu* perspective can indeed make a contribution to the position of women in leadership.

Introduction

The power and fascination with *Ubuntu* have a long history within academic and social discourse, both nationally and internationally. According to Praeg the use of the concept of *Ubuntu* has gained momentum since the Cold War, when most of the other ideologies that were used as alternatives to capitalism lost their energy. In what he calls the "global imaginaire," (Praeg 2014, 248), *Ubuntu* came to the fore as an ideology reminding us of our common humanity. In this regard, many different peoples contributed to the momentum gained by *Ubuntu*.

One of the main proponents of *Ubuntu* was Archbishop Desmond Tutu, who wrote that "Ubuntu is very difficult to render into a Western language … It is to say, 'My humanity is caught up, is inextricably bound up, in what is yours' " (Tutu 2012, 34-35). Du Toit (2004, 33) sums up this aspect of African thought when he

---

[1]   *Ubuntu* is used with a capital letter in the initial part of the article. Later on, a distinction is made between use of the concept with a capital letter and a small letter.

writes: "In Africa, a person is identified by his or her interrelationships and not primarily by individualistic properties. The community identifies the person and not the person the community. The identity of the person is his or her place in the community. In Africa it is a matter of 'I participate, therefore I am'. ... *Ubuntu* is the principle of 'I am only because we are, and since we are, therefore I am.' "

The purpose of this paper is to examine the relationship between *Ubuntu* and leadership. The primary research question is: Can one speak of *Ubuntu* leadership? If so, what does it entail and what might be gained by employing the concept in leadership discourses in Africa and particularly South Africa? To answer the question, I want to progress in three steps. First, we will examine the way that scholars use the concept of *Ubuntu* leadership or leadership in the spirit of *Ubuntu* by exploring the semantic field of the concept and by comparing it with Western approaches to leadership. Second, a critical investigation of the concept viewed through the lens of alternative heuristic devices will reveal that the notion of *Ubuntu* (or *Ubuntu* leadership) is ambivalent and therefore open to misuse, easily contributing to the exclusion of certain groups – especially women – in social activities. Third, we will discuss a case study concerning the absence of women from positions of leadership in a specific denomination in Malawi as an example of such exclusion. Finally, the concept of *Ubuntu* will be revisited to consider whether there are credible possibilities for making use of the concept in national and international discourses on leadership.

Ubuntu versus Western approaches to leadership

To gain a better understanding of what is meant when speaking about African leadership, Van Zyl maintains that it is necessary to take the changing context of Africa, the African value system and specifically *Ubuntu* into account (Van Zyl 2009a, 30). He makes use of the insights of Shonhiwa (2006) and Khoza (2005) to make the following summary of the African cultural value system that includes *Ubuntu*. According to these scholars, one finds in Africa a preference for collectivism above individualism, where leadership enjoys respect from people, especially when seen from a spiritual point of view. There is great emphasis on seeking consensus in cases where people are trying to solve complex problems, and a parallel dislike of dissension. Humility and an attitude of service as part of the spirit of *Ubuntu* are expected from followers, rather than a critical attitude challenging decisions. The result is that one finds an inherent trust and faith in the just conduct of persons that are in positions of leadership, and therefore also an absence of critique. The forefathers and the history of a group play an important role in decisions concerning the future. The structure of society is quite often hierarchical, where the acceptance of authority plays an important role.

According to Mbigi (2005, 58) and Khoza (2005, 23), a Western worldview looks different. Within such a worldview, the individual is the hero who acts as the saviour of communities and organisations through individual independence and courage. Van Zyl (2009a, 33) summarises this approach with the following slogan: "I am because I, the individual hero, dream and do." Such an attitude leads to a situation in which the leader concentrates on his or her own interests and by doing so also serves society and the community in the best way. Within such a worldview one often encounters a hierarchy that regulates conduct with strict rules about the interaction of people at different strata within an organisation or group. Each level of leadership has strict and specific targets that have to be achieved. One also often encounters a very formal way of giving account of responsibilities and tasks.

Broodryk (2006, 88), for example, describes the differences in the following way: "The difference between the African and Western life approaches is based on the 'we' (African inclusiveness) versus the 'I' (Western exclusiveness) styles. In Africa, group spirit is regarded as more valuable than individual aspirations. This explains the collective spirit or brotherhood of Africans."

Although these kinds of comparisons immediately make sense to many and help one to understand something about the essence of *Ubuntu* in comparison with Western worldviews, it is also a case that dualistic approaches of this nature result in considerable contestation, even more so when it comes to linking it with leadership. It is also the case that an understanding of *Ubuntu* that operates within such a simplistic approach can easily lead to different forms of exclusion and even serious gender discrimination, as I will try to illustrate when I present a specific case study from Malawi. What is needed is an alternative approach to *Ubuntu* and leadership that takes into account these hurdles on the long way to *Ubuntu* leadership. For this purpose, I will make use of the argument of Leonhard Praeg (2014) in his recent volume titled *A report on Ubuntu.*

An alternative approach

Praeg is interested in the unique essence of *Ubuntu*, and makes an important distinction between what we *mean* (in terms of sense making) when we ask the question "What is *Ubuntu*?" and what we *do* (acting) when we ask the question (Praeg 2014, 12). For Praeg the focus should be on the latter, an opinion that contributes considerably to developing useful heuristic devices, as we will demonstrate in the case study below. Praeg's attention to the doing of *ubuntu* relates to his conviction that the political nature of the question should have priority over the question about the different ways in which *Ubuntu* should be understood (Praeg 2014, 12). It is his contention that the meaning of *Ubuntu* in some isolated case is not important, but that its meaning can only be properly understood with specific reference to the nature of the political context.

For this reflection on *Ubuntu* and leadership, Praeg's distinction (2014, 20, 45, 47, 52) is of vital importance. He even makes a distinction in the spelling of the word, i.e., between *ubuntu* with a lower-case and *Ubuntu* with an upper-case. When it concerns the "doing of *ubuntu*" – the cultural praxis – he uses the lower case and relates it to the cultural practices that shape people "with *ubuntu*." When it concerns the "philosophical reflections" – theories and ideologies that try to make sense of the notion in different periods and places – he uses *Ubuntu* in upper case. Praeg is convinced that for a meaningful conversation about *Ubuntu* the political context of *ubuntu* should be foregrounded and explored (Praeg 2014, 12).

For the purpose of this study the political context will be the primary concern. This is because this research took place within the field of practical theology and the central concern is the cultural praxis of leadership in the light of *ubuntu*. Secondly, the following case study will reveal in what ways the specific political context contributes to the situation in which a group of people (mostly women) is excluded from leadership because of multiple factors. This situation then influences the broader philosophical discourses on *Ubuntu* when discussing notions such as globalisation and secularisation in post-colonial Africa.

In the analysis of the case study that follows, two of Praeg's helpful approach and distinctions will be considered to discover in what ways they can be useful heuristics in considering the following case study. The first is that the question about *Ubuntu*, both conceptually and practically, is not as straightforward as it might appear. So he writes: "Ubuntu is never simply an intellectual investigation, a way of saying things, but first and foremost a way of conducting … politics, of doings things … or … ubuntu is first and foremost a political act and that our responsibility lies precisely in recognizing this priority of the political" (Praeg 2014, 5).

According to Praeg, "What is *Ubuntu*?" is not first a question but a statement about power, domination in discourses, representation and suppression and exclusion (Praeg 2014, 15). Thus he employs the slogan "Everything is politics," meaning that scientific activities concerning *ubuntu* practices must be conscious about the political nature that gives birth to conversations, epistemologies and ontological assumptions that accept certain understandings of *Ubuntu* and reject others (Praeg 2014, 11). One example he uses to illustrate this concept is how the Truth and Reconciliation Commission produced a kind of "Christianised *Ubuntu*" that portrayed African people as extremely human and forgiving. According to Praeg, this occurred at the cost of a past characterised by the hurt and pain of many victims of violence that yet protected the material *status quo* of many of the perpetrators during the years of apartheid (Praeg 2014, 18, 36).

A second and equally important aspect Praeg discusses relates to the popular proverb "I am because we are," generally ascribed to John Mbiti (1970, 141) and seen as an "African" response to the "Western" concept of personhood. In this regard Praeg states that it is interesting to see in what ways Mbiti and other African intellectuals try to give meaning to what it means to be an African (in the sense of *Ubuntu*) and in light of a modernity that was responsible for the colonisation of Africa (Praeg 2014, 102). In this regard Molefe writes: "in the process of distancing themselves from modernity and aspiring for decolonisation, Africans find themselves parasitic or complicit in the very modernity that corrupted their history and their conception of their humanity" (Molefe 2014, 159).

Following in the footsteps of Mbiti, Praeg maintains that it is first necessary for an African to understand the Western mind set in order to construct one's own identity as the "other" over and against the Western concept of personhood (Praeg 2014, 102). Arguing in this way one is dualistic, in which the Western person is seen as individualistic and the African as communitarian. The net result is that the Western text becomes the real and original text for what it means to be a person in Africa. Thus Praeg remarks: "the distinction between the fact and the copy has been so eroded to the point where it can no longer be invoked to assert a meaningful difference" (Praeg 2014, 102). The result of this style of argumentation is that many scholars from Africa are dependent upon Western archives and libraries to make sense of African personhood and identity.

In what follows, these two notions of Praeg's work will be used as lenses to consider the research of Phoebe Chifungo (2014) on leadership within the Church of Central Africa Presbyterian (CCAP).

An African case study

The title of Chifungo's study is *Women in the CCAP Nkhoma Synod: A practical-theological study of their leadership roles*. Its purpose was to take a closer look at the diminished position of women in leadership in the CCAP Nkhoma Synod in Malawi. Part of her study was an empirical analysis conducted among members of the so-called *Chigwirizano cha amai* (the Women's League) as well as with some elders and ministers in different congregations that belong to this denomination.

In her research, Chifungo wanted to answer the following questions: 1) In what ways do historical and cultural factors as well as the way that the leaders interpret the Bible contribute to the situation of the absence of women from positions of leadership in the CCAP Nkhoma Synod,? 2) In what ways could these factors be recognised through some empirical research,? and 3) What possible al-

ternative ways exist in which the history, the culture and the Bible could be read
and interpreted? (Chifungo 2014, 233).

Chifungo's research shows that women in the CCAP Nkhoma Synod are
kept from positions of leadership because of a complex set of historical, cultural and Biblical factors. Historically, the first missionaries came to Malawi
from the Netherlands, introducing a very patriarchal form of leadership that excluded women from positions of leadership from the start (Chifungo 2014, 34-38).
She also concluded that traditional cultural beliefs were carried into church life,
e.g., that men are superior to women, powerful and in control, while women are
weaker, inferior and passive (Chifungo 2014, 64).[2]

By employing social identity theory, Chifungo (2014, 72-89) found that these
convictions and conduct of men concerning their perceived superiority are further enhanced through self-categorisation and stereotyping. Thus, the moment that
men categorise themselves as leaders within their respective communities, they
immediately compare themselves with other groups: in this case with the women
belonging to the *Chigwirizano cha amai*. This leads to the further stereotyping
of women as weak and without power and therefore not suitable for positions of
leadership.

Her research showed that the most important factor contributing to the si-
lencing of women's voices by the church was the way in which leaders read and
interpreted the Bible (Chifungo 2014, 45). Texts such as 1 Cor. 14:34-35 and 1
Tim. 2:11-12 were interpreted and used in a fundamentalist ways to keep women
from living out and developing their God-given talents of leadership. In response
Chifungo proposes a new model for interpreting the Bible consisting of a combination of literary, socio-historical and theological-rhetorical aspects (Chifungo
2014, 165). Chifungo stays hopeful that through a re-reading of the texts in this
way the Chewa culture, the missionary and colonial past as well as the attitudes
of people might be changed towards a more positive view of women in positions
of leadership, well aware that such might still take considerable time and patience
(Chifungo 2014, 175).

---

[2] It is especially in this context that one sees *ubuntu* (with a small letter and in the political
sense) at work. In this regard it is important to understand that what is understood as *Ubuntu* in
the Nuguni language group in South Africa is translated in Malawi in the Chichewa language
as *uMunthu*, but it operates within the same semantic field. Concerning the notion of *uMunthu*,
Sindima (1995) did some ground-breaking work. Sharra (2010) writes: "The African worldview
is about living as one family, belonging to God."

Bifocal heuristic lenses

When one uses the previously discussed bifocal heuristic lenses of Praeg, it becomes clear how *ubuntu* in the political sense of the word – i.e., as a cultural praxis of power, domination and exclusion – is reflected in the leadership practices and structures of the CCAP Nkhoma Synod. We will now briefly discuss some historical factors, cultural factors and the way in which the leaders interpret the Bible.

Chifungo describes the way in which the Christian faith came to Malawi as a male-dominated movement (Chifungo 2014, 9-10). The first missionaries that arrived in the area of the Nkhoma Synod in 1889 came from the Dutch Reformed Church, with its strong patriarchal tradition. Chifungo narrates how the missionaries forced their patriarchal theology upon the new converts. One result was that, from the beginning, women were barred from positions of leadership. It was only in 1982 that the office of deacon and in 1990 the office of elder were opened for women. Chifungo also documents how missionaries undermined the strong leadership that existed among the women and did not want to allow girls to be educated beyond Grade 5.

Culturally, she illustrates how a significant change occurred within the Chewa culture (Chifungo 2014, 10-11). Employing the insights of Phiri (2000, 23-40) she shows how the Chewa culture was originally a strong matrilineal society; thus women occupied positions of leadership in both the political and religious spheres. As time progressed, this tradition gave way to a patriarchal system for numerous reasons. These include the 19th century slave trade, that influenced men to prefer marrying slave women more obedient than the Chewa women, as well as the influence of other African ethnic groups with different practices and attitudes towards women.

Lastly, Chifungo shows that the interpretation of the Bible by members and leaders of the Nkhoma Synod – especially certain New Testament texts cited above – was done from the start in a very fundamentalist way. She shows that this practice relates to a key hermeneutical problem that influenced many other practices (Chifungo 2014, 14-15). When the underlying hermeneutical approach is influenced by the historical and cultural factors noted above, it becomes very difficult to interpret the Bible other than in a fundamentalist way.

The interpretation of the Bible in this way inevitably leads to the construction of an identity that is dependent upon Western texts. Employing texts in such a colonising way as encouraged by the missionary activities of churches from the West as well as Western fundamentalist biblical methods of interpretation led to what Praeg describes as "benevolent coercion" (Praeg 2014, 65).

Praeg's bifocal heuristic lenses show how dangerous it is when *Ubuntu* (or *uMunthu*) is naively linked to leadership and the devastating results if this naive view is accepted and affirmed. These lenses reveal huge potholes on the long road to *Ubuntu* leadership, and even question whether it is plausible to speak about *Ubuntu* leadership.

Ubuntu as critical humanism

In his book, *God is Not a Christian: Speaking Truth in Times of Crisis*, Tutu (2009, 24) writes: "*Ubuntu* teaches us that our worth is intrinsic to who we are. We matter because we are made in the image of God. *Ubuntu* reminds us that we belong in one family – God's family, the human family. In our African worldview, the greatest good is communal harmony. Anything that subverts or undermines this greatest good is ipso facto wrong, evil. Anger and desire for revenge are subversive of this good thing."

It is clear that the critical component for Tutu is his theological conviction that all people are created in the image of God and that we therefore belong to one human family. He regards anything that breaks the communal harmony as wrong and evil because it goes against the very essence of human dignity.

Praeg sees how critical humanism focuses on the political praxis. He writes: "[W]ithin this frame (Ubuntu as critical humanism), the word 'critical' refers to the primacy of the political … the relations of power that systematically exclude certain people from being considered human in the first instance" (Praeg 2014, 12). The discourse on *Ubuntu* in South Africa developed within a context in which the dignity of many people of colour was denied and from Tutu's perspective were not considered part of the human family. What becomes obvious from this critical perspective is the linking of *Ubuntu* and power, which underscores the struggle of many people of colour for the recognition of their identity, legitimacy of existence, and thus their very personhood. Here we discover the positive and constructive ways in which *Ubuntu* plays a role in the struggle for human dignity and the role that community plays in the formation of a person with *Ubuntu,* i.e., a person with certain moral values and virtues (Praeg 2014, 44).

Another insight achieved when considering *Ubuntu* through the lens of critical humanism is recognizing it as a "glocal phenomenon." Praeg remarks: "To call Ubuntu a glocal phenomenon means recognizing that global discourses (Christianity, human rights and so on) give a particular expression to the meaning of local traditions such as ubuntu, but in a way that also allows the resulting Ubuntu to feed back into the global discourse as a locally based critique and expansion of those very discourses" (Praeg 2014, 37).

According to Molefe (2014, 163), in conversation with Praeg, the understanding of *Ubuntu* as a glocal phenomenon leads to the situation where both spellings of *(u)Ubuntu* can be African and un-African at the same time without being contradictory. According to him, it is only *ubuntu* that can claim to be truly African, while *Ubuntu* can be at home in African as well as global discourses by way of response, critique and engagement. In this regard, Molefe (2014, 163) makes the following observation, resonant with the study of Chifungo: "In the traditional lifestyle of a village or pre-colonial Africa, ubuntu was not a problem for thought, it was a lived experience supported by various technologies of power and symbols of community engagement. The breaking of this tradition and its recollection in the colonial space, as resistance and as expression of the struggle for liberation, plunge us into the glocality of Ubuntu."

When leadership is linked to *(u)Ubuntu* and enriched in this way, it also opens the door to new discourses on gender and leadership that must become part of the agenda of churches and academic discourses in Africa.

Conclusion

When the shared humanity of critical humanism is the starting point and is joined to *Ubuntu* as a form of a response, critique and engagement both with modernity and with troublesome notions of *ubuntu* as "benevolent coercion" – due to historical and cultural factors supported by fundamentalist approaches Biblical interpretation (Chifungo 2014, 8) – then new and creative opportunities might arise to reflect on the important role of women in positions of leadership.

It is, indeed, a long road to *Ubuntu* leadership. Whoever is concerned with simplistic notions of *(u)Ubuntu* and the ways in which *ubuntu* is very often employed in exclusive and gender-insensitive ways – e.g., in perpetuating oppressive traditional practices – should take seriously the notion of *Ubuntu* as a glocal phenomenon. So doing might not only enrich the discourse on leadership, but also promote the positions of women in roles of leadership within the African context.

When the discourse on leadership and *Ubuntu* is seen within the broader context of critical humanism, one arrives at the same conclusion as Praeg (2014, 47): "Ubuntu is neither here nor there, neither simply from 'over here' nor reducible to what is 'over there'. It is at once here and there." Seen from this angle, the discourse on *Ubuntu* leadership can help not only to shift the way of thinking in leadership discourses, but also to cultivate a consciousness among the younger generation of leaders concerning the complexity of leadership in the African context and the global world of which we are all part. It is my hope that a more nuanced way of thinking about *(u)Ubuntu* and leadership will indeed be fruitful for the conversation on the role of women in positions of leadership within the African context.

References

Broodryk, Johan. 2006. *Ubuntu: Life Coping Skills from Africa*. Randburg: Knowres.

Chifungo, Phoebe F. 2104. "Women in the CCAP Nkhoma Synod: A practical-theological Study of Their Leadership Roles." Ph.D. dissertation, Stellenbosch University.

Du Toit, Cornel W. 2004. "Technoscience and the Integrity of Personhood in Africa and the West: Facing our Technoscientific Environment." In *The Integrity of the Human Person in an African Context: Perspectives from Science and Religion*, edited by Cornel W. du Toit, 107-151. Pretoria: Research Institute for Theology and Religion, University of South Africa.

Khoza, Reuel J. 2005. *Let Africa Lead: African Transformational Leadership for 21st Century Business*. Johannesburg: Vezubuntu.

Mbigi, Lovemore. 2005. *The Spirit of African Leadership*. Randburg: Knowres.

Mbiti, John. 1970. *African Religions and Philosophy*. New York, NY: Doubleday.

Molefe, Motsamai. 2014. "Review of *A Report on Ubuntu* by Leonhard Praeg."*Acta Academica* 2014 (2): 157–164.

Phiri, Isabel A. 2000. *Women, Presbyterianism and Patriarchysm:Malawi*. Limbe: Assemblies of God Press.

Praeg, Leonard. 2014. *A Report on Ubuntu*. Pietermaritzburg: University of KwaZulu-Natal Press.

Sharra, Steve. 2010. "Teaching uMunthu for Global Peace: Reflections on International Day of Peace. *Pambazuka News*, 497. http://pambazuka.org/en/category/features/672 11.

Shonhiwa, Shepherd. 2006. *The Effective Cross-cultural Manager: A Guide for Business Leaders in Africa*. Cape Town: Struik.

Sindima, Harvey J. 1995. *Africa's Agenda: The Legacy of Liberalism and Colonialism in the Crisis of African Values* 176. http://www.isbnplus.com/9780313294792.

Tutu, Desmond. 2011. *God is Not a Christian: Speaking Truth in Times of Crisis*. Johannesburg: Rider Books.

Tutu, Desmond. 2012. *No Future without Forgiveness*. Johannesburg: Random House.

Van Zyl, Ebben S., ed. 2009a. *Leadership in the African Context*. Cape Town: Juta.

Van Zyl, Ebben S. 2009b. "The Difference between Leadership and Management." In *Leadership in the African Context*, edited by Ebben S. van Zyl, 20-39. Cape Town: Juta.

Stew, smelting or crucible? – Harnessing the spirit of *ubuntu* in South Africa

A. Roger Tucker and Maake J. Masango

Abstract

A former South Africa President has agreed that, "There is a moral vacuum in South Africa that has the potential to make the country ungovernable." It is suggested that part of the answer to this danger is a reinvigoration of the traditional 'African' spirit of *ubuntu* and its incorporation and integration within society as a whole. As such the authors share, from the perspectives of their differing backgrounds, their insights into the spirit of *ubuntu*, and what will be involved in reinvigorating it, incorporating, and integrating it into our multi-ethnic, multi-cultural society. As this process will seriously affect the non-African sector of the population the findings of a focus group drawn mainly from this sector will be considered. It concludes by suggesting that the way forward is by using a "crucible" approach. This means using the common ground of the majority religion in South Africa, namely faith in the crucified Christ.

Introduction, nomenclature

In this chapter, following Gade (2012, 485), we describe those who are descended from "black African" indigenous cultures as SAADs (South Africans of African Descent) and those who are descended from settlers, who arrived in the last 400 years as non-SAADs. We are aware that these designations may not be entirely accurate or may seem too artificial and contrived or even offensive, we apologise, and ask you to extend the forgiving spirit of *ubuntu* towards us! At times SAADs may also be referred to as "Africans" and non-SAADs as "whites," when we wish to reflect colloquial use, although in our opinion an African may be either white or black!

Historical background

Two factors have motivated our research, namely the SAAD loss of their traditional metanarrative and the consequent *ubuntu* reinvigoration project.

The traditional understanding of *ubuntu* in the SAAD culture

In the past there seems to have been a commonality in the spirit of *ubuntu*, which still exists to some extent. This commonality may be interpreted as an integrated "theology" of life emphasising a spirituality: 1) in which "who we are" and "what we do" are intimately related; 2) that emphasises dignity, enjoyment of life and relationality; 3) and the passing on a philosophy to the young occurring in a village context and is the responsibility of the whole village. Thus Mbiti reminds us that, "It takes a whole village to raise a child" (Mbiti 1977, 23). Its continuation, which involves handing on knowledge and wisdom, depends upon elders within the village becoming leaders. Towards the end of their lives, these elders then become teachers and good ancestors, especially to younger generations.

Such is the beginning of a theology of life, full of dignity, which requires that we care for each other. Caring manifests itself in the respectful and humble way elders and superiors are greeted and addressed by young ones. It would not be wrong to say that a human being is nothing but humanness or *Umuntu* (a Zulu word for a person). This idea is rendered in Zulu by the poetic phrase, "*Umuntu ngumuntu nga Bantu*," which means, a person is a person because of others (Mbiti 2012, 133). The phrase reminds us that, individuals do not exist alone, except corporately. As a result *ubuntu* brings those who are marginalised into the center of life and the community.

The concept of *ubuntu* helps us to understand that my actions affect other people who live with me. For example, if a person within a community is violated, the whole community suffers. Hankela (2013, 73-74) is right when saying that *ubuntu* means that what I do affects others. Which is to say that if one person is affected by the action of the other, the whole community is affected. If I fail to act to right the wrong, the whole community might be negatively affected.

This awareness invites us to ponder the nature of forgiveness, if we offend the other person or are ourselves offended. Thus, Tutu (1999, 35) says, "to forgive is indeed the best form of self-interest since anger, resentment, and revenge are corrosive of that *summum bonum*, that great good, communal harmony that enhances the humanity and personhood of all in the community."

The SAAD loss of a metanarrative and its results

It seems that many SAADs have now lost their concept of a life with dignity, rooted in *ubuntu*, which they initially possessed when fighting for liberation during apartheid times. Unfortunately, during those years of struggles, the value and dignity of human life was eroded. This was especially true regarding the belief that every human being is created in the image and likeness of God. As result some

SAADs lost this great gift of *ubuntu* that enhanced life and respect for humanity. In the new democracy, with its emphasis on human dignity and human rights, the community is now trying to recover the traditional concepts which, formerly in the pre-struggle era, enabled villagers and people to respect each other.

One symptom of this sense of loss is that many SAADs are now explicitly hearkening back to their African roots in powerful ways. For example, after the 1976 riots, many parents named and re-named their children with African names. This is a way of reclaiming their human dignity by abandoning English names, which is also symbolised in changing the names of cities, e.g., from Louis Trichardt to Makhado, and Pretoria to Tshwane.

The *ubuntu* reinvigoration project

The sense of loss has also initiated what we call the "*ubuntu* reinvigoration project," in which SAADs and some non-SAADs are seeking to establish *ubuntu* as an ethical and spiritual metanarrative for all of South Africa. This originated in a meeting in 1999 which occurred between the South African philosopher Augustine Shutte and then President of South Africa, Thabo Mbeki. In that meeting they spoke of:

a 'moral vacuum' in South Africa that had the potential to make the country ungovernable. Crime and corruption were just the outward signs of a sickness of the soul that was a legacy of apartheid. The separateness and conflict inevitable in a multicultural society such as South Africa had been intensified by apartheid… (now) in spite of a fine constitution and democratic elections, South Africa is threatened with disintegration. People have lost touch with the common humanity we share. A spirit of self-interest is growing. What South Africa needs more than anything is an RDP (Reconstruction and Development Program) of the spirit. (Gade 2011, 321-322)

Shutte's aim seems to have been for their idea – which we interpret as a reflection of *ubuntu* – to become a semi-official government project (Shutte 2004, 4; Gade 2011, 317). The aim was to marry "two different traditions of ethical thinking, the European and the African" (Mkhatshwa 2001, back cover). It has since been promoted by the Constitutional Court that has referenced *ubuntu* as a determining factor in some of its judgments (Gade 2011, 312).

Admittedly, this vision will not be easy to achieve. One problem is that although SAADs compose roughly 70% of South African society, non-SAADs have established and currently control the dominant educational, political, legal, commercial, industrial and governmental structures in the country. Therefore, their reaction to *ubuntu* cannot be dismissed. Furthermore, this process of integration will not be easy for them, or even for some urbanised and Eurocentrically educated SAADs, and may even heighten tensions and misunderstandings.

Such may be illustrated by a debate that occurred at the 1999 general assembly of the United Presbyterian Church of Southern Africa. The question of African spirituality and ancestor veneration became a crucial topic for African delegates at that assembly. The debate was tense and highly charged. It seemed to the SAAD delegates that most of the non-SAADs did not fully understand the nuanced attitudes that many Christian SAADs have regarding ancestor veneration. This lack of comprehension is understandable since the latter had not been SAAD language speakers from birth, and had not grown up in SAAD villages. Nevertheless, although understandable, the stance of the majority of non-SAAD delegates was hurtful in that they failed to comprehend and publicly sympathise with the struggle SAADs faced living in two cultures.

To Masango, present at the meeting in 1999, it was obvious that this debate was the result of SAADs' attempt to recapture their Africanness, and what could be construed as their lost human dignity. Their anger was fanned by the fact that the non-SAADs failed to show respect for this deep psychic need. The SAAD arguments in defending African spirituality and ancestor veneration were actually rooted in defending the concept of *ubuntu* and not in defending ancestor "worship" (as it is often misleadingly labeled by non-SAADs). In fact, SAADs were trying to free themselves from the domination of the colonial frameworks that the European missionaries had imposed upon earlier generations of SAADs. Now the present generation was living with the almost unbearable tension of an un-*ubuntu*, disharmonious dualism that had become part of their "Christian" lives. This led to them practicing an African way of life, but also trying to hold to Christian principles, which seemed foreign and Western. As a result, the interpretation of "history" became an important issue in the debate especially as regarding the missionaries and their values.

As we shall note below, the focus group discussion only appears to highlight this 'clash of cultures' and the difficulties their integration will involve, although offering a possible way forward.

The *ubuntu* focus group and its findings

Participants

The focus group, which met on 23 April 2015, was composed of eight ministers/pastors and church leaders located in Bloemfontein, a South African city in the Free State, recognised as an educational, legal and medical center. The participants were "full-time" church leaders, members of a racially mixed, minister's fellowship belonging to the Presbyterian, Methodist, and Dutch Reformed family of churches, who responded to an invitation by Tucker to share their views on the issue of *ubuntu*. Six of these leaders were from Afrikaans backgrounds, one was "colored" (of black, Khoi-san, Afrikaans, and English descent) and one was Xhosa. The gender composition was five men and three women. The presence of two SAADs was welcomed in that it meant that they could hear all contributions and challenge any wrong or blatantly prejudiced ideas. All participants had many years' involvement with the Zulu, Sotho/Tswana and Xhosa populations at multiple levels: e.g., growing up with them, living among them, ministering to them, and working with them in the structures of their denominations, in nonprofit organisations or in governmental organisations.

The focus group commenced by discussing how to define and characterise *ubuntu*. It then moved on to considering its strengths and weaknesses, and closed by considering the way forward for the *Ubuntu* reinvigoration project, about which the participants had been previously informed.

The strengths of ubuntu

Everyone in the focus group resonated with the thought "We are too imperfect to point accusing fingers at *ubuntu*!"[1] It was pointed out that non-SAAD culture has many weaknesses. For instance, non-SAAD culture is in many ways prejudiced against outsiders and those of other race or language groups. "As whites we find it difficult to really accept people of color and thus we have lost our credibility among SAADs. We are not truly accepting and loving. Afrikaans people do not accept or welcome even English speakers into their congregations!" was a comment made as an evidence of this.

It was in this light that the focus group considered *ubuntu* as "mostly a good idea" and saw it as having a positive influence in South Africa. "Many individuals practice *ubuntu* generosity and selflessness at a personal level, regardless of race of culture. This is what holds the country together" (2016: np.). The group reported that they had often seen this being lived out in SAAD communities. It was stated that, "If we, as whites, really practiced *ubuntu* no household will go without a head, and no hungry person without being fed." Perhaps the most outstanding strength was that *ubuntu* is very visibly evidenced in the way that those in black (sic) cultural groups "enjoy being with each other." They find joy and relaxation by meeting together, rather than being energised "through going off by themselves to seaside beaches, as in the European community."

Another *ubuntu* strength concerned its leadership ethic that teaches, "a king's or chief's power and position is only because of the will of the people and he has to submit to their will." Thus such leadership should lead to good governance and harmony. This was particularly symbolised in the exemplary, forgiving behavior

---

[1]   Quotation marks here indicate actual comments by focus group participants.

of Nelson Mandela. This undoubtedly helped "save South Africa from a conflagration in 1993 after Chris Hani's (the popular and gifted leader of the communist party) assassination."

The weaknesses of ubuntu

The focus group perceived real weaknesses with *ubuntu*, both inherently and in its realisation in a modern, urbanised, technological society that is no longer a village, such as South Africa is rapidly becoming today. These weaknesses are its: 1) indeterminacy; 2) traditional selective application; 3) stifling of enterprise, advancement and social development; 4) inconsistent leadership practice; 5) sanctioning of criminality and inefficiency; 6) repression of an individual's conscience and opinion; 7) putting social harmony before justice and accountability (in commerce, business and government); and, 8) its inflexibility.

Its indeterminacy

The focus group clearly agreed that the *ubuntu* concept is ill-defined and little understood at a cognitive level. Contributing to this vagueness is that most of the academics who have studied it and written about *ubuntu* are mostly of non-SAAD origin. "They do not speak black (sic) languages and have not been brought up in the culture of those influenced by *ubuntu*. Thus they will never correctly or fully understand it because it is lived rather than taught." An added difficulty is that, "[*Ubuntu*] is over idealised being a vague romanticised idea that has not been quantified." More confusingly this romanticisation "has been used by many whites (sic) to unrealistically romanticise our rainbow nation."

One result of this confusion is that it gives SAAD people an excuse to behave unethically, because there is now no commonly accepted standard of right or wrong. This was emphasised by the comment, "When there is a choice between greed and *ubuntu*, greed wins." Another result is that individuals or communities "use the indeterminacy of the *ubuntu* ethic as a manipulative tool to avoid punishment" for malfeasance. The (usually rural) community who traditionally punish malfeasance themselves, "may 'invent' the idea that punishing that particular crime is not in the *ubuntu* ethic."

Its selective application

Although many have been surprised at the recent outbreaks of xenophobia in South Africa, and the reasons for this are no doubt complex, yet one of the culprits is undoubtedly the traditional "village" selective application of *ubuntu*. For many SAADs its principles do not apply to those outside one's own tribe or language group. As the group noted, "It does not cross the boundaries between language groups and tribes" and "Different tribal groups will always call those of another group 'outsiders' and never accept them." This will seriously hinder harmony within South African multi-cultural society, especially as the size of the economic cake to be shared around is getting smaller in a rapidly growing population, leading to a struggle to get "your" share.

It may stifle personal development

The economic situation in South Africa is unlikely to improve as much as it potentially could, since *ubuntu* often stifles personal self-advancement and social development. As the focus-group shared, "*Ubuntu* does not allow for excellence or permit accountability in South Africa." Only the chief or certain favoured individuals will be allowed to be more successful because of the communal respect given to them as representative figureheads. Individual ambition and advancement through personal effort (education, hard work or skill) are often frowned upon and may accrue the jealousy and condemnation of the less successful. Another manifestation of this is a sometimes undue respect for age means that whatever an elder says dominates, even if he or she is perceived by the local community as obviously wrong. Young people do not contradict elders. The words of chiefs and kings carry inordinate weight even if it is recognised that they are advocating immoral actions such as xenophobia or are against beneficial development.

Its inconsistent leadership practice

"What many leaders do in South Africa is inconsistent with the *ubuntu* ethic." "*Ubuntu* should always engender servant leadership but it often does not." If these were a few comments from the leaders we engaged then it could be put down to the failings of human nature. Unfortunately, this inconsistency is not the case, "it being a mark of African (sic) leadership as a whole." Thus, despite its professed servant-leadership philosophy *ubuntu* seems, more often, to encourage an autocratic leadership. Group members characterised the attitude of much African leadership as, "The leader is always right." It is suggested that this is a result of a tension between two opposing leadership ideas found in *ubuntu*; that of seeking the good of the group as opposed to that of respecting age and authority. Often authority's undue demand for respect seems to overrule servanthood.

The sanctioning of criminality and inefficiency

This has implications for the supervisory discipline needed in all areas of industry, business, government, education, service delivery and non-profit organisations (such as churches) necessary for governing a modern country and enforcing the law. Those influenced by the *ubuntu* ethic find it very difficult to sanction laziness, inefficiency or criminal practices such as corruption or to accept such sanctions. It is regarded as disrespectful, inharmonious, and bringing an unacceptable loss of face. Moreover, social groups try and protect their "own" from punishment being correctly meted out by the State or other organisations, because of the selective nature of *ubuntu*.

Its repression of an individual's conscience and opinion

Such attitudes are exacerbated by the fact that *ubuntu* imposes such a strong group pressure to conform to the values and decisions of the group mind, so that even when an individual disagrees with these, his or her strong personal convictions are not verbalised out of fear of retribution or from respect for *ubuntu's* traditional values. This will sometimes lead to a form of hypocrisy in which one's personal convictions expressed in private conversation are repressed in later conversations in order to appease others, making SAADs sometimes appear hypocritical or untrustworthy to non-SAADs. Thus a "SAAD will often agree with you in a personal conversation but then agree with a completely different opinion in accordance with the consensus of his or her own 'tribal' group or family."

Its emphasis on social harmony defeats justice and accountability

The relational aspect of *ubuntu* may lead to deliberate evasions of the justice needed to order an efficient technocratic, national society as distinguished from a village society. Under the *ubuntu* ethic, guilt for a crime is imputed not only to the individual but also to the whole community and the family. "It is a 'shame' society and the individual conforms to its rules so as not to bring shame upon the community or family." The respect for others that *ubuntu* inculcates, unfortunately, means that an individual does not want to shame them by exposing their wrongdoing. "Respect for age and patriarchy also means that the accusations of a wronged younger person or woman will either not be voiced or else assertively repressed by the family or community."

Another manifestation of this emphasis on social harmony is that respect for age sometimes weakens discipline in the South African National Defence Force, "because an older soldier will often not obey or listen to a younger superior non-com or officer, with serious implications for its efficiency."

Its inflexibility

Lastly, and perhaps with greatest significance, the focus group concluded that "In the past the traditional community structures which underpinned *ubuntu* are now disappearing." Many in the SAAD community are influenced by the precepts of Western education, materialism, individualism, globalism, pluralism and modernity. Thus the whole concept of *ubuntu* in South Africa is "under considerable strain and tension," causing much confusion and inconsistency.

It is an arguable question whether the spirit of *ubuntu*, because of its traditional foundations, will be able to survive, cope with or modify its precepts and practices in the light of this tension. The problem is that those who promote *ubuntu*, such as the elders and traditional leaders, "often adhere rigidly to tradition." As the focus group agreed, "Tradition rules" in *ubuntu*. This makes the *ubuntu* code very resistant to change. When an ethical or judicial decision is made, tradition is virtually always determinative. It thus, often, enslaves people to traditions that are inappropriate to a modern, urbanised, industrialised society. As a result, "It has an element of oppression and prevents people listening to the truth." I would interpret this comment to mean that *ubuntu* is perceived not to be able to be adapted rationally to the truths and realities of today's world. This would be the case, as the group shared, with such "traditions as regarding the role of women in society; what happens when they are raped; and the inheritance and marriage practices which penalise and oppresses them, making them vulnerable to abuse."

The way forward – "Stew, smelt or crucible?"

Our conclusion is that there are considerable differences between SAAD and non-SAAD ethical codes. The focus group discussion revealed some non-SAAD values that, although they may be honoured more in the breach than the observance, are those against which *ubuntu*'s perceived weaknesses and strengths were judged. These non-SAAD values include the importance of individuality, the need to speak the truth despite the cost, expressing personal convictions, individual initiative and advancement, the need for accountability, and submission to institutional chains of command, the moral priority of exposing sexual abuse, the equality of the sexes, the virtue of "newness and change," leadership directed toward the welfare of the governed, and their universal application.

As a result of this study it is suggested that it would probably be most productive for the *ubuntu* reinvigoration project to commence tackling three areas: 1) the codification of *ubuntu* and its modification to adjust to the reality of the new South Africa; 2) influencing the current political and governmental system to make the concept of *ubuntu* less adversarial; and 3) similarly influencing the current legal system also to make it less adversarial. It would seem that because of its current and historical influence in South African society that the church, along with its members, may be able to play an important role in implementing this process.

Incorporating *ubuntu* into our legal and governmental institutions

The adversarial approach of non-SAAD law courts and politics is contrary to the spirit of *ubuntu* and therefore offensive to SAAD political parties such as the African National Congress and their constituency. The government needs to be held accountable but with much greater respect being shown towards its members. The adversarial approach of the legal system needs to be amended to show far more respect from attorneys in court toward the accused and complainants.

Unfortunately, it is the direct experience and anecdotal evidence acquired by these authors that South African law often tramples over community consensus and the principle of harmony and unnecessarily shames people who value *ubuntu*. Thus, there is considerable dissatisfaction among many SAADs with the way that the South African "Roman Dutch" law is applied. (Its very name indicates that is of European origin.) This dissatisfaction is not surprising since the *ubuntu* moral philosophy has a fundamentally different basis from that of the European moral philosophy.

... (one) respect in which African morality characteristically differs from an Aristotelian or other Western moral philosophy concerns the way it defines a positive relationship with others, namely, in strictly communal terms. One is not to positively relate to others fundamentally by giving them what they deserve, respecting individual rights grounded on consent, participating in a political sphere or maximizing the general welfare, common themes in Western moral philosophy. Instead, the proper way to relate to others, for one large part of sub-Saharan thinking, is to seek out community or to live in harmony with them (Metz and Gaie 2010, 275).

This means that South African law which is ordinarily concerned with the "letter of the law", is adversarial, and it is often perceived that those who can hire the best lawyers win their case or avoid prosecution. In fact, it is the opinion of Nicholson (2015), the Dean of the law faculty at The University of the Free State, that although there have been instances in the last ten years when judgments have relied upon the precepts of *ubuntu*, that more often they rely upon the Aristotelian legal framework. This is serious because a legal system will not work in a democracy unless "humanity has a role to temper the law with justice" (Nicholson 2015) and in South Africa humanity is inextricably linked with *ubuntu* in the eyes of the majority of its citizens.

The *ubuntu* inflexibility issue

Traditional SAAD rural village life is fast disappearing from South Africa. The contemporary urban SAAD, of all socio-economic categories, is now facing problems never before encountered or even imagined. There are no traditional precedents in *ubuntu* about what should be done in these situations in order to live harmoniously and respect others. In many townships life is just a struggle to survive, without any time to think about how to enjoy it or live holistically.

The problem is crucial since these authors believe that South African society as a whole is at a crucial tipping point: a term that the Oxford Dictionary of English (2016, np.) defines as, "the point at which a series of small changes or incidents becomes significant enough to cause a larger, more important change." The change we envisage is that the many small moral deteriorative changes in SAAD society, leading to the abandonment of the spirit of *ubuntu,* could become so great that the whole ethical/spiritual system will break down completely and, in effect, cease to exist. This catastrophic "tipping point" transition – the culmination of many small changes – is known in dynamic systems theory, as hysteresis (Scheffer 2009, 250ff), and as Scheffer comments, "hysteresis is important because… this kind of catastrophic condition is not so easy to reverse" (Scheffer 2009, 20).

So where might we begin with *ubuntu* reinvigoration? To answer this, the authors pick up on a comment made by one member of the focus groups concerning where to begin, how it would be done and who would do it.

Stew, smelt or crucible?

A member of the focus group commented that, "*ubuntu* is just one factor in being South African. Account has to be taken of the other cultures." He suggested that the government's efforts to incorporate *ubuntu* into the national ethic in order to promote harmony is like "making a stew as opposed to producing a product through smelting." This analogy electrified the group.

He defined a stew as "a random mixing of ingredients that are thrown into a pot and cooked together in the hope that the outcome is good, edible and tasty, which it may not be except by chance!" In contrast he defined the smelting process as "the careful scientific addition of selected ingredients to form a molten mixture which when cools produces a scientifically planned solid substance." In other words, when you make a stew anything can be the result, whereas when you smelt you know what you want the intended outcome to be, and select the substances you want to add to the smelt accordingly.

At the moment adding *ubuntu* to the prevailing non-SAAD ethic, which is also embraced by many middle class SAADs, would be like making a stew because the ingredients of *ubuntu* are undefined. Moreover, the non-SAAD ethic is so different from the *ubuntu* ethic – as should be clear from the group discussion – that there is no guarantee the two will ever mix. As one member commented, "*ubuntu* does not belong to whites and cannot be adapted to white (non-SAAD) culture and we have no right (sic) to adopt it anyway."

If there is ever a chance of the two ethics being merged then the only hope of success is by using a smelting process. The first step is to define *ubuntu*, not as it is "romanticised" in some academic philosophies, but how it works in practice. Ideas then need to be selected that will complement the weaknesses of the non-SAAD ethic and vice-versa, presumably with much negotiation and discussion.

However, another member then suggested that a "crucible" approach was needed. A crucible is a ceramic or metal container in which metals or other substances may be smelted. The crucible is then tipped and the desired pre-formed mould filled with the resulting liquid compound, allowing it to cool and solidify to the requisite shape. The point of the metaphor is that the English "crucible" has its origin from the Latin *crux* meaning a "cross." Only the transforming power of the gospel will enable SAAD and non-SAAD cultures to be integrated and *ubuntu* to be consistently put into practice on a pan-African basis. This will require the two strengths of each to be discerningly mixed through the power of the cross of Christ and rooted in the gospel since, "True *ubuntu* flows from a heart of love towards God and others." This was further emphasised thus: "The motive for practicing *ubuntu* must be the desire to be Christ-like not because it is our culture."

Conclusion

We finally conclude by referring back to the original conversation that purportedly started the *ubuntu* reinvigoration project. Our research appears to indicate that the project in itself is insufficient to lead to a moral reformation in South Africa. The moral reformation desired needs to take account of both non-SAAD and SAAD cultures in the context of a modern industrial and technocratic, urban society, and involve surrender of cultural pride at the foot of the cross, which can only be accomplished through the church. Then furthermore for *ubuntu* to become truly effective there needs to be a consistency between its philosophy and practice sufficient so that it can be discerningly combined with the non-SAAD ethic. Therefore, it is suggested that the *ubuntu* reinvigoration project be specifically embraced by the church in Southern Africa by establishing a multi-cultural, ecumenical panel in order to examine, codify and merge the two ethics in a manner that will impact the preaching of the gospel, emphasise the cross, influence Christian discipleship and impact society in general at all levels, in SAAD and non-SAAD congregations.

References

Gade, Christian. 2011. "The Historical Development of the Written Discourses on Ubuntu." *South African Journal of Philosophy* 30 (3): 303-329. http://0-content.eb scohost.com.wagtail.ufs.ac.za/

Gade, Christian. 2012. "What is Ubuntu? Different Interpretations among South Africans of African Descent." *South African Journal of Philosophy* 31 (3): 484–503. http://0-content.ebscohost.com.wagtail.ufs.ac.za/ContentServer.asp?

Hankela, Elina. 2013. "Rules of Reciprocity and Survival in Negotiating Ubuntu at the Central Methodist Mission in Johannesburg." *Journal of Theology for Southern Africa* 147: 73–89.

Mbiti, John S. 1977. *Introduction to African Religion*. Nairobi: Hennemann.

Mbiti, John S. 2012. *Concepts of God in Africa*. Nairobi: Acton Publishers.

Metz, Thaddeus, and Joseph Gaie. 2010. "The African Ethic of Ubuntu/Botho: implications for research on morality." *Journal of Moral Education* 39 (3): 273-290. http://www.informaworld.com

Mkhatshwa, S'Mangaliso. 2001. Back cover, *Ubuntu, an Ethic for a New South Africa*. Pietermaritzburg: Cluster Publications.

Nicholson, Caroline. 2015. "Justice, Righteousness and Terry Pratchett." *Rethinking Righteousness and Justice in Society*. Lecture, University of Free State, August 25, 2015.

Scheffer, Marten. 2009. *Critical Transitions in Nature and Society*. Princeton: Princeton University Press.

Shutte, Augustine. 2001. *Ubuntu, An Ethic for a New South Africa*. Pietermaritzburg: Cluster Publications.

Tutu, Desmond M. 1999. *No Future without Forgiveness*. New York: Doubleday.

III. PRACTICING UBUNTU:
INTERNATIONAL PERSPECTIVES

Postcolonial parallels: Practicing *ubuntu* in a divided landscape

Lynn Bridgers

Abstract

This chapter explores the post-colonial parallels in the divided landscapes of South Africa and the state of New Mexico in the United States. Both areas have more than one layer of colonial rule in a land of diverse indigenous peoples. New Mexico's indigenous peoples were colonised first by the Spanish, then by an Anglo American culture. South Africa's indigenous peoples were colonised first by the Dutch and later by the English. These histories create a dynamic post-colonial context as all three groups interact with each other and the layering effects of their colonial and religious histories. This chapter employs post-colonial theory to explore parallels in those contexts and the need for *ubuntu* to interact respectfully and create or continue a workable pluralism.

Postcolonial parallels

The genesis of this chapter began when I attended my first International Academy of Practical Theology in 2001. It was held in Stellenbosch, just outside of Cape Town. The complexity of South African culture seemed strangely familiar to me. I then began to realise parallels between New Mexico, where I was born and raised, and South Africa. Both had indigenous peoples native to the land. Both had multiple colonisations. Both have multiple languages. Both have smaller governing cities to the north, Pretoria and Santa Fe, and larger more commercial cities to the south, Johannesburg and Albuquerque. We start by looking at the indigenous peoples of both lands.

Indigenous peoples/tribes

Currently New Mexico has twenty-two tribes. Nineteen of the tribes are pueblos, the oldest tribal communities in the U.S. (New Mexico Tourism, undated). New Mexico is also home to nomadic tribes – the Jicarilla Apache, and Mescalero

Apache – as well as the Navajo Nation. Historically the Ute, the Comanche and the Jocome, Jano and Soma tribes have also lived in New Mexico (American Indians 2015).

In South Africa the word "tribe" became associated with a pejorative connotation under apartheid. In 1993 and 1994, when the country came out of apartheid, many South Africans reclaimed their ethnic heritage and began to take pride in their ancestry (South Africa History Online 2015). The interim constitution in 1993 recognised nine languages along with Afrikaans and English as official languages. Those languages include Zulu, Xhosa, isiNdebele, sePedi, seSotho, seTswana, siSwati, tshiVenda, and xiTsonga (South Africa History Online 2015). Thus both areas have a layering to different cultures and different languages, including the languages of their colonisers.

First colonisation

New Mexico was first colonised by the Spanish. The first Spaniards came to New Mexico under the leadership of Francisco Vazquez de Coronado in 1540. He and about 400 Spaniards explored the area and stayed until 1542. Spanish colonisation of New Mexico began in earnest in 1598, when Juan de Onate established the first capital at San Juan de los Caballeros.

In 1680, the indigenous peoples of New Mexico drove the Spanish out of New Mexico with a rebellion known as the Pueblo Revolt. Twelve years later, in 1692, the Spanish recolonised New Mexico, an event known as the *reconquesta* (New Mexico Office of the State Historian 2015).

South Africa's first colonisation began in 1602, when Chamber Representatives of the Netherlands Parliament granted a founding charter to the Dutch East India Company (Dutch: *Vereenigde Oost-Indische Compagnie*, or VOC), to begin establishing a trading empire in the East. In 1652 the company established a station on the Cape for their VOC shipping fleets on the way to and from India (South African History Online 2015).

Second colonisation

While New Mexico came under control of the Mexican government briefly from 1821 to 1846, the second substantive colonisation came in 1846 when Brigadier General Stephen Watts Kearny led the occupying forces of the United States of America (U.S.). First as a territory, and later as a state, New Mexico has remained under the jurisdiction of the U. S. government ever since (New Mexico Office of the State Historian 2015). English replaced Spanish as the "official" language of the area, but in reality it was simply layered on top of the existing Native American languages and Spanish.

South Africa's second colonisation could be seen as starting in 1795, when the British took over the Cape. Although the Dutch temporarily regained control of the Cape – known for three years as the Batavian Republic – the British would eventually occupy the Cape again and remain in control throughout the 19th century.

It is interesting to note that in one period of history the Flemish and the Spanish came under the dominion of a single sovereign. Charles V (d. 1558) inherited sovereignty over the Flemish from his paternal grandmother, Mary of Burgundy (d. 1482). He inherited sovereignty over Castile from his maternal grandmother, Isabella of Castile (d. 1504) and the crown of Aragon from his maternal grandfather, Ferdinand II of Aragon (d. 1516). Had those alliances remained intact, the colonisation of both New Mexico and South Africa would have been undertaken by the same empire (Elliott 1990, 148-149).

Colonial aftermath

Postcolonial theorist Leela Gandhi points out that since the 1980s "postcolonialism has taken its place alongside poststructuralism, psychoanalysis and feminism as a major critical discourse in the humanities" (Gandhi 1998, viii). Scholars in postcolonialism have explored the impact and legacies of colonial systems and their effects on both the coloniser and the colonised.

A colonial past often calls on us to confront both the positive and the negative consequences of colonialism. On the part of the coloniser this can take the form of exalting the benefits of such a past while denying the underside of colonialism, the abuse of power and the abuse of the colonised. Accordingly, Gandhi reminds us: "If postcoloniality can be described as a condition troubled by the consequences of a self-willed historical amnesia, then the theoretical value of postcolonialism inheres, in part, in its ability to elaborate the forgotten memories of this condition. In other words, the colonial aftermath calls for an ameliorative and therapeutic theory which is responsive to the task of remembering and recalling the colonial past" (Gandhi 1998, 7-8).

Postcolonial scholarship, then, seeks to reclaim those voices that were "lost" under the triumphalism of the coloniser. Gandhi notes, "Colonialism, then, to put it simply, marks the historical process whereby the 'West' attempts systematically to cancel or negate the cultural difference and value of the 'non-West' " (Gandhi 1998, 15).

In the process of rediscovering "lost" voices and experiences, and looking behind the curtain of triumphant coloniser, we find a revised history and begin to recognise the complex relationship between coloniser and colonised. Gandhi explains, "... we might conclude that the forgotten content of postcoloniality reveals the story of an ambivalent and symbiotic relationship between coloniser and colonised" (Gandhi 1998, 11). Remembering the colonial past, as Homi Bhabha writes, "is never a quiet act of introspection or retrospection. It is a painful remembering, a putting together of the remembered past to make sense of the trauma of the present" (Bhabha 1994, 63). We use postcolonial theory then, not only to remember and reconceptualise the past, but also to understand our present, with all the hurt and abuse that continue to shape the way we live today.

A workable pluralism?

I first heard the term "workable pluralism" several decades ago in a lecture given by Mexican writer Carlos Fuentes when he was speaking at Popejoy Hall in Albuquerque. At the end of his lecture, Fuentes chided his New Mexico audience for not exporting the most important asset they had: their workable pluralism. While there are still deep pockets of resentment and pain at times in New Mexico, for the most part New Mexico has achieved a workable pluralism in which its diverse citizens are recognised and honoured.

Historian Lenn A. Goodman writes: "A workable pluralism demands a certain self-restraint and mutual accommodation. Push openness too hard and it turns impotent, powerless to defend itself and without a principle to defend" (Goodman 2014, 25). A workable pluralism honours the tension between diversity and identity. It recognises the diverse voices and histories of the members who make up the culture, recognises the need for tolerance and respect for the "other." Yet at the same time it encourages members to take pride in and to honour their own specific identity, not to have it dissolve into the collective.

Robin Murphy Williams explains "A workable pluralism is possible for one thing because... the sharpness, strength and permanency of ethnic boundaries are highly variable characteristics.... Ethnic collectivities are not firmly fixed units; they emerge and disappear; their boundaries shift (and change in kind) not only over time but from situation to situation" (Williams 1977, 373).

This fluidity of ethnic collectivities can be seen in New Mexico, in part, in the consistent inter-marriage between Native American, Hispanics and Anglos, or whites. Most families have what is called a "coyote marriage," or a marriage between an Hispanic and an Anglo. Many members of the pueblos have Spanish surnames, evidence of inter-marriage in the past. One often encounters Native Americans who have married Anglos or vice versa. Simply put, it is much harder to sustain stereotypes and uninformed ignorance when a member of a different ethnic group is part of your family.

The need for *ubuntu*

Recognising those qualities which sustain a workable pluralism can help us to understand the need for *ubuntu* in a post-colonial setting. The term itself dates back to the 19th century, although it has come into wider usage since the end of apartheid. The word is made up of "*ubu*," the prefix that forms abstract nouns, and "*ntu*," meaning person or human being. The closest English translation would be "humanity."

There are many different meanings ascribed to the term *ubuntu*, but Michael Onyebuchi Eze emphasises the intersubjectivity implicit in the concept. He is worth quoting at length.

A person is a person through other people' strikes an affirmation of one's humanity through recognition of an 'other' in his or her uniqueness and difference. It is a demand for a creative intersubjective formation in which the 'other' becomes a mirror (but only a mirror) for my subjectivity. This idealism suggests to us that humanity is not embedded in my person solely as an individual; my humanity is co-substantively bestowed upon the other and me. Humanity is a quality we owe each other. We create each other and need to sustain this otherness creation. And if we belong to each other, we participate in our creations: we because you are and since you are, definitely I am. The 'I am' is not a rigid subject, but a dynamic self-constitution dependent on this otherness creation of relation and distance. (Eze 2010, 190-191)

Ubuntu became better known, in part, as a result of the writings of Archbishop Desmond Tutu. In his 1999 book *No Future Without Forgiveness,* he wrote: "A person with Ubuntu is open and available to others, does not feel threatened that others are able and good, based on the proper self-assurance that comes from knowing that he or she belongs in a greater whole and is diminished when others are humiliated or diminished, when others are tortured or oppressed" (Tutu 1999, 73).

Ubuntu is a strong counter-balance to the West's emphasis on individuality. The West generally thinks of the person as a sole entity, separated from others. Philosophical emphasis is on the agency the person embodies and moral choices the person embraces. Each person is viewed as unique, with due deference given to maintaining a sense a personal space, and keeping an appropriate distance from other individuals.

The definition of individuality itself includes a "total character peculiar to and distinguishing an individual from others," and "separate or distinct existence" (Merriam Webster 2015). This silo approach stands in direct contrast to the intersubjectivity of *ubuntu*. Individuality is, if you like, a vertical definition of the person. *Ubuntu* emphasises the horisontal dimension of the person, the relational dimensions of people's lives. In this sense *ubuntu* is more similar to the ethos

of many Native American beliefs. Vine De Loria, writing on the differences between a native view of religion and a Christian view, explains: "When we turn
from Christian religious beliefs to Indian tribal beliefs in this area, the contrast
is remarkable. Religion is not conceived as a personal relationship between the
deity and each individual. It is rather a covenant between a particular god and
a particular community. The people of the community are the primary residue
of the religion's legends, practices and beliefs. Ceremonies of community-wide
scope are the chief characteristic feature of religious activity. Religion dominates
the tribal culture, and distinctions existing Western civilisation no longer present
themselves" (DeLoria 2003, 194).

Ubuntu not only counterbalances the West's emphasis on individuality and
separateness, but can help to counter the pain of remembering a past fraught with
colonisation and abuse. The post-colonial setting of New Mexico is built upon the
abuse of Native Americans by early Spanish soldiers and settlers. It is built upon
the displacement of Native peoples from their traditional land. It rests upon the
subsequent displacement by Anglos of New Mexico Hispanics from lands their
families had held for generations. As noted above, Homi Bhabha has reminded us
that postcolonial remembrances is "a putting together of the remembered past to
make sense of the trauma of the present" (Bhabha 1994, 63).

This sense of connectedness aids one in coming to terms with historical injustice and atrocity. The Native peoples of New Mexico have known the genocide
imposed on them by their colonial conquerors, yet have come to a perspective
that allows them to continue in meaningful ways. As the dedication in Joy Harjo's
book *How We Became Human* reads, "For my sisters and brothers, by blood and
by love. For my allies, and for my enemies. For my heart" (Harjo 2002, dedication). By transcending the division between oneself and one's enemies, one heals
one's own heart.

Ceremonies are used to overcome these divisions and achieve the right balance. As Kenneth Lincoln writes of the culture of Laguna Pueblo and the work
of Leslie Marmon Silko: "All this ceremonial behavior ensures the natural way
of things, the right balance of communal energies – pairing and coupling and
adjoining necessary to peace and prosperity in a demanding environment where
enemies, witches, ghosts, evil spirits, and plain bad luck have just as much a place
as tribal proprieties and blessings of the good spirits and general goodwill of the
people" (Lincoln 2007, 121).

Similarly, *ubuntu* emphasises the collective, the connection of one to all of the
community and ultimately to the world. Tutu understood this dimension of *ubuntu*
writing, "We think of ourselves far too frequently just as individuals, separated
from one another, whereas you are connected and what you do affects the whole

World. When you do it well, it spreads out; it is for the whole of humanity" (Tutu 1999, 73).

The post-colonial present of South Africa is built upon years of slavery and the physical abuse of slaves at the hands of white slave owners. It is built upon the struggle between Dutch and English for primacy. It is built upon the cruelty and injustice of apartheid. There is pain in such remembering, and post-colonial theory has assured us of the painful process of remembering a colonised people.

This is why both landscapes can benefit from *ubuntu*. They can benefit, in part, by the emphasis that each of us is connected to the "other." They can benefit by recovering a lost sense of humanity. They can benefit by the emphasis on kindness and humanity toward others. There is a real need for *ubuntu* in such landscapes. As novelist Barbara Kingsolver has observed: "The legacy of colonialism is a world of hurt and cross-pollinated beauty, and we take it from there" (Kingsolver 1995, 193).

References

American Indians in New Mexico. 2015. Native American Tribes of New Mexico, http://www.native-language.org/nmexico.htm.

Bhabha, Homi. 1994. *The Location of Culture*. London: Routledge.

DeLoria, Vine. 2003. *God is Red: A Native View of Religion*. Golden, CO: Fulcrum Publishing.

Elliott, John H. 1990. *Imperial Spain: 1469-1716*. New York: Penguin Books.

Eze, Michael O. 2010. *Intellectual History in Contemporary South Africa*. New York: Palgrave.

Gandhi, Leela.1998. *Postcolonial Theory: A Critical Introduction*. New York: Colombia University Press.

Goodman, Lenn A. 2014. *Religious Pluralism and Values in the Public Sphere*. Cambridge: Cambridge University Press.

Harjo, Joy. 2002. *How We Became Human: New and Selected Poems, 1975-2001*. New York: W.W. Norton & Company, Inc.

Kingsolver, Barbara. 1995. *High Tide in Tucson*. New York: HarperPerennial.

Lincoln, Kenneth. 2007. "Southwest Crossings: Lucy Tapahonso and Leslie Silko." *Speak Like Singing: Classics of Native American Literature*. Albuquerque, NM: University of New Mexico Press.

Merriam Webster. 2015. "Individuality | Definition of Individuality by Merriam-Webster." http:www.merriam-webster.com/dictionary/individuality.

New Mexico Office of the State Historian. 2015a. "Mexican Period." http://newmexicohistory.org/historical-evens-and-timeline/spanish-colonial.

New Mexico Office of the State Historian. 2015b. "Spanish Colonial Period." http://newmexicohistory.org/historical-events-and-timeline/spanish-colonial.

New Mexico Tourism Department. Undated. *The Native New Mexico Guide*, Indian Tourism Program, 491 Old Santa Fe Trail. Santa Fe, NM.

South African History Online. 2011. "History of slavery and early colonisation in South Africa timeline, 1602-1841." http:www.sahistory.org.za/topic/history-slavery~--and -early-colonisation-sa-timeline-1602-1841.

Tutu, Desmond. 1999. *No Future Without Forgiveness.* New York: Image Books.

Tutu, Desmond. 2015. "Ubuntu Women Institute USA with SSIWEL as its First South Sudan Project." http:uwi-usa.blogspot.be/2012/01/umbutu-brief-meaning-of-african-word.html.

Williams, Robin Murphy. 1977. *Mutual Accommodation: Ethnic Conflict and Coopera-tion.* St. Paul, MN: University of Minnesota Press.

Critical *ubuntu*: Rethinking the role of subjectivity

Hans-Günter Heimbrock und Trygve Wyller

Abstract

In this chapter we elaborate on ideals of *ubuntu* within the frame of Western Practical Theology. Two case studies, one on perceived racism in Peru and one on the church's work with migrants in Pietermaritzburg, focus on pitfalls regarding the interplay between participation and belonging. By means of field research and using the methodology of life-world theory the chapter shows that critical reflection on subjectivity and connected-ness together, has liberating potential. By reflecting on preconditions and limitations in practice, practical theology reinterprets the ideal task of Christian churches, namely to provide spaces for those in need.

Methodological points of departure

In this chapter the goal is to comment on and contribute to the *participation and belonging* aspect of *ubuntu* (see Kumalo 2015; Tutu 1999; Shutte 2004). *Ubuntu* has often been criticised for being too narrow and community centered and there-fore lacking the transcending strength of a critical theory and practice. This chap-ter aims to reflect (and act!) more in depth on what *participation and belonging* means. Life-world analysis and spatial approaches can contribute to a more radical and critical interpretation of *belonging and participation*. A critical juridical anal-ysis of the use of *ubuntu* in South African court sentences has shown that *ubuntu* is by nature rooted in the life-world (Bennett 2011). Methodologically we engage critically with the concept of *ubuntu* from a practical-theological perspective.

Simanga Kumalo emphasises the religious core of *ubuntu* (Kumalo 2015, 20). Rooted in African traditions, the modern distinction between religion and non-religion is not relevant in this context. However, Kumalo does suggest that *ubuntu* expand its scope by fostering connections with traditions and liberating practices other than those from its own past. One such tradition could be the practical-theological discussion of the last few decades. *Belonging and participation* play a central role in traditional *ubuntu*. Who you are relates closely to where you belong. This is often contrasted with the focus on subjectivity and individuality in Western modernity. However, such an almost essentialist contradiction should be reevaluated. Here methodological discussions in practical theology can prove to be useful.

Though practical theology necessarily emphasises *belonging* in religious and ethical theory and practice, its perspective is dialectical. It picks up on the impulse from Christian faith of the dynamics of human beings as subjects in relations, both to God and to one another. The German practical theologian Henning Luther (1992, 257) puts it as follows: "Denn nicht Vergegenwärtigung von Kirche, sondern die Gegenwart von Religion im Subjekt ist das eigentliche Thema der Praktischen Theologie" ("Not the representation of the church, however the presence of religion within the human subject is the original theme of Practical Theology"). In this tradition subjectivity and relationality (belonging) are not contradictory positions.

The starting point for any pastoral praxis is not the existence or the mission of the church (participation/belonging) and its task to transmit teachings and ethical rules. This is what Edward Farley calls the "clerical paradigm" (Farley 1975). Its task is rather to unveil the core of religion as facilitator for human practice, giving space to individuated subjectivity. Subjectivity is not a fixed and given entity, however fragile. It evolves through mutual recognition, but is not completely conceptualised as social relation. Individuated subjectivity consists of formational processes which transcend social relations. It includes experiences of inner difference and duality, an awareness of similarities and otherness, existential estrangement. Traditional religious language expresses this existential experience of difference as "sin," "reconciliation," and "grace." Related subjectivity and its theological implications have been explained in Chicago theologian Bernhard Meland's (1969) systematic theology. This interpretation of faith and related religious practice is clearly in opposition to the Cartesian idea of the ultimate self-giving of the subject. It is also in opposition to the unlimited individuality of late-modern Western societies and their social values which contradict the gospel of the "kingdom of God." However, it inscribes in practical theology the experience of the fragility of subjectivity as a self-critical stance towards one's Christian personal and professional praxis. For Edward Farley the objective is "to see how faith apprehends God as a reality not coincident with human subjectivity" (Farley 1975, 223). Any diaconical praxis which aims to benefit and liberate the other in the name of the gospel, should also care for the persons who do the caring and should take heed of their various motives for doing so.

Practical theology as practical ecclesiology has the ideal of "church for the Other" (Bonhoeffer 1997). Christian communities should not only care for their internal praxis, but should look beyond themselves, participate in everyday life and culture, influencing issues of human dignity. The task is to critically reconstruct the actual social practice of congregations in light of qualified subjectivity. How do congregations engage to help the poor, refugees and other victims of our times on the basis of the Christian message? Does this contribute to the development of even more individuated subjectivity?

To deepen these research questions could be one way of following Kumalo's suggestion to look for other liberating traditions to further develop *ubuntu*. The following two cases will illustrate the critical, liberating potential of practical theology to think simultaneously in terms of subjectivity and connectedness. Perceiving the other paradoxically requires a continued reflection on what subjectivity means in practical theology, both methodologically and substantially.

With the focus on human dignity, this chapter makes a connection between *recognition of the other* and practical theology as *art of perception* (cf. Failing and Heimbrock 1998). This can pave the way to a better Christian praxis in which respect and inter-subjective sensitivity are not only ethical convictions, but also a practical habit which manifests in all interaction. Some years ago, in a bi-national research project "Perceiving the Other: Case Studies and Theories of Respectful Action," we used perceptive praxis to enhance the professional competence of those engaged in Christian praxis (Wyller and Heimbrock 2010). In order to develop a suitable method for this very practical research, we take our epistemological point of departure from phenomenology and theory of life-world. These provide methodical tools to deal critically with one's own subjectivity, social involvement and spatial embeddedness.

For the purposes of these case studies it is necessary that the researchers locate themselves. The researcher in the first case is Hans-Günter Heimbrock from Frankfurt, Germany and in the second case Trygve Wyller from Oslo, Norway.

Perceived racism: A case study

In the first case study Hans-Günter Heimbrock relates an event that took place in 2014 in Peru, South America. In December of that year the department store Saga Falabella launched its Christmas campaign. In an advertisement of children's toys four pretty little blonde-haired white-skinned girls each hold a doll with blonde or red hair. The dolls are white-skinned as the girls. The dress of the girl and the doll she is holding are the same.

This photo unleashed public outcry in the national and social media. Within five days a petition with 30 000 subscriptions was collected. The famous Peruvian writer and playwright Eduardo Adrianzen wrote on Twitter:

Could anything be MORE RACIST in Peru than the Saga Falabella Christmas catalogues? It can't be. No. In the USA and Europe there is much more racial variety than in these photos, I swear. Pretty little girls, yes, but how many Peruvians do they represent? 1%? (too much?). The rest of us can't shop at Saga: it isn't for us. Seriously, the people who approved these catalogues must live on Narnia or in some arch-Caucasian country that exists only in their minds. Should we impose fines on RACISTS or would it be better to send them for urgent psychiatric care?

"Teun A. van Dijk author of a book on racism in Latin America, told the BBC that almost all Latin American countries share an ideal of physical beauty that is unattainable for the vast majority of their people – 'white, blond, and blue-eyed. You don't need a lot of research for this,' he said. 'Everybody in Latin America knows it' " (Anglin 2014). The company Saga Falabella reacted quickly, withdrew the photo and published an extended apology.

"According to our values, we respect and appreciate diversity in the broadest sense, and we ensure that there is no discrimination in our approach," the company said in a statement. "We regret that the design of one part of our commercial communication has caused conflict for not having adequately represented the diversity that is present in the rest of our campaign." The company also told the BBC that the rest of their holiday campaign features children from Colombia, Chile, Peru and Argentina" (Simon 2014).

The National Department of Culture welcomed this.

At first glance, the situation seems clear: there are actors, there are victims, and there are advocates. There is a photo, which led to protest because it was re-garded as disrespectful to 99% of Peruvian people who were forced to see some-thing that was offensive to them.

I (Hans-Günter Heimbrock) did not have the opportunity to interview anyone from Peru about the catalogue. I could not observe anyone looking at the internet catalogue and their reaction to it. I am a white male member of a dominantly white skinned society with German as my first language. I am not directly involved in the sort of racism and violation of human rights which was criticised. I am not familiar with the everyday discrimination against indigenous people in Peru and especially against the female majority. The incident in Peru does not involve me personally. I have no experience of my personal dignity being harmed or violated. I run the risk of responding to the situation with moral indignation at others' faults.

My reconstruction of the case began with the media campaign as a social praxis "out there." I did not pay attention to the interactive visual dynamic between me and them. However, when the focus is also on the researcher as a subject, my own perceptive process and experience in my life-world come into play. The photo in the catalogue is part of a larger composition of texts and pictures formatted as an advertisement. The page on which the product appears is clearly marked so that the product can be ordered and bought via the internet. The content consists of four girls dressed up the same as the doll in expensive clothing to impress and attract the viewer. It is an artificial situation. They were told to look into the camera and smile. The effect is rather unnatural. They do not look at me. They are not individuals who can be encountered in their concrete lifeworld. There is no interaction among them either. They stand there as isolated beings. Each girl has a different expression. There are traces of individuality, but visual elements make their individuality invisible for the purposes of the advertisement.

In a Western consumerist cultural context the praxis at stake is a rather trivial life situation. Leafing through catalogues, skipping pages, doing it at a certain speed, I do not expect high quality art, just advertisements, a world framed and sorted in terms of goods to buy. Only sufficient attention is needed in order to buy and pay. An eye-catching picture aims to seduce the prospective buyer at a glance. The photo is openly instrumental. It lacks any originality and uniqueness, although the four girls do exist in flesh and blood somewhere out there.

Perceiving the particular photo without knowing the background and context, I felt insulted by the fact that these girls' toys promote a one-sided and problematic gender model regarding women. I did not perceive a racist element tied to skin color.

A critical focus on subjectivity provides insights as to the subject's limitations. It is not completely my personal, individual, intended way of perceiving other per-sons that was activated in this simple situation, but rather a number of socialised patterns. It is also not a purely rational process. Perceiving is a mix of choice, desire, being attracted and affected. This case is one perspective, one atomic element, in the universe of everyday praxis. Through all kinds of social and cultural codes, it has an impact on our worldview and perception of the other. This means that a normative impulse rooted "only" in context and in belonging, would not be sufficient. One needs more than *belonging and participation*, because sometimes it is belonging that blinds one to other relevant aspects.

Looking back on the reflections on the incident in Peru, there is an obvious discrepancy between the discourse about the picture on racism and the perception of the photo. What is even more important for practical theology: there is a qualitative difference between being involved in an *ethical discourse* on human dignity and getting *involved as a subject* who attempts to perceive foreign human beings in their concrete situation. The normative implications of such perception cannot be clarified without referring to life-world, in this particular case: referring to the different life-worlds, the one here and the one there.

Church for "the foreigner": A case study

The second case, that of Trygve Wyller, is from a context geographically very different from the first. Migration, undocumented migrants and asylum-seekers have become a political predicament both in the North and South (Anderson 2014; Snyder 2012). Recently Europeans have witnessed how many anonymous individuals come to Europe from Africa, Syria and Iraq. Europeans tend to forget that there are asylum-seekers, refugees and undocumented people on all continents, not the least in Africa. Migration is global. The problem in Europe is the illusion that this problem is only local and in their neighbourhood (Levitt and Glick-Schiller 2004).

Churches and faith-based organisations are among the most active to provide support regarding this global migration, whether in the South or the North. They aim to improve the lives and conditions of refugees, undocumented migrants and asylums seekers (Groody 2008). In this rather dramatic and exposed context, it is important to develop research methodologies that are more than instrumental or victim-oriented (Wyller 2016b). The question of subjectivity, liberation and life-world is relevant to migration studies in the area of practical theology.

In Pietermaritzburg, a South-African town one hour's drive north of Durban, as in most of the South African cities there are a significant numbers of people from neighbouring African countries such as Malawi, Zimbabwe and the Democratic Republic of the Congo. Tourists might not notice them but locals do. The majority of them have small barber shops, cafes, and the like. The locals call them "foreigners."

In June 2015 I met some groups of Congolese refugees, asylums-seekers and undocumented migrants in Pietermaritzburg. Two ministers of refugee congregations who work mainly with Congolese and a Congolese PhD student were present as helpers. The migrants had experienced much violence and aggression. Some would gladly return to the Congo is they had the opportunity, but there was none. The experience of segregation and lack of generosity of South-African communities were painful and humiliating to them. With the prevalent tribal wars going on in Congo, that as not a safe place either. The majority, therefore, were obligated to stay in South Africa.

The one minister was from the Pentecostal tradition and the other defined his ministry as ecumenical. Even though there were confessional differences between them, they had much more in common. They both ministered to Congolese migrants. The pastor from the ecumenical ministry wanted to be respectful of the traditions, culture and customs of the refugees. He therefore did not want to enforce his own congregation onto them and expect of them to leave their denomination of origin. He aimed at a ministry in which people of different traditions and denomination can gather to worship in their own language and culture. He said: "I did not want the church to be a specific denomination, because the refugees came here from different religious traditions. I want the group to be such that they can start their own church and continue with their beliefs and ways." He also did this work for missionary reasons. In order to be able to reach out to people, he could not have a specific denominational ministry. Therefore, his ministry had to be ecumenical. The decision to work in the native language and respect the ethnic culture of the people was part of what he called his "mission strategy." He was taught this strategy at a training center for evangelists somewhere on the African continent.

During the week the pastor attends to social issues concerning migrant people and invites them to Congolese, ecumenical services in a local church building on Sunday afternoons. The service takes place in the afternoon, so that the migrants, should they choose to do so, can attend the morning services of the local Pietermaritzburg churches of their own denomination. The ecumenical afternoon service attends to ethnic and cultural aspects. It follows a regular structured liturgy of a word of welcome, much local music and singing, sermons, testimonies and prayers, offerings, and information. After the service there are biscuits and mineral water in the church room. In a way the service is similar to other mainline Protestant services in South Africa. The clothing, language and music are not the same and contribute to maintaining a strong cultural identity. This seems to be the main goal of the service.

In these services there are drums, women carry small children on their backs and wear clothing from their homeland. It feels to them as though they are in the Congo for that short time, even if they are in the city of Pietermaritzburg, the former British capital of the colonial province of Natal. This is a life-world experience, but only in a church context. The churches emphasise cultural belonging. The question of this article is how to address such traces of a strengthened subjectivity in such a ministry or church context.

In a 2010 article Jennifer Greenburg discusses Congolese migrants in Johannesburg. Her point of departure is what she calls "the spatial politics of xenophobia," referring to the spate of xenophobic violence in 2008. For Greenburg the implicit politics of xenophobia is spatial: "The violence and cultural racism to which migrants are subjected, combined with volatile housing conditions, has the effect of continually displacing migrants within the city" (Greenburg 2010, 67). The reason for this displacement is that racist aggression makes it impossible for migrants to stay in one place for an extended period. They are not safe in any one place in the long run. Moving becomes the permanent trajectory of refugee people. "Migrant trajectories within the city point to the production of a new relationship between race and space through which the violent racism to which migrants are subjected at the same time as they are forced to remain constantly on the move" (Greenburg 2010, 67).

Following other migration scholars, Greenburg points to the significance of Pentecostal churches for the refugee population in South Africa. On the one hand, the spatial politics of xenophobia is to reduce the spatial belonging and force migrants to remain on the move, never settling in a permanent space. On the other hand, religion takes people back to spaces. Her research shows that "Pentecostal churches are some of the most important sites at which urban space is being reconfigured ... The church is one of the everyday practices that produce migrants' spatial and racial experiences of the city" (Greenburg 2010, 78).

My limited fieldwork in Pietermaritzburg in 2015 confirms Greenburg's findings. However, it is not only in the Sunday services that space is "reconfigured." The reclaiming of the downtown streets by means of migrant small businesses also counts as such. Though migrants themselves were the entrepreneurs, pastors played an important role behind the scenes. In this way, churches contribute to a reclaiming of space. This includes secular spaces. In order to investigate this, the researcher becomes involved in concrete spatial practices. The Sunday service is a religious space that has a strong secular, not only religious, impact. Inside the religious church space a new cultural secular subjectivity is developed, sometimes as a secular space inside the religious. Everyday life during the week can be seen as important secular spacing, which also contributes to increased subjectivity and self-confidence. Religious practices could open up new cultural and religious spaces for "foreigners," for the stranger, the migrant, the "insignificant other." These new spaces have ecclesiological significance (Wyller 2016a).

Life-world and *ubuntu*

Neither of the case studies is from an explicit "*ubuntu* context," even if the second is located in South Africa. Neither makes explicit use of *ubuntu* philosophy. However, we do think that these two cases illustrate the basic expectation of *ubuntu* that "the good life" is attained in community, and that communal experiences contribute to identity formation. These findings also contribute to the discussion on methodology in practical theology.

The two cases present a different understanding of subjectivity. In both, however, subjectivity is clearly not the opposite of participation and belonging. On the contrary, participation and belonging form the core of subjectivity. The liberating tendencies of this becomes clear in both cases. However, with critical reflection on participation and belonging, there is also a flipside. There is also some ambivalence. Success is not automatically guaranteed.

The first observation is that the researcher has an impact on life-world studies. The researchers could not come to a normative position without having themselves become part of the life-world that was investigated. This is valid for both cases, even though the life-world in the first case is partly virtual. The second case presupposes that the researcher is invited in and becomes a part of the community. However, his subjectivity remains rooted in his own particular life-world. When two subjects are present, this does not constitute a methodological problem. Quite the opposite: it is part and parcel of life-world studies. This again ties in with *ubuntu's* strong emphasis on community, which could be called a life-world. Articulating, reflecting on and deepening the meaning of a shared life-world, requires an active subject. Therefore, a critical engagement with the concept of *ubuntu* also requires reflection on the position of the subject in community based ethics, theology and normativity. The subject is conceptualised as entering into a life-world or community and participating in it with solidarity and openness. However, in the first case the subject was not rooted in that life-world. That poses an ethical question. Reflection on the limitations of participation in a life-world is needed when both *ubuntu* and practical theology are discussed. In both cases the most radical and critical perspectives in the interpretation come from a reflection rooted in the contextualised life-world experiences of the researchers.

The second observation is a "spatial confirmation" of the first. The second case definitely shows that migrants re-spatialise public space by means of the Pentecostal services and social practices. In a way one could say that the churches provide a space for others. This again means that communitarian practices (such as in the migrant churches) are *ubuntu* practices among and with the refugees.

However, two levels of subjectivity are manifest in the two cases. First level subjectivity is the level of the researcher and his or her life-world. The second is the level of the participants in practice. In the two cases this means the ethical discourse on racism concerning the photo and the refugees in the services. In the first case, self-critical reflection on the life-world can lead to a normative rethinking of the racist presence in the photo. Though the researcher from a Western life-world initially lacks this perspective, the reflexive process can lead the researcher to an awareness of injustice regarding the subjects in the photos. These should be substituted with native, non-white, indigenous children, as the commercial business company did after the protests. So the lack of a "true" subjectivity on the level of the practice itself, is a second important interpretation of this case.

This second level is also evident in the refugee case. Life-world oriented research and the participant observer in the life-world also discover an increased significance of the migrants as subject. They themselves are often more significant than the church community as an organisation. Though the aim of the ministries and pastors' work is community building for refugees, it is through the migrants' own performing and practicing of self-identity and subjectivity in the new life-world context, that the goal is reached. So a "Church for Others" (Bonhoeffer) is not first of all to provide church space, but to provide a space that the migrants others can appropriate for themselves. The church is for others. When the church disappears the participants will take the lead.

As in the first case, traces of a critical understanding of *ubuntu* can also be found here. There is definitely a connection to community, but one which equips its members to perform as subjects, not necessarily only in the community itself. From a practical-theological perspective one can add that the researcher with a critical awareness of the limitations of his or her own life-world, also needs a theological eye to discern this change of subjectivity. One needs a trained eye to discover empirical theological practices. The goal is not the church, but rather the freedom and dignity of human beings and societies. If this is not their aim, churches are not truly church, but an institution serving its own interests. This conclusion can be drawn from both a critical discussion on *ubuntu* and practical theology.

Ubuntu is often interpreted as a fundamental ethical call towards humanity and universal interconnectedness. This is valuable as a regulative idea, a "metanorm" (Bennet 2011, 46), especially with regard to the particular historical development of societies and churches. This should be complemented by critical empirical reflection. In our view, the contribution of practical theology is a critical rethinking of the practice of *ubuntu* with its focus on participation and belonging. It divulges hidden preconditions if this practice and develops realistic hope-filled theological perspectives. The practice of *ubuntu* should not be exclusively conceived as ethical (cognitive) discourse. Reflecting on human beings in their concrete and spatial life-world situations is also a productive source for directing our sense of human dignity and our theology.

References

Adrianzen, Eduardo. 2011. https://twitter.com/adrianzeneduard.

Anderson, Ruben. 2014. *Illegality, Inc.: Clandestine Migration and the Business of Bordering Europe*. Oakland, CA: University of California Press.

Anglin, Andrew. 2014. "Peru: Retailer Pulls Catalogue Featuring Blue-Eyed, Blonde-Haired Models." *Daily Stormer.* http://www.dailystormer.com/peru-retailer-pulls-catalog-featuring-blue-eyed-blonde-haired-models/.

Bennett, Tom. 2011. "Ubuntu, an African Equity." *Potchefstroom Electronic Law Journal* 14 (4): 30-61.

Bonhoeffer, Dietrich. 1997. *Letters and Papers from Prison*. New York: Touchstone.

Failing, Wolf-Eckart, and Hans-Günter Heimbrock. 1998. *Gelebte Religion wahrnehmen: Lebenswelt –Alltagskultur –Religionspraxis*. Stuttgart: Kohlhammer Verlag.

Farley, Edward. 1975. *Ecclesial Man: A Social Phenomenology of Faith and Reality.* Philadelphia, PA: Fortress Press.

Greenburg, Jennifer. 2010. "The Spatial Politics of Xenophobia: Everyday Practices of Congolese Migrants in Johannesburg." *Transformation: Critical Perspectives on Southern Africa* 74: 66-86.

Groody, Daniel and Gioacchino Campese, eds. 2008. *A Promised Land, a Perilous Journey: Theological Perspectives on Migration*. Notre Dame, IN: University of Notre Dame Press.

Kumalo, Raymond. 2015. "Practicing Ubuntu." Paper, International Academy of Practical Theology, Pretoria, South Africa.

Levitt, Peggy, and Nina Glick-Schiller. 2004. "Conceptualizing Simultaneity: A Transnational Social Field Perspective on Society." *International Migration Review* 38 (3): 1002–1039.

Luther, Henning. 1992. *Religion und Alltag: Bausteine zu einer Praktischen Theologie des Subjekts*. Stuttgart: Radius.

Meland, Bernhard, ed. 1969. *The Future of Empirical Theology*. Chicago: The University of Chicago Press.

Mnyandu, Michel. 2003. "Ubuntu as the Basis of Authentic Humanity: An African Christian Perspective." In *Mission is Crossing Frontiers: Essays in honour of Bongani A. Mazibuko*, edited by Roswith Gerloff, 304-313. Pietermaritzburg: Cluster Publications.

Setiloane, Gabriel. 1986. *Introduction to African Theology 14.* Trenton, NJ: Red Sea Press.

Shutte, Augustine. 2004. *Ubuntu: An Ethic for a New South Africa*. Pietermaritzburg: Cluster Publications.

Simon, Yara. 2014. "Saga Falabella Accused of Racism after 'Third Reich' Reminiscent Peru ad features Only Blode Girls." *LatinPost.* http://www.latinpost.com/articles/27332/20141208/saga-falabella-accused-racism-third-reich-reminiscent-peru-ad-features.htm

Snyder, Susanna. 2012. *Asylum-seeking, Migration and Church*. Burlington, VT: Ashgate.
Tutu, Desmond. 1999. *No Future Without Forgiveness*. New York: Doubleday.
Wyller, Trygve. 2016a. "Heterotopic Ecclesiology: Critical Reflections on What the Church on the Margins Might Mean." *Diaconia: Journal for the Study of Christian Social Practice* 1: 42-55.
Wyller, Trygve. 2016b. "A Spatial Power that Dissolves Itself: Space, Empathy and Theology – when the Colonised Enter the Empire." In *Heterotopic Spaces: Spaces of Others*, edited by Hans-Joachim Sander, Kaspar Villadsen, and Trygve Wyller. Göttingen: Vandenhoeck & Ruprecht.
Wyller, Trygve, and Hans-Günter Heimbrock, eds. 2010. *Perceiving the Other: Case Studies and Theories of Respectful Action*. Göttingen: Vandenhoeck & Ruprecht.

Because we are: Practical theology, intersubjectivity and the human brain

David Hogue

Abstract

The emerging interdisciplinary field of cognitive social neuroscience, or interpersonal neurobiology, is increasingly engaging significant issues of personhood and relationality. U.S. psychologist Allan Schore observes that psychotherapeutic models are undergoing a paradigm shift from individualised notions of patient and therapist to "a relational two-person psychology" (Schore 2012, 6). He notes that "more so than the cognitive mechanisms of interpretation and insight, relational-affective processes between patient and therapist are at the core of the change mechanism." Such shifts parallel important developments in other disciplines, including practical theology. Social contexts and intersubjective space both shape, and are shaped by, human brains. This chapter explores intersections between interpersonal neurobiology and theological anthropologies that embrace belonging, mutuality and reciprocity as central dimensions of human identity by drawing on Schore's descriptions of intersubjectivity, Clifford Geertz's description of religious and cultural ordering of the affects, and several central claims of *ubuntu* theology.

Introduction and context

The deeply communal nature of personhood that lies at the heart of *ubuntu* theology challenges the more sharply individual paradigm of most Western cultures. And yet emerging work in psychoanalytic thought and in interpersonal neurobiology provides a potential bridge between these competing value systems. Cognitive social neuroscience describes the significant ways in which social context shapes the human brain and the ways in which the brain shapes social relationships. Of particular value is the encyclopaedic work of clinical psychologist Allan Schore, beginning with his 1994 classic, *Affect Regulation and the Origin of the Self: The Neurobiology of Emotional Development*. In addition to multiple journal articles and other publications, he followed that text with two newer volumes in 2003 on affect regulation, first regarding "disorders of the self," and secondly the "repair of the self." Most recently his 2012 volume on the *Science of the Art of Psychotherapy* has provided an even richer description of the deep human interactions that are critical to the healing of persons with a history of childhood trauma.

I propose that there is an implicit theological frame to this work that stands in significant dialogue with the theological themes that emerge in *ubuntu* theology as expressed in Desmond Tutu's work. Schore, of course, had no such purpose and denies any claim that his descriptions apply to all human beings in all circumstances. His is not a claim to describing human nature, let alone a theological treatise. Nonetheless, his observations of the contained intimacy of the therapeutic relationship does point to deeper issues in our comprehension of human nature, sin, and salvation.

The sharp contrast between cultural contexts such as the United States and Europe that emphasise the individual and competition with those of Asia and Africa where the family, the community, and cooperation shape identities is by now quite familiar to most, nearly to the level of cliché. The oft-repeated phrase "It takes a village to raise a child" or the Native American proverb "If you want to go fast, go alone. If you want to go further, go with others" are often invoked to demonstrate a communal web in which persons grow in contrast to the rugged individualism of Western societies. *Ubuntu* and other communal theologies are not without critique, of course, nor are Western theologies without their redeeming and redemptive qualities. There is a temptation to romanticise other cultural groups' emphasis on belonging, and to stylise the "rugged individualism" in Europe and North America. Some critics have, therefore, pointed to the ways in which individual differences and initiative can be stifled or even punished in cultural settings. While most in the West would acknowledge that two of the profoundest needs of human beings, universally, are to *be* and to *belong* – to live fully into one's individuality but consistently remain engaged in the relationships that give life its meaning – we also acknowledge that Western social and cultural scripts dictate, sometimes subtly, the priority of the individual. Self-sufficiency is seen as the hallmark of true maturity, particularly for men. Thus, there is value in thinking more deeply about the role of relationships in human identity and wholeness.

The goal here is to place in conversation claims in emerging work at the intersection of developmental neurobiology, attachment theory, and psychoanalytic thought with our relational theologies, i.e., those that increasingly highlight the critical nature of belonging, of shared humanity, and of the social matrices that shape both our individuality and our relationships. I suggest that these trends give further credence to the theological claims that we are not alone and that we live in God's world.

Three historical developments

Three notable shifts in fields as diverse as psychotherapy research, cognitive psychology, neuroscientific studies and literary theory converge to provide an intriguing platform from which to reconsider our understanding of human suffering and healing: 1) the recognition of the *centrality of affect* in human relating and functioning, and 2) the growing emphasis on *intersubjectivity*. The third development concerns the reemergence of attachment as a schema that describes the unique intersubjective experiences necessary for the developing infant to develop capacities for integrating thought and feeling, or as Allan Schore would describe it, affect regulation.

Affect and attachment

Psychoanalysis – which has profoundly shaped practices of pastoral care, counseling and psychotherapy in the U.S. for over a century – has undergone significant modifications from a drive theory focused especially on sex and aggression, through an emphasis on cognitive ego processes and more recently to a focus on the fundamental human drive for relationship that appears in the object relations and self psychology schools of thought developed by psychoanalyst Heinz Kohut (e.g. Kohut 1971). Classical psychoanalysis as developed by Freud and his early followers came to be known as the "talking" cure, and while emotion was a critical dimension of that theoretical frame, the emphasis was on verbalising feeling and on rendering the unconscious conscious. As various psychotherapies developed over the 20th century a competing school of behaviourism promised a quicker and more measurable resolution of emotional distress through carefully constructed systems of reward and punishment, sidestepping theories about the internal functioning of the mind/brain and treating it instead like the proverbial black box. Somewhat later cognitive theories prioritised the role of thought in shaping behavior and feeling and produced a variety of strategies to assist sufferers in restructuring cognitive schemata. These schools are very much alive in the cognitive-behavioral treatments encouraged and supported by health insurance companies that value measurable, efficient outcomes.

In recent decades the importance of affect, emotion, and feeling has reappeared. Antonio Damasio's (1994) popular book *Descartes' Error* documented the inadequacy and emptiness of purely rational processes in the brain/mind and the critical role of feeling and emotion in a flourishing life. Neuroscientists such as Jaak Panksepp (1998) are making detailed studies of emotional processes central to their empirical theoretical work. Affect theory has an even broader appeal as political, economic and literary theories move to account for the role of emotion in human decision-making processes.

Such a shift has also prompted a return to the mid-20th century work of John Bowlby (1969) and attachment theory – an arena that set the early stage for bridging the divide between psychology and biology: a move that had motivated Freud's early work in neurology. Noting the similarities between humans and other mammalian species in child-rearing, Bowlby argued that infants bond with consistent parental figures in an emotional attachment that may be dependable or not in responding to the child's felt needs. When the caregiver is emotionally attuned to the infant's internal affective world an intersubjective space is created that gradually enables the child to order her chaotic emotional experiences, tolerate temporary ruptures in relationships through emotionally reconnecting, and establish a coherent sense of self.

Psychologist Allan Schore has carefully outlined key developments during the first months of life. In a child's first twelve months, the nurturing parent mirrors the infant's inner emotions of joy, excitement, sadness, and pain, matching them and giving both verbal and physical expression to them on the child's behalf (Schore 1994). The mother helps strengthen and consolidate the child's awareness of his own feelings by *amplifying them*; by reflecting the child's feelings visually and tactilely she helps bring order to otherwise chaotic feelings and responses and also helps make them an integrated dimension of the child's emerging sense of himself. Touching and mutual gaze are primary arenas for parent-child communication.

The central nervous system undergoes critical structural changes during this period. The sympathetic (arousal) branch of the autonomic nervous system develops during these months. This system prepares the child to face threats later in life but also provides the neural platform for excitement and exploration. A very specific circuit in the right frontal lobe of the brain (the orbitofrontal cortex, or OFC, located just behind the eye) forms a vital connection between the emotion-generating-and-detecting limbic system with the developing frontal lobes of the neocortex (Schore 1994). Cortical structures between the prefrontal lobes and the limbic system help regulate emotional responses from the limbic system by introducing order, inhibiting undirected emotional responses, and shaping more appropriate "prosocial" expression. "Affect regulation" is the term used to describe this maturing process. Schore reports an intriguing correlation between brain development and the child's social environment, noting that infants who experience secure attachments develop thicker neural connections between the right prefrontal cortex and the limbic system, which then appears to correlate with later attachment relationships. Thus, neuroscientists highlight the critical interaction between genetically-driven brain development and the social environment in which children develop, providing mounting evidence that our experiences with significant others in our lives actually shape the brain itself (Schore 1994; Siegel

1999). That is, the social environment shapes the brain as much as the developing brain shapes human experience.

Schore (1994) outlines in exquisite detail the development of this neural bridge between the rational, problem-solving neocortex and the emotional limbic system. When the infant's experiences are accurately perceived and sensitively acknowledged, this brain circuit (OFC) thickens and the child develops feelings of security and attachment. The child also forms patterns of connecting to important others that will facilitate relationships of love and care later in life. On the other hand, when caregivers are mis-attuned with the child's experience, insecure or avoidant attachments result. These early patterns of attachment are literally built into our brains and influence our relationships throughout life.

Since newborn infants lack verbal comprehension, all significant communication in these years is non-verbal, relying on touch and vision, as well as the prosody of the caregiver's voice. That is, it relies primarily on the brain's right hemisphere. The parent and child's right (non-linguistic) hemispheres are constantly communicating with each other. More importantly, the mother's brain is taking into itself the chaotic and unformed feelings of the infant, ordering them, and then offering them back to the child. She is "loaning" the child the use of her more mature right hemisphere as the infant struggles to organise her experience of a new world. When the child's developing ability to walk is supported by caregivers, the child gradually learns to balance excitement and exploration with a sense of safe harbour – exploration alternating with security. These descriptions of human development underscore the social connections vital to the very formation of personhood.

Intersubjectivity

Our growing sensitivity to the inherent tension between individuality and connectedness, between being and belonging, mirror in interesting ways shifts occurring in pastoral theology's cognate areas of psychoanalytic thought and the neurosciences. Variously called *relational* or *intersubjective* psychoanalysis, these approaches share a classical view that particular forms of human suffering – i.e., psychopathologies and particularly mood and character disorders – stem from early relationships with primary caregivers which then shape, for better or for worse, significant relationships throughout the rest of life. Relational psychoanalytic theories go even further in locating the source of healing within the relationship created between therapist and client. Treatment involves creating an intersubjective space between analyst and analysand that is shaped by those early relational templates and seeks to provide a "corrective emotional experience" (Schore 2012, 140) that can promote fuller human relationships in other spheres of life. The social intimacy of the therapeutic setting, therefore, establishes an emotional space shaped by both therapist and client that becomes the avenue for disclosing and addressing the concerns of the client. Stolorow and Atwood, for example, critique the "myth of the individual mind" inherent in a theory that locates problems of living within the patient to be analysed by an objective observing therapist. They argue that such a paradigmatic myth – as an organizing assumption – alienates individuals from nature (specifically the body), from social connections, and from subjectivity itself. Intersubjectivity in their terms is a sphere of mutual influence. All human experience, they argue, is intersubjective in ways that appear quite congruent with some claims of *ubuntu* theologies (Stolorow and Atwood 1992, 7-28).

Schore sees this attachment process reemerging in long-term psychotherapeutic relationships and, therefore, seeks to define intersubjectivity within that context. For Schore, *intersubjectivity* identifies a primarily unconscious, non-linguistic, affectively-charged, right hemisphere-to-right hemisphere communication between therapist and client that mirrors early parent-child interactions and seeks to provide a corrective emotional experience. "An intersubjective field is more than just an interaction of two minds, but also that of two bodies, which – when in affective resonance – elicit an amplification and integration of both CNS [central nervous system] and ANS [autonomic nervous system] arousal" (Schore 2012, 93). It must be noted that Schore's focus here is on intense, in-depth therapeutic work with moderately to severely impaired patients, particularly those suffering from personality disorders like borderline personality often resulting from severe neglect and abuse during infancy and childhood. There are significant dangers in extrapolating from pathological states to common human experience, as is the difficulty of translating from individual or dyadic interactions to larger group experiences. Yet, the model of affect regulation theory provides critical insights into intimate human relationships, and these insights can help inform our understanding of the larger social networks that bring relationship and self-definition.

According to Schore, attachment disorders in intense emotional encounters result in two distinct forms of experience involving each branch of the autonomic nervous system (Schore 2012, 71-117). In states of high, stressful emotional arousal, stimulation of the sympathetic nervous system produces feelings of fear and terror, triggering the common "fight-or-flight" response. The patient experiences fragmentation of the sense of self, since these feelings cannot be tolerated and incorporated into a felt unity. These intense feelings are in essence split off from the self. As Schore notes, fear and arousal (a.k.a., anxiety) have received much more attention in research and clinical work than the equally troubling response to emotional stress of emotional collapse and withdrawal. He describes this experience as *dissociation*, which involves a collapse of the implicit self and triggering of the parasympathetic branch of the ANS. Such collapses are experienced as *shame* and *disgust*.

Schore then sees the patient's distress as rooted in an incapacity to experience strong affect without either fragmenting or dissociating – a failure of "affect regulation." Clinical work with such patients focuses on increasing the window of affect tolerance by working at the boundaries of that tolerance. Several features of this work are significant. First, it is an *interpersonal venture*, supported by the relatively more mature right hemisphere of the therapist who is able to remain in an interpersonal space with the patient at the edges of tolerable experience and so create a container for the patient to increasingly experience the distressful feelings. Integration and regulation then become possible.

It is again important to note the significance of attachment relationships in early life. Since perfect attunement is never possible (nor even desirable as the infant matures) and ruptures of emotional resonance are inevitable, caregivers will inevitably err on occasion in matching the child's emotional state, be distracted from attending to the infant's distress or joy though exhaustion or busyness, or otherwise disrupt the emotional connection. Such rupture and repair are inevitable; in fact, it is in the repair of such empathic breaks, followed in a timely manner by reestablishment of the emotional connection, which serves the process of healing. Such claims will be familiar to those acquainted with the work of Heinz Kohut (1998).

Given his concern with patients with early trauma, it may not be surprising that Schore prioritises unconscious right hemisphere functioning, since this echoes the likely engagements during early infant development. What his model lacks, for our purposes, is an appreciation of the linguistic linear functions of the left hemisphere, along with the conscious thought and careful planning that such structures support. For instance, in this model speech content plays no significant role. What does matter is the non-verbal structures of the communication that neither party acknowledges: tone, prosody, amplitude, etc. (Schore 2012, 127).

Beyond the intimate? Communities of belonging

These descriptions of intense psychotherapeutic interactions provide a crystallised view of key processes that underlie, to varying degrees, all human relationships of engagement. At least two significant leaps, however, must be addressed if we are to move from the intense interactions we have been describing between two persons, particularly in settings of human suffering and a search for healing. First, to what extent can we relate Schore's particular brand of (clinical) intersubjectivity to our understanding of human relationships of care more broadly? Can we in fact apply them to all or at least most human interactions, perhaps diluted in intensity but relying heavily on unconscious, automatic right-hemisphere-to-right hemisphere communication? Can we discern a domain of emotional engagement that leads variously to a sense of commonality and understanding or to suspicion and hiddenness? We must guard against generalising from persons or relationships that are "broken" to those who are whole. Nonetheless, does not diagnosis at its best lead to treatment? Does not "illness" presume some image of health? Does not a critical appraisal of sin, in most of its definitions, point toward salvation? Secondly, what tentative theological claims, if any, can we make about the human condition? What models of care from our religious traditions might provide the deeper metaphors of our living together that can shape our response to human relationships?

Don Browning helpfully distinguishes between the purposes of theology and the function of psychological systems. "It is the task of theology, I would argue, to look forward, think *prospectively*, and project the goals of life. It is the task of the clinical psychologies... primarily to think *retrospectively* and help us analyze the interaction between biology and early parental and social influences in the formation of the self" (Browning 1987, 219). I would differ only in suggesting that these approaches do not stand in isolation, and in fact require each other if we are to achieve a fuller account of human suffering and redemption. There is no vision of the future without memory of the past (Hogue 2003). And it is here that the contributions of *ubuntu* theology can be helpful, mediated through the insight of anthropologist Clifford Geertz.

Some of these claims will appear self-evident or even simplistic. Nonetheless, I want to suggest that they add further depth to our most cherished (or avoided) comprehensions of human existence; these claims all provide important observations about an overarching theme of theological anthropology – the *imago Dei* – a term frequently invoked by Archbishop Tutu himself (Battle 1997, 5). In what ways do our traditions suggest that we "bear the image of God?" In the words of the Psalmist "What are human beings that you are mindful of them, mortals that you care for them? Yet you have made them a little lower than God, and crowned them with glory and honour" (Psalm 8:4, 5; cf. also Hebrews 2:6-8a).

First, Schore's work, along with volumes of supporting research, provides an additional reminder of our profound embodiment. While strict mind-body dualisms are justifiably under attack, we cannot replace the thick meanings that the word *soul* sparks in our own religious consciousness; instead, those challenges prompt us to revisit the complex and culturally shaped understandings of soul that we have inherited through our biblical and theological traditions. Our physical and social worlds shape our souls (who we most profoundly are) from the very beginnings of life, and those worlds are, in turn, shaped by our souls. Here we find important correlations with *ubuntu* theologies. For Tutu, for instance, the separation of body and soul makes no sense, since in much African philosophy, according to Michael Battle, "an African concept of personality called *seriti* ... identifies a life force that makes no distinction between body and soul" (Battle 1997, 50). Here *ubuntu* theology is more closely aligned with Hebraic understandings of the inviolable unity of mind/soul and body (Murphy 2006).

Second, our understanding of the roles of feeling and emotion in human relationships, in the building and healing of communities, and in relationship with the Divine stands in need of rethinking. Particularly in the West, our Enlightenment heritage has led to a worship of logic over emotion, "cold reason" over passion, observation and analysis over participation, and control over engagement. While few would argue that we human beings would be well served by abandoning our left hemispheres and the deliberate, reflective thought they support, it is more than likely that we have treated the passions as troublesome beasts to be tamed rather than full partners in the flourishing of life. If the term "affect regulation" calls to mind Plato's charioteer too quickly, we may seek more adequate language that reflects the integration of thought and feeling, of human wholeness and relatedness that Schore appears to hold out for patients in psychotherapy.

It is here too that the role of our religious communities can be seen as a broader social structure of which the psychotherapy consultation room is an echo. Alternatively, it could be argued that the analyst's couch has become a repair for cultural and religious failures. It is here that we find the beginning structures of a bridge between the intimate, dyadic experience of parenting and psychotherapy to the broader arena of culture. Decades ago anthropologist Clifford Geertz spoke of the role of religion in the integration of feeling, grounded in an evolutionary understanding of the human brain. Describing emotions as "cultural artifacts," he nevertheless went on to claim that "[t]he management of the individual's emotional economy becomes, therefore, his primary concern, in terms of which all else is ultimately rationalised" (Geertz 1973, 135). In what might be a prescient description of Schore's affect regulation, he notes that "[t]he individual's proximate aim is, thus, emotional quiescence, for passion is crude feeling, fit for children, animals, madmen, primitives, and foreigners" (Geertz 1973, 135). While we might take issue with his description of "quiescence" and certainly with his labeling of classes of human beings, the notion of unintegrated affect sounds familiar. The remedy he observes in cultural practices has a clearly therapeutic tone: "In order to make up our minds we must know how we feel about things and to know how we feel about things we need the public images of sentiment that only ritual, myth and art can provide" (Geertz 1973, 82). In words that bridge the apparent divide between affect regulation and cultural processes, Geertz declares, "... it is a matter of giving specific, explicit, determinate form to the general, diffuse, ongoing flow of bodily sensation; of imposing upon the continual shifts in sentience to which we are inherently subject a recognizable, meaningful order, so that we may not only feel but know what we feel and act according" (Geertz 1973, 80). Finally, Geertz provides an additional bridge to *ubuntu*-thought when he declares "that some of the more important developments in neural evolution which occurred during the period of overlap between biological and sociocultural change may turn out to consist of the appearance of properties which improve the performance capacity of the central nervous system but *reduce its functional self-sufficiency*" (Geertz 1973, 76, italics mine). Because we are, I am.

Third, these theological and clinical observations cohere in pointing to an *essential relatedness* of all human beings. The forms and shapes and quality of those relationships vary across cultures, genders, and individuals; relationships vary in the degrees to which they promote harm or wholeness and intimacy. Even when they do harm, however, they remind us of the critical dimension of human engagement, of the futility of self-sufficiency, of the desperate need for the other without which life itself is diminished. Our needs for intimacy, and our terror of being alone, are rooted in the deepest recesses of our bodies. We are social creatures from the moment of birth, created in relationship, and it is the breath of relationships that supports life itself. A number of years ago, in a *Zygon* article entitled "Cry For The Other," pastoral theologian James Ashbrook suggested that the roots of faith and of our religious imagination grow from the experience of separation as infants. "The cry for the other, then, arises out of the experience of distance between ourselves and those with whom we are connected, those upon whom we depend for safety and satisfaction .... That consciousness releases the imaginative powers of the infant and later the creative powers of the adult" (Ashbrook 1994, 299). While that consciousness may begin in separation, it cannot be sustained there. We are not simply our brains or even our bodies. We *are* our connections.

Such a claim might suggest further implications for our understanding of the *imago Dei*. Have we looked in the wrong places for the marks of such an image? In considering human capacities for symbolisation or language, or in the production of religious art, might we be asking too much of the individual human being to bear that image alone? Might the very heart of the *imago Dei* in fact consist in the "we" rather than the "I"? For Tutu, as an example, the individual makes no sense; self-sufficiency falls short of full humanity, and it is our interconnectedness with others that bears the divine image. In his words, "we can be human only in community, in koinonia, in peace." (Battle 1997, 5) To those Western voices who would say "resist thinking of yourself as others see you, be who you truly are inside" Tutu would respond, "Persons are ends in themselves only through the discovery of who they are in others" (Battle 1997, 43).

The ancient command to "forsake not the assembling of yourselves together" reminds us not only that are we more than individual brains and bodies, but Paul's metaphor of the church as the body of Christ takes on renewed importance. We become bodies within the body, giving and receiving, playing our roles and relying on others to play their roles, bound to each other in an identity that transcends any one of us, or any part of the body. In our worshiping together we are "embodying our souls" and "ensouling our bodies." As a result, our liturgical practices are also embodiments of our belonging in ways that parallel Tutu's deep spirituality.

References

Ashbrook, James. 1994. "The Cry for the Other: The Biocultural Womb of Human Development." *Zygon* 29 (3): 297-314.

Battle, Michael. 1997. *Reconciliation: The Ubuntu Theology of Desmond Tutu*. Cleveland, OH: Pilgrim Press.

Bowlby, John. (1969) 1982. *Attachment*. New York: Basic Books.

Browning, Don. 1987. *Religious Thought and the Modern Psychologies: A Critical Conversation in the Theology of Culture*. Philadelphia, PA: Fortress Press.

d'Aquili, Eugene, and Andrew Newberg. 1999. *The Mystical Mind: Probing the Biology of Religious Experience*. Minneapolis, MN: Fortress Press.

Damasio, Antonio R. 1994. *Descartes' Error: Emotion, Reason, and the Human Brain*. New York: G. P. Putnam's Sons.

Geertz, Clifford. (1973) 2000. *The Interpretation of Cultures*. New York: Basic Books.

Hogue, David A. 2003. *Remembering the Future, Imagining the Past: Story, Ritual, and the Human Brain*. Cleveland, OH: Pilgrim Press.

Kohut, Heinz. 1971. *The Analysis of the Self: A Systematic Approach to the Psychoanalytic Treatment of Narcissistic Personality Disorders*. New York: International Universities Press.

Murphy, Nancy. 2006. *Bodies and Souls, or Spirited Bodies?* Cambridge: Cambridge University Press.

Panksepp, Jaak. 1998. *Affective Neuroscience: The Foundations of Human and Animal Emotions*. Oxford: Oxford University Press.

Schore, Allan. 1994. *Affect Regulation and the Origin of the Self: The Neurobiology of Emotional Development*. Hillsdale, NJ: Lawrence Erlbaum Associates.

Schore, Allan. 2012. *The Science of the Art of Psychotherapy*. New York: W.W. Norton.

Siegel, Daniel. 1999. *The Developing Mind: How Relationships and the Brain Interact to Shape Who We Are*. New York: Guilford Press.

Stolorow, Robert, and Atwood, George. 1992. *Contexts of Being: The Intersubjective Foundations of Psychological Life*. New York: Routledge.

Communal identities and collective trauma: A practical-theological exploration into Indonesia's 1965-1967 anti-Communist massacre

Joyce Ann Mercer

Abstract

This chapter asks how *ubuntu*-like values underlying Indonesia's relational, collectively based cultures might sustain collective trauma and prevent reconciliation by encouraging silence around painful events. Using a case study from narrative research with survivors of Indonesia's 1965-1967 massacre, in which nearly a million people died during the Suharto government's actions against the Communist Party of Indonesia, I explore the collective sanctioning of silence amid a national culture of stigma around survivors who frequently did not even tell their stories to family members, resulting in decades of silence. The chapter inquires about the possible conditions for reconciliation in such a context.

Introduction

Ubuntu, the indigenous African philosophical concept undergirding anti-apartheid and the ongoing construction of a new nation, opens spaces for social transformation through links with restorative justice, reconciliation, and pro-social values (Himonga, Taylor and Pope 2013, 376-380). Yet *ubuntu* is not without its critics (cf. Cornell 2010, 395-397; Himonga, Taylor and Pope 2013). *Ubuntu* brings possibilities for individual wellbeing to be subsumed under easily manipulated, implicit demands for group cohesion. Most critics recognise *ubuntu* as far more complex than simplistic reductions to social cohesion. Nevertheless, the communitarian features of *ubuntu* – among its most commonly cited aspects along with its near-parallels outside of South Africa – are vulnerable to distortion. This chapter will bring a critical lens to the communitarian themes within *ubuntu*, by examining how such themes functioned in Indonesia's anti-communist massacre, the "1965 Tragedy." This traumatic event in Indonesia's history exemplifies how the same dynamics that give rise to *ubuntu*'s constructive power also can be harnessed in the service of oppressive regimes.

Ubuntu in Indonesia?

Indonesia does not appear to have a precise conceptual or linguistic corollary to *ubuntu*. However, collectivist notions of personhood operate across Indonesia's diverse cultures that parallel core communitarian meanings within *ubuntu*. Indonesian social understandings of selfhood bear close similarities to Desmond Tutu's expression of *ubuntu* as an antithesis of the western Cartesian notion, "I think therefore I am." Tutu offers alternative sayings – "I am because we are," "I am because I belong" – as expressions of South African subjectivity at the heart of *ubuntu* (Tutu 1999, 31). *Ubuntu* emphasises community, relationality, and dignity formed collectively.

Indonesian peoples similarly hold a strongly collective sense of identity, seeing selfhood constituted in and through community. Yet Indonesia's mid-twentieth century history reveals how dynamics underlying a positive social construction of selfhood also can be manipulated to contribute to harm. These dynamics include the subsuming of individual agency beneath norms of social cohesion, and a tendency toward conservatism that maintains unjust hierarchies and status inequalities in the name of social harmony (cf. Cornell 2005, 395). Both played a key role in authorizing Indonesia's collective silence and the ensuing social trauma of the country's 1965-1967 anti-communist massacres during which 500,000 to 1,000,000 people were murdered.[1]

This chapter is based on a small study of ten interviewees. In 2014 I was studying women peace-builders' work in Indonesia. I conducted research in Indonesia because religious leaders and scholars there with their wealth of experience dealing with religious pluralism and conflict have important insights from which United States (U.S.) scholars can learn. Additionally, I lived and taught for several years in the Philippines, which acquainted me with the regional context of religious violence. During my Indonesian research I unexpectedly encountered stories about the 1965 tragedy. By the end of my larger study, I had interviewed ten persons who were either victim-survivors or family members of victims of the 1965 events. The interviews employed a combination of English and Bahasa Indonesia, with translation help when needed. Due to space constraints, this essay utilises one victim-survivor's story as a case study to tell the story of the 1965 tragedy in which mass atrocity met with collective silence.[2]

---

[1]   The number of victims is contested; these figures come from sources both external and internal to Indonesia (cf. Anderson and McVey 1971; Nadia et al. 2007).

[2]   Besides appreciation for those who willingly told their stories, I am indebted to Indonesian colleagues who facilitated connections with interviewees, assisted with translation, and provided hospitality: Linna Gunawan, Mery Kolimon, Septemmy Lakawa, Tabita Christiani, and Hennie Wattimena.

Before conducting this research, I knew almost nothing about the massacre that Indonesian people still tend to narrate in hushed tones. I quickly came to recognise my own government's complicity in these horrendous events. Recent work by historians demonstrates how the U.S.A. seriously encouraged and supported the "extermination" of Indonesia's Communist Party, part of Cold War fears about the "domino effect" of communism in Southeast Asia (Simpson 2008). I engage in this research as a U.S. practical theologian acknowledging the suffering furthered by my country's participation, and working in solidarity with theologians and church leaders concerned about healing, peace and justice in their Indonesian communities. That healing remains impaired by open wounds of collective trauma from the events of 1965.

Socially sanctioned suffering

In October 1965 on the small island of Sabu in Indonesia, soldiers entered the home of Tommy, a respected, 25-year-old school principal, and his wife Gema.[3] They arrested Tommy, charged him with being *PKI* or a member of the *Partai Komunis Indonesia* – the Communist Party of Indonesia. Eyewitnesses later reported that Tommy and thirty others arrested that night were forced to dig their own mass grave before being executed.

Local militia returned to Gema's home, claiming she was a member of *Gerwani*, a women's organisation accused of colluding with the *PKI* in an alleged coup attempt against the government. The soldiers, in an act of gendered aggression intended to humiliate, cut off Gema's hair. She was forced to report daily for "dirty, hard labor," where she and other women were paraded in public view to be heckled as *Gerwani anging* (Gerwani dogs/bitches). Eventually released from this daily labour, she was required to report to the police monthly; was not allowed to be employed; her children were excluded from schooling; and she had no support. Gema says that she was treated with utter contempt by most people in her village, save a few neighbours who gave her food in exchange for laundry work. She and her four children often went hungry.

From 1965-1967, versions of this story repeated all across Indonesia. Beyond those murdered, countless others were arrested, subjected to humiliation, and tortured. Family members of those killed or arrested lived out the rest of their lives under conditions of severe constrictions, due to laws requiring them to bear a mark on their identity cards designating them as relatives of former political prisoners.

In Indonesia's "official" historical narrative, the killing of six military generals and a lieutenant during what the government terms the abortive coup attempt of

---

[3]   Pseudonyms are employed for all interviewees.

30 September 1965 justified the mass genocide. This official history also accused *Gerwani* women with seducing the generals and castrating them while dancing naked around them. The dangerous threat the *PKI* and *Gerwani* supposedly posed to Indonesia became the rationale for military and paramilitary groups to arrest, torture, and even kill anyone suspected of association with these groups. A blanket of silence covered what now has come to be known as the "1965 tragedy." From 1965 until 1998, when President Suharto was forced from office in a wave of violent conflicts, only the official version of the story could be told (Farid 2005; Ariati 2012; Leksana 2009).

Many victim-survivors did not even tell their own family members about their experiences. As Gema related,

I am 74 years old now and my memory is good.... For 48 years I kept this story to myself. I can tell you the story now because ... [since 1998] we can speak more freely without fear. At that time, though, I could not even cry for my husband, because I would be arrested. I could say nothing. My husband was killed, and they took me to do hard labor, and I could say nothing about his death. We could not protest. We had to be quiet. And all around us, everyone knew what was happening but no one said anything.

Domestic terror

When the victim-survivors of the 1965 tragedy told their stories, they generally spoke as if these events were current. They also spoke about living among the very people who carried out the violence. Gema wept, describing the arrest and death of her husband:

My husband was taken from the hospital that the military used as a jail. They spent a whole day preparing to bury the ones they would kill. There are two men who took my husband to be massacred. We knew them, of course. It is a small place. The killing went like this. The soldiers had a list of names, including my husband's. They called them one by one to step over to the hole, and the gun was already ready to shoot them. After shooting them, they just kicked their bodies into the hole. I was not there. I know about it because I heard this story from the two men who took my husband at night. One was his student. Ten others were neighbours who were in the military. They told me, "The ones in charge say if we don't do that [participate in the arresting of suspected *PKI*] we will be killed ourselves." But they didn't tell me why they took my husband.... My house is not too far, I could hear the [sounds from digging the] hole that became the grave and I could hear the sound of the shooting. There were thirty-one men shot in front of the hole, including my husband.

I asked her if she knew the others who died. She emphatically replied, "Yes, I know them all. Many were teachers." With eyes closed, she then proceeded to recite the full names of each of the 31 men killed that night. "The Army pushed community members to watch the execution. And then no one spoke about it."

For Gema, the silence surrounding the death of her husband is juxtaposed with the intimacy of his murder – she knew those who took him away, those directly responsible for his death, and those killed alongside him. Like situations of domestic violence, closeness of relationships only intensifies the injury and betrayal of victim-survivors. In Gema's village, neighbours, colleagues, and students willingly or unwillingly participated as perpetrators of the violence. The wider community knew what was happening and who were the actors, yet kept silent.

The special evil of women

Many victims of Indonesia's mass murders were men, because they were more likely to be associated with the *PKI*. Nevertheless, women were also victims of this anti-communist pogrom: many were arrested, some were executed due to actual or alleged associations with *Gerwani*: a feminist organisation established in the 1950's as a "movement of conscious women" in Indonesia. The story of *Gerwani* women's alleged role in the September 30 coup, which somehow gained wide popular support as a factual account, involves the specific targeting of women, and particularly women reaching beyond the constraints of prescribed gender roles. Wierenga argues that the slander against *Gerwani* provided the spark that ignited the mass murders and repression:

All through the New Order [i.e., Suharto's presidency] the word *Gerwani* was associated with allegedly unspeakable sexual perversions. People lowered their voices when referring to the "evil mothers of *Gerwani*." The police treated women activists harshly and often sexualised their violence against them... [Even in the 1990's with the rebirth of feminist organisations,] women's political activism was still associated with moral depravity" (Wierenga 2011, 547).

Gema, arrested as a *Gerwani* member despite her protestations against any affiliation, described her arrest:

When [police] came to my house to arrest me, they cut my hair, saying, "You are *Gerwani*." I don't know anything about *Gerwani* or *PKI*. In any case before that time *PKI* was legal, a legal political party in our country. We didn't know anything about what happened in Jakarta on 30 September 30 1965. But we didn't do protests or ask why, because in that moment we must be silent or die. Many women came under arrest and had their hair cut. Our children almost could not go to school at all, because the government said they are the children of *Gerwani*.... Yes, there is a *Gerwani* organisation in Sabu but I don't know anything about it. I already have many things to do with my children so there is no time to join another organisation.

In the requirement of hard labor, we just followed orders, we could do nothing about it.... I felt almost hopeless. But my tears and my faith to God sustained me.

God helped me and God knew we were not guilty. We were afraid to lift up our face to others in the street. If we did that, they would say many bad things about us. I felt so much shame but I kept it inside.... If we wore the good clothes they blamed us – because they say that we are going to be stylish like a "bad woman." We were not wearing shoes or anything on foot to go to church, we had to cut our hair. For the Sabunese woman, hair is like a crown – so having to cut it is punishment to make the woman ashamed. The woman who cuts her hair is just like a prostitute, a bad woman. Yes, we had to do that because we didn't have any choice. I had to go to work with these changes of my body for my children, even though I felt shame about what my body looked like. The community including my family didn't want to socialise with us anymore, because if they did, they were afraid they would be shamed along with us.

What possibly could allow neighbours to stand back in silence and allow such treatment of their own community members? Gema's description of humiliation through the forced cutting of her hair, demonstrates the targeting of *Gerwani* women in a particularly sexualised act of aggression, intended to disrupt a growing national feminist moment (Wieringa 2011). After the "extermination" of *Gerwani*, a new government-endorsed women's organisation formed, centered around affirming women's roles in the home as support to their husbands. Both the suppression of *Gerwani* and the building up of new nationalist women's organisations emphasising women as the wives and "mothers of the nation" (Martyn 2005, 65), was dependent upon the erasure of protest and difference beneath a dominant discourse subordinating women. Certainly this silence happened due to fear of further violence. It also happened as persons with strongly communally situated identities avoided challenging the dominant direction of the larger group. The ability of those in power to manipulate such *ubuntu* – like communal loyalties to national and communitarian identities fostering group cohesion thus supported collective silence.

The sounds of silence

Gema's story illustrates several forms of silence resulting from the 1965 mass murders. First is the silence of victims: "We could not say anything"; "I could not even cry for my husband or I would be arrested." The silence of victim-survivors reflects the harsh reality of their powerless position. Arrested, tortured, threatened with death or with harm to their family members, such dangers procured the silence of many like Gema and muted their protests. For women accused of membership in *Gerwani*, sexual harassment and communal public shaming of them worked further still to procure their silence. Silence became a functional form of resistance to annihilation in the face of severe repression by the government in families associated with *PKI* and/or *Gerwani* (Farid 2005, 13). Alongside the silence of arrested victim-survivors stands the total silence imposed on those who were murdered. Taken suddenly and violently from their homes at night without opportunity to speak to their families or plead their cases, these victims of torture and killing were buried in mass graves, often with no word to their families about their deaths or the places of their burials.

A second kind of silence in Gema's narrative concerns those coopted into participation as perpetrators. Moral injury resulting from perpetrating violence effectively silenced their capacities to speak out against what was happening because they were implicated: Gema's neighbours could not refuse to participate or else they would be killed. Friends, neighbours and – in some cases like Gema's – even victims' family members feared that associations with political prisoners would lead to their own stigmatisation. They became perpetrators of a structural and social form of violence in their shaming and shunning of victim-survivors, colluding with the group as a means of protecting their own survival. In this kind of silence, the fear of becoming a fellow victim functioned to silence opposition to immoral actions. It is important not to underestimate the effects of living in a military state on the decisions and ethical stances of people (Farid 2005, 14). At the same time, such corporate silence about the atrocities allowed violence to continue unchecked.

The third silence in Gema's story involves the social contract of silence about the very existence of the mass murders in Indonesia. Official discourse focuses only on the "danger" of the *PKI* and *Gerwani* to the Indonesian nation, and the heroism of the governmental and military personnel who saved the nation from these "threats." There is no reporting of mass killings, arrests, torture, sexual harassment and stigmatisation perpetrated on so many people.

In an event of such vast proportions, many in Indonesia had to be aware of what happened, since many knew someone arrested or killed. They became bystanders to massive, state-sponsored violence. Yet they remained silent. I do not mean to suggest that there were not perfectly valid reasons for bystanders to keep silent: they too, after all, were living in the midst of this police state. I simply note the widespread social agreement not to acknowledge mass murder as a significant form of silence.

There is a fourth form of silence: the international community to this day remains silent about Indonesia's murders. Unlike Bosnia, Rwanda, or Nazi Germany, there has been no expression of moral outrage from the international community about the murder of a million Indonesians by their own government in the 1960's. There has been no public acknowledgement that these murders even happened, a situation particularly egregious in the case of the U.S., where documents show that my country had an important role in encouraging what occurred (Simpson 2008).

To some extent, these silences all rest on constructions of personhood-in-society that privilege (and enforce) *ubuntu*-like values of belonging, not standing out, harmony, and cohesion characteristic of Indonesian society.

Silence as a theological problem

In what ways does silence in the aftermath of Indonesia's 1965 tragedy constitute a theological problem? Recent theories on collective trauma offer helpful perspectives, as does the work of theologian and ethicist Elizabeth Vasko (2015) on "bystanders." As noted above, the existence of collective trauma and bystander silence both benefit from social dynamics privileging group-sanctioned behaviors in what I call the "broken side of *ubuntu*."

Trauma to the social body

Traumatic experiences start with some kind of originating even – a typhoon, violent conflict, the shock of loss, sexual assault – that creates a sense of threat to a person or group's well-being and/or existence, overwhelming their ability to cope. This sense of threat undermines their ability to make sense out of what is happening. Judith Herman, considered by many the "mother" of U.S. trauma studies, notes: "Psychological trauma is an affliction of the powerless. At the moment of trauma, the victim is rendered helpless by overwhelming force... Traumatic events overwhelm the ordinary systems of care that give people a sense of control, connection, and meaning... The common denominator of psychological trauma is a feeling of 'intense fear, helplessness, loss of control, and threat of annihilation'" (Herman 1997, 33).

As Gema's testimony illustrates, the dual experiences of her husband's state-sponsored murder and her own arrest and dehumanising treatment constituted atrocities that left her feeling fearful and helpless. Her sense of herself as agent and actor in her own life was erased; the things that gave her a sense of meaning no longer seemed to hold.

Most theological attention to trauma focuses on individual trauma sufferers (Rambo 2010; Jones 2009; Hess 2009). While it is appropriate to understand the impact of trauma on individuals like Gema, it is crucial to remember that her traumatisation did not occur in isolation but was part of a widely shared experience affecting (and continuing to affect) an entire society. Trauma at the level of the social body often takes place within, and is facilitated by structural injustices such as colonialism, racism, sexism, classism, and heterosexism – ignored in trauma perspectives focused only on individuals.

Collective trauma refers to trauma experienced at the level of an entire society or group within a society. Jeffrey C. Alexander refers to this phenomenon as "cultural trauma": "Cultural trauma occurs when members of a collectivity feel they have been subjected to a horrendous event that leaves indelible marks upon their group consciousness, marking their memories forever and changing their future identity in fundamental and irrevocable ways" (Alexander 2013, 1).

Collective trauma constitutes trauma to the "social body," in which the sense of helplessness, loss of control, and erasure of meaning occur for all who belong to the affected group whether or not they personally experienced the traumatising event. "As individual trauma damages the inner structure of a person, collective trauma damages the structures of a community... Collective trauma ruptures social ties, undermines community, and destroys previous sources of support" (Veerman and Ganzevoort 2001, 5). Gema's description of a community fractured by the participation of neighbours and relatives in violence, including widespread stigmatising of political prisoners and their families, mirrors what Veerman and Ganzevoort name. If collective trauma "damages the structures of a community," then it is logical that such communities are particularly vulnerable to the dynamics of in-group solidarity and out-group exclusion. In Gema's community, silence enforced by implicit norms to conform, functioned both to form and to express these exclusionary dynamics.

Dipak K. Gupta uses the phrase "collective madness" to describe "an extreme case of a group of people's collective identity gone wild" (Gupta 2001, 11). Gupta views this phenomenon as a potential byproduct of the pursuit of a collective imagination in such societies, when there develop no boundaries in the ways people seek shared ideology. He notes that collective madness is largely invisible to those affected by it, who see themselves as simply doing what any reasonable person would do.

Gupta's description is apt in the case of the 1965 Indonesian tragedy and the silence that followed. Undoubtedly the most effective cause of silence in the wake of this widespread atrocity happened not in the internal, psychological experiences of individual people, but in the Suharto government's ability to leverage the sense of collective identity to procure widespread acceptance of their version of the events of 30 September 1965: rendering mass violence reasonable. That version involved construction of the *PKI* and *Gerwani* as threatening and dangerous, and the subsequent "necessity" of huge social stigma attached to any association with persons accused of involvement with these groups.

The silence of bystanders

Elizabeth Vasko looks at the phenomenon of "those who aid and abet perpetrators (oppressors) through acts of 'omission and commission' " (Vasko 2015, Kindle

127). "Silence is performative. It shapes the stories we tell about ourselves, the divine, and others... It functions to create the perception of communal agreement" (Vasko 2015, Kindle 1368-1381). Focusing on bystanders disrupts false victim-perpetrator binaries, as it changes the question from "Why did you let this happen to you?" or "Why did you do this to him/her?" to "Why did we let this happen in our community?" Vasko theologically bases her framework on claims that our relationships with God cannot be separated from our relationships with people; that alienation from the neighbour – especially the suffering neighbour – is alienation from God (Vasko 2015, Kindle 750). In Indonesia, large portions of the society became bystanders to mass murder. The dynamics of relationally oriented identities, unattenuated by a strong justice norm, underwrote this bystander group behaviour and silence.

Toward a constructive proposal

Communitarian, social notions of selfhood also have many positive aspects, particularly when contrasted with the excessive individualism of the West. Yet, either position can be manipulated, particularly when idealised. What if, instead of framing *ubuntu*'s communitarian aspects as idealised forms of selfhood, we might continue to value personhood formed in and through communities, but from a perspective emphasising mutual obligation under norms of justice? Such a perspective includes relationships among strangers, persons with distinctive needs, and even enemies. Areas of incommensurability are not simply erased in the press toward a harmonious state of communal agreement. At times it will be important to give primacy to social notions of selfhood, and at other times to more individual notions. The norms for adjudicating which perspective to emphasise in a given context include (restorative) justice that privileges and advocates for the most vulnerable, and holds those exercising power accountable. This proposal is resonant with that of feminist legal philosopher Drucilla Cornell. Cornell offers a more robust understanding of *ubuntu* – one that might be up to the challenge posed by Indonesia's situation in the aftermath of collective silence and trauma. Drawing on South African Justice Mokgoro's legal interpretation of *ubuntu* as it appears in the new South Africa's constitution, Cornell writes:

The concept of a person in uBuntu is an ethical concept. A self-regarding or self-interested human being is one that has not only fallen away from her sociality with others; she has lost touch with her humanity. One crucial aspect of doing justice to such a person is that we who are participating in an ethical community help that individual get back in touch with himself or herself. Thus, cohesion and harmony are not the ultimate good because they must always be submitted to the doing of justice (Cornell 2010, 393).

While Cornell situates her more refined understanding of *ubuntu* in legal justice, I locate the theological grounding for a more complex notion of communal identity in Jesus' redefinition of "neighbour" in the Gospels. Jesus frames neighbour-care as extensions of love and relationship toward those to whom I explicitly am *not* related. The story of Jesus' interactions with the Samaritan woman at the well (John 4: 1-42) is but one example of this ethic. It is true that the Christian Gospel critiques radical individualism (like U.S. capitalism) that puts one's individual self above all concern for community and collective wellbeing. Yet this same Gospel simultaneously critiques the abandonment of personhood that happens when collective affiliation demands that persons' distinctive needs are absorbed into an uninterrogated social identity.

Such a perspective brings several implications for transformative practice in the case of the continuing impact of Indonesia's 1965 tragedy. I conclude by identifying these, understanding that each deserves further development in subsequent scholarship. A more adequate form of *ubuntu*-community in Indonesia is needed that honours the social body without the need to sacrifice individuals for its existence. Victim-survivors need to have spaces to tell their stories, and to lament. There is no requirement of granting forgiveness in order to have acknowledgement of victim-survivors' suffering. In this new community, the Indonesian government and the broader "society of bystanders" to the events of the 1965 program should offer formal apologies and set up public processes for acknowledgement and reparations. Finally, the wider international community, especially the U.S. government, must acknowledge complicity in the mass killings. Along with public apology and actions to make amends (e.g., support for present day survivors), people of faith in the U.S. must work for changes to foreign policy, and maintain commitments to stand with victim-survivors.

References

Alexander, Jeffery C. 2004. "Toward a Theory of Cultural Trauma." In *Cultural Trauma and Collective Memory*, edited by Jeffrey C. Alexander, Ron Eyerman, Bernard Giesen, Neil J. Smelser, and Piotr Sztompka, 1-30. Berkeley, CA: University of California Press.

Anderson, Benedict R. O'G, Ruth Thomas McVey, and Frederick P. Bunnell. 1971. *A Preliminary Analysis of the October 1, 1965, Coup in Indonesia*. Interim Reports Series. Ithaca, NY: Cornell University.

Ariati, Ni Wayan Pasik. 2012. "The Indonesian Massacre of 1965 and Contemporary Reconciliation Efforts in Indonesia," Paper, International Symposium on Conflict and Resolution, Kigala-Rwanda. June 9-13, 2012.

Cornell, Drucilla. 2010. "Is There a Difference That Makes a Difference between Ubuntu and Dignity?" *Southern African Public Law* 25 (2): 282-399.

Farid, Hilmar. 2005. "Indonesia's Original Sin: Mass Killings and Capitalist Expansion, 1965-66." *Inter-Asia Cultural Studies* 6 (1): 3-16.

Gupta, Dipak K. 2001. *Path to Collective Madness: A Study in Social Order and Political Pathology.* Westport, CT: Praeger.

Herman, Judith Lewis. 1997. *Trauma and Recovery.* Rev. ed. New York: Basic Books.

Hess, Cynthia. 2009. *Sites of Violence, Sites of Grace: Christian Nonviolence and the Traumatised Self.* Lanham, MD: Lexington Books.

Himonga, Chuma, Max Taylor, and Anne Pope. 2013. "Reflections on Judicial Views of *Ubuntu.*" *Potchefstroom Electronic Law Journal* 16 (5). doi: 10.4314/pelj. v16i5.8.

Jones, Serene. *Trauma and Grace: Theology in a Ruptured World.* Louisville, KY: Westminster John Knox Press, 2009.

Leksana, Grace. 2009. "Reconciliation Through History Education: Reconstructing the Social Memory of the 1965-66 Violence in Indonesia." In *Reconciling Indonesia: Grassroots Agency for Peace,* edited by Birgit Brauchler, 175-191. New York: Routledge.

Martyn, Elizabeth. 2005. *The Women's Movement in Post-colonial Indonesia: Gender and Nation in a New Democracy.* New York: Routledge.

Mercer, Joyce Ann. 2015. "Pastoral Care with Children of War: A Community-Based Model of Trauma Healing in the Aftermath of Indonesia's Religious Conflicts." *Journal of Pastoral Psychology* 64: 847-60. doi: 10.1007/s11089-015-0654-4.

Nadia, Ita F., Karen Campbell Nelson, Sawitri, and Rina Widyawati. "Women's Human Rights Monitoring Report, Gender-Based Crimes against Humanity: Listening to the Voices of Women Survivors of 1965." Jakarta: Komisi Nasional Anti Kekerasan Terhadap Perempuan/National Commission on Violence Against Women, 2007.

Rambo, Shelly. 2010. *Spirit and Trauma: A Theology of Remaining.* Louisville, KY: Westminster John Knox Press.

Simpson, Bradley R. 2008. *Economists with Guns: Authoritarian Development and U.S.-Indonesian Relations, 1960-1968.* Stanford, CA: Stanford University Press.

Tutu, Desmond. 1999. *No Future without Forgiveness.* New York-London: Doubleday.

Vasko, Elisabeth T. 2015. *Beyond Apathy: A Theology for Bystanders.* Minneapolis, MN: Fortress Press. Kindle edition.

Veerman, Alexander L. and R. Ruard Ganzevoort. 2001. "Communities Coping with Collective Trauma." Paper, International Association for the Psychology of Religion, Soesterberg, Netherlands, September 28-30, 2001.

Wieringa, Saskia Eleonora. 2011. "Sexual Slander and the 1965/66 Mass Killings in Indonesia: Political and Methodological Considerations. *Journal of Contemporary Asia* 41 (4): 544-565. doi: 10.1080/00472336.2011.610613.

Reconfiguring Manithaneyam in the context of injustice, inequality and violation of personhood of manual scavengers

John Mohan Razu

Abstract

Manual scavengers as part of the divisions of labourers created by the system of caste are faced with one of the most horrendous challenges that confront their human dignity and personhood. Their forcible occupation has been legitimised and reinforced by the heinous system of caste that continues to dominate the Indian social structure. Abused and deprived of their human dignity, their dreams and hopes have not been translated into reality for centuries. Hence, this chapter examines and analyses the practical challenges that the manual scavengers face from a perspective called Manithaneyam. In Tamil language it means essentialising humanity as its core working principle by pitching humaneness at the centre consequently leading to common humanity. Manithaneyam as such implies cultivating the right conditions for personal and communitarian ethic of co-existence respecting each other with equality and quality of life within the parameters of equitable and egalitarian rubrics of institutional frameworks.

Rationalisation of the theme

As an Indian hailing from a downtrodden social category, the social milieu I belong taught me innumerable lessons. My existence, thought processes and consciousness have also been shaped by the social milieu that the Dalits[1] as a community experience. I learned from them the abiding value of simple human decency and civility. I have rebelled against the oppressive and exploitative ideologies, doctrines, philosophies, theologies and values that de-humanise and segregate the

---

[1] Those who belong to outside the caste system (varnas) are called by different names. The government in its notifications and gazettes use Scheduled Castes (SCs). Those against whom some of the terms and names used found them derogatory insinuating instead started using Dalit(dal) which means in Hebrew and Sanskrit as oppressed, exploited, dissected, torn apart so on and so forth. Dalits are meant as those oppressed communities experiencing discrimination because of their status enumerated in the system of caste.

people as "we, the people and you, the other"; "we, the touchable, and you the Untouchable"; "we, the main-line, and you the by-lane." I am a firm believer of the enlightenment ideas of freedom, justice, democracy, human rights, equality, equity and inclusivity as those universal normative principles that everyone practices and follows, but the reality portrays just the opposite. There have been visible representations of many in the academia, church and society who justify the system of caste, hierarchy and difference, against which I take a stand.

Nelson Mandela of South Africa and B.R. Ambedkar of India are part of egalitarian thinking. They subscribed to the rationale that each of us is born with equal value and worth, and so entitled to dignity and equality. Their radical and progressive ideas had created ripples in their time and in return provided the ethical grounding, intellectual rigour and moral prowess for further development. Their ground breaking ideas thus gave the momentum to anti-apartheid struggles and Dalit human rights movements. Since then, the ideals of equality, fraternity and liberty have inspired millions of Dalits in India, South Africa and the world at large to struggle against all forms of inequality and discriminatory practices.

Caste system and inequalities

The age-old maxim of equality has become the universal norm now it is premised upon the notion: "All human beings are born free and equal in dignity and rights." Although we find this ideal almost in all the international and national covenants and also in the preambles of the Constitution, the concept of equality is under attack and faces opposition whenever people try to translate it in concrete terms. Therefore, it makes many to wonder whether "Equality has become the 'endangered species' of political ideals." And yet, there are people who continue to strive for equality and human dignity.

The terrains of the Dalits present mixed picture of caste atrocities and discriminatory practices, hopes and aspirations. Though their formats and forms keep changing, the severity, intensity and veracity of oppression continues due to the Hindu Scriptures that reifies, justifies and legitimises the caste schema. For instance, the loyalty of Hindus to the theodicy of Karma, a theory which provides metaphysical explanations and legitimisation of each individual's social situation and the sufferings as said by Max Weber in his seminal work on *Protestant Ethic and the Spirit of Capitalism* was complete and unassailable rendering any change of heart and attitude of Hindus towards the so-called "untouchables." This pessimistic analysis impelled particularly B.R. Ambedkar, the architect of India's Constitution, a Dalit by birth who decided to totally sever with the ideological, theological and religious mores of Hinduism as the only way to ensure social and spiritual emancipation of the so-called "untouchables."

B.R. Ambedkar makes a succinct analysis of the philosophy of Hinduism from the point of view of justice discloses clearly the ways with which "Hinduism is inimical to equality, antagonistic to liberty and opposed to a fraternity" (Moon 2014, 66). He explores further by digging deeply into these concepts and comes out candidly that,

Fraternity and liberty are really derivative notions. The basic fundamental conceptions are equality and respect for human personality. Fraternity and liberty take their roots in these two fundamental conceptions. Digging further down it may be said that equality is the original notion and respect for human personality is a reflexion of it. So that where equality is denied, in other words it was enough for me to have shown that there was no equality in Hinduism. But as Hinduism has not been examined so far in the manner I have done. I did not think it sufficient to leave it to implication that Hinduism was denial of Fraternity and Liberty as well (Moon 2014, 66).

Hinduism is the root of discrimination

Having examined the basic philosophy and tenets of Hinduism, B.R. Ambedkar categorically opines that, "For in Hinduism inequality is a religious doctrine adopted and conscientiously preached as a sacred dogma. It is an official creed and nobody is ashamed to profess it openly. Inequality for the Hindus is a divinely prescribed way of life as a religious doctrine and as a prescribed way of life; it has become incarnate in Hindu Society and is shaped and moulded by it in its thoughts and in its doings. Indeed, inequality is the Soul of Hinduism. And he thought could happen only by a change of faith" (Moon 2014, 66). B.R. Ambedkar probed and dissected Hinduism so deeply and thus exhumed the inherent contradictions and riddles entrenched in Hinduism.

His vision of religion was that it should accord primacy to morality, and not God. For him, religion must be in accordance with science, which is a synonym for reason. Religions which surrender reason to transcendental gods and dogmas are an anathema. It must recognise the fundamental tenets of liberty, equality, and fraternity; religion must not sanctify and ennoble poverty. Ambedkar valued human beings and morality as the means of all things. "If these conclusions are sound, how can a philosophy which dissects society in fragments, which dissociates work from interest, which disconnects intelligence from labour, which expropriates the rights of man to interests vital to life and which prevented society from mobilizing resources for common action in the hour of danger, be said to satisfy the tests of Social Utility" (Moon 2014, 71).

B.R. Ambedkar systematically peeled Hinduism layer by layer and unpacked the inherent contradictions and thus exposed the riddles. So, "The philosophy of Hinduism therefore neither satisfied the test of social utility nor does it satisfies the test of social utility nor does it satisfy the test of individual justice" (Moon 2014, 71). Hence, Hinduism for Ambedkar could never be considered as the religious heritage of the Dalits, because of its peculiar scheme that stratifies people because of the fact that "... Manu preached the sanctity of the Varna ... is the parent of caste ... In the scheme of Manu the Brahmin is placed at the first in rank. Below him the Kshatriya ... the Vaishya ... the Shudra and ... is the Ati-Shudra (the Untouchables). This system of rank and gradation is, simply another way of enunciating the principle of in-equality so that it may be truly said that Hinduism does not recognise equality ... Manu has introduced and made inequality the vital force of life" (Moon 1989, 25).

Hinduism is built on the solid foundation of caste. This being the foundational principles of Hinduism, the only option left for Ambedkar was to rip open the fallacies, riddles, and irrationality of Hinduism by intensifying and deepening the in-built contradictions by pointing out: "... In Hinduism you will find both social inequality and religious inequality imbedded in its philosophy. To prevent man from purifying himself from sin!! To prevent man from getting near to God!! To any rational person such rules must appear to be abdominal and an indication of a perverse mind. It is a glaring instance of how Hinduism is a denial not only of equality but how it is denial of the sacred character of human personality" (Moon 1989, 36).

Caste system and social stratification

Caste is a vicious form of social stratification. It revolves around creating differentiation between human beings by segmenting those who are bound to control the materiality of production and those who by virtue of being born as "untouchables" are required to contribute labour for menial jobs. Those who are at a higher rung of caste are regarded as inherently pure, intelligent, and worthy of respect as the rungs descend are inherently impure, stupid, dirty, dumb and worthless. Therefore, "The spirit of caste unites these three tendencies, repulsion, hierarchy, and hereditary specialisation" (Bougle 1958, 64). As pointed out in caste there is no division of labour, but divisions of labourers. Certainly all these tendencies form the basis of caste system incarnating as hierarchy. Therefore,

To begin with the notion of hierarchy implicated in the caste system tends to relativise inequality. While it is obvious that you cannot have hierarchy without inequality; social anthropological modes of caste stress the systemic nature of this inequality: almost everyone in the system is unequal with respect to almost everyone else, being above some groups and below others. Because everybody is unequal they are also in a certain sense equalised by this fact. For instance, in the most sophisticated theoretical model of the caste system we have, that of Louis Dumont, the key feature is the subordination of the

(Kshatriya) king to the (Brahmin) priest. This means that even the highest secular power (the king) requires religious sanction from the priest; and even the caste with the highest ritual rank (Brahmin) is subject to the secular power of a caste of lower rank. Thus, the anthropological understanding of caste as hierarchy blunts the sharp edge that inequality often acquires in other contexts (Deshpande 2003, 102-103).

The ideal of caste cannot be construed as mere ideal because the ideal those dominant castes speak will have to be tested by its results. B.R. Ambedkar offers the following conclusion: "1) Caste divides Labourers, 2) Caste disassociates work from interest, 3) Caste disconnects intelligence from manual labour, 4) Caste devitalises by denying to him the right to cultivate vital interest and (5) Caste prevents mobilisation. Caste System is not merely division of labour. It is also a division of labourers" (Moon 1989, 67). B.R. Ambedkar, by critically analysing Hinduism, penetrates into the fallacies of Hindu Society and brings to the fore layer by layer the latent aspects of it. Intensifying his logical and scientific analysis, B.R. Ambedkar elaborates,

Civilised society undoubtedly needs division of labour. But in no civilised society is division of labour accompanied by this unnatural division of labourers into water-tight compartments. Caste system is not merely a division of labourers – which is quite different from division of labour – it is an hierarchy in which the divisions of labourers are graded one above the other. In no other country is the division of labour accompanied by this gradation of labourers ... This division of labour is not spontaneous, it is not based on natural aptitudes. Social and individual efficiency requires us to develop the capacity of an individual to the point of competency to choose and to makes his own career. This principle is violated in the Caste System... (Moon 1989, 67-68).

Terrains of the manual scavengers

Vidisha, the thriving trade centre of ancient India, is the well-known tourist attraction maintains the banned practice of manual scavenging. It is still a forced occupation for several Dalit families. Over 200 families in this district continue to bear the brunt of caste discrimination through the practice of manual scavenging. For instance, "Every morning, I go to eight to ten households, collect the garbage in a straw basket and dump it a mile away from the village. When it rains, the water oozes through the basket over to my hair," says Guddi Bai (38) of Nateran tehsil (The Hindu, 16.12.2010). The waste she is talking about is human excreta, euphemistically called "night soil." Guddi belongs to the Valmiki community, relegated by the caste system to practice manual scavenging as their traditional occupation.

Vidisha District Collector Yogendra Sharma accepts that the practice still continues. He says that "All these families have alternative livelihood options; most of them fall under the category of Below Poverty Line (BPL). The only reason, I understand, they are still doing it for generations, because it is easy money for them compared to jobs that require hard work like agriculture," says Mr. Sharma, the Collector. What else can we expect from Sharma? The job she is doing since her marriage she gets around 20 to 50 kilos of grain annually, a few old clothes on occasion. When asked, why doesn't she quit then? "If we quit, the upper caste women ridicule us by saying "Tum to panditaain ho gayi ho" (you seem to act like a Brahmin woman) (The Hindu 16.12.2010). It is dehumanising, but the patron-client system has given its legitimacy and sanction. It has firmly entrenched into the psyche of those who benefit and make the Dalits to perform this degrading job in the name of descent and occupation.

However, manual scavenging exists in many States despite an Act of Parliament banning it. "Shameful," "degrading," "disgusting," "obnoxious," "abhorrent," a "blot" are some of the words used to describe "manual scavenging." It just means, people lifting human excreta with help of the scraper with their bare hands and carrying the load on their heads, hips or shoulders. Over the years, many commissions have been set-up; laws have been enacted; millions of rupees spent to eradicate manual scavenging, but even after six decades of Independent India, the nation continues to dehumanise, degrade and shame the Dalits, in particular the Valmikis (Dalits). Governments in several States have staunchly denied in Courts the existence of manual scavenging, but the ground reality shows the naked practice of it.

Experiences of Dalit women who are involved in manual scavenging correspond to the lived experience of each other's inter-subjective world. The experience and understanding are to be mediated for which language plays an important and vital role. Dalits do express their feelings, sufferings, pain, pathos and hope in varied ways. Thus, the language of the Dalits, their idioms, and narratives are to be brought to the centre for any discourse on Dalits. Making the Dalit women to carry the shit of others; watching these women who undergo the traumatising process as they carry human excreta in bamboo baskets which gradually slip into their mouth and yet continuing the practice for centuries tantamount to the pathological sick mind-set.

These experiences are not isolated, but cumulative. These are the real life experiences that the scavenging communities face in their day-to-day existence. Are there any methods that would measure, qualify and understand what is happening to them in their psyche?

However, articulating the experience in a proper context still requires language and theory. After all, a dalit cannot tell (if we accept Guru's argument) how a non-dalit experiences the sight of a dalit woman carrying human excreta. His response cannot be anticipated and taken as a priori in the sense that he/she would not bother. Even if it seems natural, there is reification involved in which the ideology of caste has been so powerfully internalised that something inhuman is perceived as natural (Judge 2010, 6).

The so-called "upper castes" perceive these as natural. It is also interpreted that the physical and mental labours as two functions juxtaposed with each other in which Brahmins are supposed to do the mental work and Dalits the physical labour. "What lies beneath this purity-pollution is the hierarchical separation of the manual labour from that of the non-manual (Judge 2010, 6)." Within this scheme, jobs are clearly delineated based on caste. "The so-called upper castes" would look at Dalits who carry human excreta as something normal and natural because they are indoctrinated with the ideology of caste that justifies the means.

Squalid conditions beyond human habitation

For Dalits, their locales play the most crucial role. Context does emphasise not just one part of the reality, but all. Context presents concretely all the dimensions. Hence, context not only gives rise to holism of the milieu, but also pre-empts the arguments put forth against it. Context portrays all the features sufficiently for the analysis, interpretation and theorising. Face-to-face encounters and periodic visitations with the manual scavenging communities unfolded the inherent contradictions and fallacies of Hinduism which happened to be their religion and their belief systems is entrenched.

In a horrifying incidence that killed three unprotected manual scavengers namely, Kutti Prasad, Nagendra and Ravi, due to suffocation as they were working in a septic tank in Kolar Gold Fields (KGF) in Karnataka brought to light our society's heinousness. A house owner who hired these three who belong to the scavenging community to clean the septic tank and when they failed to come to the surface, the house owner reported to the fire brigade who rushed to the spot, by then they were dead and their bodies were removed from the septic tank. Kutti Prasad has two sons (Ajit and Nitish) studying 6th and 4th standards, Nagendra was married two years ago and has a month old child, while Ravi got married just three months ago.

Karnataka's former Urban Development Minister S. Suresh Kumar in his routine visit had visited KGF on the 21st of June, 2011 and had promised to rehabilitate those who were involved in manual scavenging. When I visited after that, i.e., in November and December, 2011, nothing had changed and the inhuman practice continues. The terrain is just 100 kilometres from Bangalore. However, the district administration in the beginning of the year 2011 gave alternative employment to nearly 140 manual scavengers as daily wage labourers in the municipality for three months, but stopped them from work abruptly saying that the job was temporary in nature and due to lack of funds they should be terminated from work. The Commissioner of the Municipality asked them to take loans from the Ambedkar Corporation, but the manual scavengers demanded work.

For the sake of subsistence whoever calls them to clean the cesspool or sewerage or septic tank they attend to them. One day, a group of three men received a call from a private house owner to remove night soil. Accordingly, they went to the spot and was about to start their work. As one of them by name Prasad was standing at the edge of the septic tank slipped and fell into the tank, and the other two jumped into the cesspool to rescue him. Along with him, they also died of suffocation. This incident had happened during the last week of October, 2011. Almost all the dailies had flashed this horrifying news. In an exclusive interview with one of the leading dailies, *"The Times of India"* as soon as this incident took place, on the 25th October, 2011, Kutti Prasaid had explained the circumstances which were forcing his community members into this inhuman practice. "We don't have any other alternative. Manual scavenging is the only work we know and no one gives us better jobs."

He further said that "In Kennedy Telugu 6th Main along, there are 109 families and at least one member of each family works as a manual scavenger. Many people are dead, a few are handicapped, yet the others continue their work." As usual the bureaucracy and casteist mind-set go all out by giving all sorts of excuses and defences. In the same interview to TOI, Robertsonpet City Municipality Commissioner V. Balachandra said "though the civic body had taken steps to create awareness among safai karmacharis against engaging in manual cleaning of tank, they had violated the directions of the civic body." He went on adding that "despite awareness programmes, safai karmacharis engage in such jobs due to pressure from middlemen who want to make money through such work." The fact of the matter is the practice of the divisions of labourers rooted in the system of caste that the casteist psyche does not want to accept, but keep offering flimsy excuses.

In Kolar District alone some decades ago about 50,000 Adi-Andhras migrated and have three settlements. Within the activity of manual scavenging, there are clearly demarcated areas with which each one has a specialised activity such as headers, lifters, scrapers, loaders, and disposers. This community is both with Hindu as well as Christian. Their problems have further precipitated due to the closure of mines. So, many commute to Bangalore in search of job. Those who got converted to Christianity do not enjoy the reservation privileges. Those who belong to Christianity are widely spread out to the Church of South India (CSI), Baptists and non-denominational viz. Indian Pentecostal Assembly, Assembly of God and other para-churches. Their economic and educational profiles remain way behind compared to other communities.

The next striking narrative comes from Bangalore, the Silicon Valley of India, the Premier Outsourcing Hub; the Cosmopolitan City with other dubious distinctions is plagued with manual scavenging. Within the proximity of the Silicon Valley, a place called as Electronic City, known also as Silicon hub sewerage disposal is practiced. Nearby to the Silicon hub, a small colony called as Rammurthy Nagar, a group belonging to the manual scavenging community is involved in manually removing human excreta from publicly maintained cesspools. Waste is transported on busy roads and is dumped at a convenient spot, usually in one of city's lakes. Those who are involved over 600 of them engaged in this occupation use simple methods. Their only tools are a few drums, buckets, and pickup vans to transport the filth. Residents who reside in and around the city of Bangalore, have to make phone calls to have their cesspits cleaned or blocks cleared.

When asked for the details, Vincent, a 28-year-old who has been cleaning cesspits for over five years said that many in Bangalore call them over cell phones whenever their sewage tanks or pits gets filled up they go in batches to attend the work. They work in batches of three. One gets into the pit and then hands over the filled bucket to another standing on the edge of the pit. He in turn hands over to a person on the pickup van who empties it in one of the drums of the van. For this, they charge between Rs. 700–Rs. 900 to clean a single pit. Having come to know of this heinous practice when the Times of India reporter by name T.S. Srinivas succinctly described his conversation and observation in a column entitled "Scavenging is Big Business" (September 3, 2010, 1, 4).

On several occasions particularly in Nellore and Ongole Districts of Andhra Pradesh, I observed that those women when they carry the water oozes through the baskets and passes through their hair and then touches their lips and sometimes enters into their mouth. As the men enter into the septic tanks the gas and smell that they inhale, and when they clean the sewerages and septic tanks the sight they see, materials on which they stand and hold in their hands raise a number of questions. If we re-capture those terrains and bring them before our eyes it chills and in the process numbs our body, it creates nausea, it raises our hair, and it shames us. The topography of these communities who are involved in manual scavenging evokes yearnings for dignity and equality. In Hinduism they did not get, and so, they embraced other religions such as Christianity or Buddhism or Islam. But, did Christianity live up to their expectations.

Inequality and equality examined

The social structure of the Indian society revolves around caste within which each individual is measured by the social status (caste) premised on binaries (purity and pollution) to which she/he belongs. If we go by that standards caste then automatically becomes the measuring rod to value and qualify individuals, groups and communities. In this scheme how could anyone expect equality? Rather, it promotes, difference, hierarchy and stratification leading to inequality and people as unequal. Therefore, according to B.R. Ambedkar, "Inequality is the soul of Hinduism. The morality of Hinduism is only social. It is unmoral and unhuman to say the least. What is unmoral land unhuman easily becomes immoral, inhuman and infamous. This is what Hinduism has become. Those who doubt this or deny this proposition should examine the social composition of the Hindu Society and ponder over the condition of some of the elements in it" (Moon 2014, 87). However, for centuries political philosophers have been grappling with the term "equality" that elevates those who fall at the lowest ebbs or outside the scheme of caste hierarchy, differentiated and marginalised. "Equality" as an ethical principle and a political concept should be made to work because it is rich in meaning and essence because,

At the heart ... the notion of equality lays the conviction that each person is of infinite, and hence equal, worth and should be treated as such. This means that being human is far more important than differences of colour, gender, class, creed, wealth, intelligence, nationality and so forth. This conviction should colour our attitudes and relationships and should shape social structures, which are networks of relationship and distribution. We recognise other people's equal worth by our attitude towards them, out treatment of them, our relationships with them and our regard for them, and also, rather more indirectly, but very significantly, in the way a society and its distribution of resources of all sorts are organised. To affirm human equality is both to say something important about what human beings are, and also how relationships and social institutions should be arranged, and how we should behave to one another (Forester 2001, 30).

So, equality is an all-embracing and holistic concept because it adds an important value that cuts across other considerations and thus pervades into political, social, economic and cultural domains. Basically equality is a far superior category than others because it revolves around two key questions: What is the ground for affirming that equality is good, desirable and proper? What is the basis of equality? For both these questions the underlying principle that governs all of us is that all human beings per se are equal on grounds of our common humanity. Equality does not function on the basis of social, economic, cultural and political distinctions and considerations as part of its valuation. So, what is the starting point and from where do we start with?

How do we create equality in a stratified and hierarchical society? Or at any rate reduce the injuries of inequality? Reducing inequality almost requires narrowing the economic and social divides because of the fact that "(t)he norms relating to social inequality determine the distribution of resources among individuals, families and groups. Unequal distribution causes high and low positions and other dysfunctional consequences... There is constant structuring and re-structuring of social inequality. Inequality is a 'relational' rather an 'absolute' phenomenon.... Also criteria such as income, occupation, education and competition alone cannot explain the entire gamut of social inequality" (Sharma 1995, 16).

The system of caste is merely an ideational phenomenon but effectively explains, reifies and justifies the notions of hierarchy and difference and in the process legitimises inequality. By doing so it insulates normative or valuational aspect of hierarchical relations of those born within the system of caste. Inequality that operates in the social structure of the Indian society is structural and thus permeates the existential conditions and differential distribution of and access to resources. Inequality that is present in India is premised on norms that justify inequality and the forms, manifestations and degree of inequality keep evolving, changing and influence social relations. Nevertheless, amidst a maze of definitions we need to articulate clearly how inequality affects different layers of society. The following will help us to derive clarity on this aspect:

Inequality reduces economic efficiency and traps societies in bad development paths through inequality-perpetuating institutions in three ways:

- *Inequality* reduces the participation of vulnerable and disenfranchised people in the political processes, both directly and indirectly. This in turn reduces the livelihood that poor people have access to education, health care, and other services that would contribute to growth.
- *Inequality* can hinder the establishment of independent and impartial institutions and the enforcement of binding rules, because they might reduce the benefits of the privileged.
- *Inequality* makes it easier for the wealthy to hold out in political bargaining, either directly or through capital flight. It therefore makes it more difficult for societies to respond quickly and optimally to external shocks (World Development Report 2003, 89).

Manithaneyam: A categorical imperative

In an inhuman and stratified Indian society, Manithaneyam is a viable and feasible component, a process and a praxis that restores those who are dehumanised as non-entities or non-persons relegated to menial occupations such as manual savaging. Manithaneyam has to do with restoring the sense of humanness and instils awareness within those who treats others as lesser humans. The caste-minded oppressors continue to perpetuate the system of caste and in the process stripped people of their worth as humans and tear away their personhood and in such appalling landscape Manithaneyam enables them to become humans and persons from such dehumanising forces.

Everyone is born free and thus enjoined with basic human rights. The Constitution of India guarantees to its citizens basic rights that insulates personhood, dignity and equality. Despite these, dehumanisation in varied forms and degrees exist nakedly all over the world within which caste manifests as the highest form of apartheid function in effective ways in India. In such a de-humanised Indian milieu manithaneyam could certainly become a tool and a proposition. There are some engaged in establishing a just, humane, egalitarian and inclusive embedded with equality, dignity and fairness invoke manithaneyam since it bound by these intrinsically linked as constitutive elements of manithaneyam. So, the concept of manithaneyam is central and pivotal to the dignity and self-esteem of manual scavengers.

In the Tamil literature I find Thiruvalluvar who wrote Thirukural (form of couplets) that convey noble thoughts. Some of the Thirukurals exposits the essence and significance of manithaneyam. Thirukural is considered to be a book of ethics for the ordinary folks, the administrators, kings and the ascetics. It indeed offers an universal perspective. It also affirms our ability and responsibility to lead ethical lives of fulfillment that leads to the greatest good of humanity. Thiruvalluvar was a rationalist informed by science and motivated by compassion. The couplets talk about all facets of life including the goals of life that embarks from human needs. Thiruvalluvar categorically asserts that humanity must take the responsibility of whatever happens in the society.

However, the section on virtue is entirely dedicated towards moral values and ethical behavior. Thiruvalluvar believed in the equality of all human beings, and denounced any system that dehumanises. He declares "All human beings are equal by birth but distinctions arise only because of different qualities of their actions" (Kural 972). He emphasises the importance of love and compassion in several kurals. He says "Love is the quintessence of life, without it, a man (sic) is nothing but a frame of bones covered with skin" (Kural 80). He substantiates that "The soul is born with the body because of its inborn bonding with love" (Kural 73).

He categorically states that everyone should have empathy for his/her fellow human beings. He wonders if one cannot treat others' suffering as his/her own, what benefit one gained from intelligence (Kural 315). He invokes reason by comprehending "Why does a man (sic) inflict upon other human beings those things he found harmful to himself?" (Kural 318). Thiruvalluvar's idea of equality, empathy, avoiding evil thoughts, harsh words and harmful deeds towards others are based on rules of socially acceptable good conduct and ethical behaviour of any rational human being.

In Tamil it goes this ways: "*Anbum, aranum uddaithyin illvalkai, panbum payanum adu.*" If love and virtue in the household reign, then the life manifests perfect grace and blessing. In another thirukural "*Anbin vazlya thuir neli akthi-*

laku anbuthol pootraudambu" which means bodies of loveless man are like bony
frame clad with skin. Then is the body seat of life only then love resides within.
That body alone which is inspired with love contains a living soul. "If void of it",
"the body" is just the bone.

   Manithaneyam encompasses the rich ethical values that ought to be the governing principles of any individual, community or even society. Manithaneyam
touches the core of humanity that respects human esteem, human dignity and human rights. In the case of manual scavengers their self-esteem is torn apart and
self-dignity is thrashed by making them to remove the excreta. The very thought
and act of those who involve a sizable population belonging to a Dalit community with that type of job tantamount to gross injustice. The caste-stratified Indian
society in the name of "karma" and "caste duty" offers all kinds of justification.
Nonetheless, there are no ethical basis and moral justification for treating a community as manual scavengers for centuries. It should be condemned and annihi-
lated.

References

Ambedkar, Babasaheb and Vasant Moon. 1989. *Dr. Babasaheb Ambedkar Writings and
    Speeches,* Vol. 5. Bombay: Government of Maharashtra.
Bouglé, Célestine. 1968. "The Essence and Reality of the Caste System." *Contributions
    to Indian Sociology*, 2(1): 7-30.
Deshpande, Satish. 2003. *Contemporary India: A Sociological View,* New Delhi: Viking.
    102-103.
Forrester, Duncan. 2001. *On Human Worth*. London: SCM Press.
Judge, Paramjit S. 2010. *Changing Dalits: Exploration across Time*. New Delhi: Rawat
    Publications.
Shalizi, Zmarak and the World Bank. 2003: *Sustainable Development in a Dynamic
    World- Transforming Institutions, Growth and Quality of Life*. World Development
    Report. Washington, DC: World Bank; New York: Oxford University Press.
Sharma, K. L., and Yogendra Singh. 1995. *Social Inequity in India: Profiles of Caste,
    Class and Social Mobility*. Jaipur: Rawat Publications.
Singh, Mahim Pratap. 2010. "Enslaved by Tradition: The Manual Scavengers of Vidisha."
    The Hindu, December 16.

Race, religion, and health among African-descended young women

Evelyn L. Parker

Abstract

African-descended young women ages 15-24 who experience Intimate Partner Violence (IPV) are at risk for HIV/AIDS. Churches are silent about this co-occurring health risk and fail to bring hope to the lives of these young women. A realised hope for IPV victims is wholesome relationships rooted in the African ideal of *ubuntu*. A critical *ubuntu* takes into account practices of sexism and patriarchy in congregations. African-descended churches can practice critical *ubuntu* and thus prevent IPV and HIV/AIDS through "Women and Girls Lamenting and Learning Together," a four-step educational program for congregations.

Introduction

The health of African-descended late adolescent girls is at risk in the United States of America (U.S.) and South Africa. Specifically, there is a co-occurring health risk for girls who experience Intimate Partner Violence (IPV) and the high potential for HIV/AIDS infections in these contexts. While governmental and non-government agencies have noticed this health risk among adolescent women and girls and make recommendations for prevention, African-descended communities and churches are silent about the problem. These contexts tend to avoid addressing the problem of IPV and only recently started to address the prevention of HIV/AIDS infections.

This chapter considers the health and well-being of African-descended young women, ages 15-24 years, by focusing on the intersectional nature of IPV and HIV/AIDS infections among African-descended female adolescents, and proposes a vision for ecclesial practices in African-descended churches in the U.S. and South Africa. IPV is the key term for consideration of young female health at the intersection of IPV and HIV/AIDS. The Center for Disease Control defines IPV as

...actual or threatened physical or sexual violence or psychological and emotional abuse (when there has been prior physical or sexual violence or threats thereof) directed toward a current or former spouse, boyfriend or girlfriend, or dating partner. The term *violence* usually describes specific assaultive acts whereas abuse usually connotes a dynamic within a relationship...relationship violence [is] any attempt to control and dominate another person resulting in harm. IPV includes violent acts, threats, and/or abusive (controlling) behaviors within a sexual relationship or otherwise intimate relationship (Teitelman et al. 2007, 69).

I will primarily use the term Intimate Partner Violence in this paper but on occasion will interchange IPV with Gender Based Violence (GBV). "The term *gender-based violence* refers to violence that takes place against members of the opposite sex, who may or may not have a romantic relationship, and is influenced by prevailing gender norms" (Teitelman et al. 2007, 69). Because the age cohort of 15-24 female adolescents who are African-descended is the focus of this paper the social locations of girls from the U.S. must be distinguished from those in South Africa. African-descended girls (ages 15-24) in the U.S. refers to girls in the U.S. census data who self-identify as African American. This group may also include black-white mixed-race girls who, like President Barack Obama, identify as African American. Borrowing from the nomenclature of South African theologian Beverley Haddad, African-descended girls (ages 15-24) in South Africa refers to girls who are black or "indigenous African South Africans" and classified as "coloured under the apartheid racial system" (Haddad 2013, 20).

In September 2013 the World Health Organisation reported that "adolescent girls and young women ages 15-24 were twice as likely to be at risk for HIV infection compared to boys and young men of the same age group" (World Health Organisation 2013). The high risk of HIV was associated with unsafe and often unwanted or forced sexual activity. This health fact is related to partner and non-partner violence and the larger health issue of violence against women and girls. Some predominately African-descended churches in the U.S. consider acknowledgement of the problem of IPV, education for the community, and support for both victims and perpetrators (Jordan 2002) viable solutions to IPV. There are non-governmental organisations, such as the Balm in Gilead, that engage in HIV/AIDS prevention in the African American community. In South Africa some churches are involved in HIV/AIDS intervention through education, spiritual counseling, sermons, and dramas. However, there is no indication of church involvement concerning intervention efforts of gender-based violence and its connection to HIV/AIDS in either African American churches or South African churches. African-descended churches are suspiciously silent about gender-based violence, not to mention its relationship to HIV/AIDS. Violence and HIV/AIDS are co-occurring health risks for black girls and women, particularly on my focus group – black girls in the United States and South Africa.

This paper has three movements. First, I will highlight statistics concerning violence, HIV/AIDS and gender-based violence, specifically IPV. Second, I will consider the theological implications of GBV and HIV/AIDS. Finally, I propose a vision for ecclesial practices in African-descended churches in the USA and South Africa.

Statistics on IPV and HIV/AIDS

The whole continent of Africa is widely known for its HIV/AIDS pandemic, particularly the high rates of HIV/AIDS in South Africa. While not an epidemic, HIV/AIDS is highest among same gender loving males in the U.S. (CDC 2014). Adolescents present the highest number of new cases of HIV/AIDS in both South Africa and the U.S. A 2014 report from the Center for Disease Control (CDC) – whose headquarters is in Atlanta, Georgia – provides a graph titled "Diagnoses of HIV infection among adolescents and young adults aged 13-24 years, by Race/Ethnicity, 2009-2013 [in] the United States and 6 Dependent Areas that include Whites at approximately 18% and Hispanics at 20%" (CDC 2014). Of all ethnic groups Black/African Americans are 60%, which is 40% higher than Hispanic/Latino, and much higher than Whites, Asians and all other ethnic groups in the U.S. (CDC 2014). Adolescent male-to-male sexual contact is about 73% to 79% over the 2009-2013 period (CDC 2014). Black/African American adolescents 13-19 years account for 67% of new HIV cases yet they are 14% of the total U.S. population. Black/African American adolescents 20-24 years account for 57% of new HIV cases and 15% of the total U.S. population (CDC 2014). Black females in the same age cohorts account for 81% and 89% respectively (CDC 2014). Clearly, HIV infection is disproportionate for black adolescents in the U.S., particularly black female adolescents. HIV infections among black adolescent females are primarily from heterosexual contact (CDC 2014).

It is well known that in the U.S. one in four women are victims of gender-specific violence (Women of Color Network 2006). For women of colour, high rates of poverty, poor education, limited job resources, language barriers, and fear of deportation increase their difficulty finding medical help and support services (Women of Color Network 2006). An estimated 29.1% of African American females are victimised by IPV in their lifetime (Women of Color Network 2006). They experience IVP at a rate 35% higher than that of white females, and about 2.5 times the rate of women of other races (Women of Color Network 2006). However, they are less likely than white women to use social services (Women of

Color Network 2006). Black women die at higher rates of IPV-related homicide when compared to their white counterparts (Women of Color 2006).

While current data is not available, African American women typically comprise about 70% of black congregations. Religious convictions and a fear of shame or rejection from the church may contribute to their inclination to remain in an abusive relationship.

Black girls' sexual health, emancipatory hope, and *ubuntu*

Emancipatory hope means "...the expectation of freedom from the dominating forces or racism, sexism, and classism, and the assumption of agency in God's vision for this liberative process" (Parker 2003, 75). This form of Christian hope is compromised when African-descended adolescent females are victims of IPV and HIV/AIDS. The interlocking systems of domination – racism, sexism, and classism – increases the vulnerability of black girls to IPV and HIV/AIDS when they are poor, female, and persons of colour. Research has shown the relationship of socioeconomic status of South African youth to sexual-risk behavior.

SES [Socioeconomic status] is likely to have a particularly significant effect on gendered sexual-behaviour outcomes and, among South African youth, low SES has been found to have more consistent negative effects on female risk behaviours than on male risk behaviours... For young women, lower SES has been found to be associated with earlier sexual debut..., higher reporting of transactional sex..., and coerced sex..., higher risk of early pregnancy..., having multiple partners..., lower chances of secondary sexual abstinence..., and lower instances of condom use at last sex... (Rogan et al. 2010, 356).

Socioeconomic status demonstrates how class is related to the intersection of IPV and HIV/AIDS, thereby demonstrating the convoluted and complex nature of the problem. Hope that liberates us from the interlocking oppressions of racism, classism, sexism and heterosexism is found in God's gift of relationships. For the purposes of my project I focus on relationships between heterosexual young African-descended women and their intimate partners. This idea is one of my "recent turns" in concretising the idea of *emancipatory hope*. This caused me to wonder – if as Christians our hope is in God – where then is that hope realised in the sociohistorical moment of African-descended girls who experience IPV? African womanist systematic theologian Dr. Isabel Phiri supports this new turn in my thinking about emancipatory hope. She writes, "...African women theologians' understanding of eschatology, says the expected new life of wholeness should be experienced here on earth just as it is yet to come" (Phiri 2004, 34-35). As such, African-descended girls should experience "life in all its fullness as demonstrated in Jesus Christ" (Phiri 2004, 34-35). Quoting Susan Rakoczy,

Phiri describes the embodiment that womanist theologians envision as realised eschatology. Stating her position, Phiri writes: "We live in a time of realised eschatology, of the already and yet to come. The future is here and yet to come, we strain forward with expectation to shape the new worlds, new relationships, new ways of ministry and new community, new ways of being women in societies and cultures. We see the new and yet long for so much more" (Phiri 2004, 44).

Just as Jesus ushered in the reign of God through his life and ministry so that his contemporaries could experience the promises of God – life in all its fullness – we too, as disciples of Jesus Christ through the power of the Holy Spirit at work in the world today, should expect God's promise of fullness of life in *this* world as we wait for the world to come. To expect fullness of life, wholesome and healthy living that pours out of God's grace, is *emancipatory hope*. Hope of this nature is found in wholesome relationships, specifically intimate relationships of heterosexual young African-descended women. To be clear, God's gracious hope-filled gift of wholesome relationships is not afforded to young women who experience IPV and thus are at risk for HIV/AIDS.

Wholesome relationships for African-descended young women are an aspect of the African worldview of *ubuntu*. This worldview or spirituality emphasises the "relational self" and inter-subjectivity. "I am because we are, and since we are, therefore I am" (Appiah 1992, 13). *Ubuntu* also connotes, "A person is a person through other persons" (Appiah 1992, 13). *Ubuntu* is most prevalent in traditional African communities. However, some scholars have argued that remnants of traditional African ideology, such as *ubuntu*, are traceable in African-descended people in the Americas. Professors Sterling Stuckey and Peter Paris are two noted scholars that make this claim. In his book *The Spirituality of African Peoples*, Paris argues that a person is the embodiment of moral virtue. He writes, "African understandings of *person* is always expressed in social terms because the process of becoming a person can only occur within the confines of the family, which. . . includes both contemporaries and predecessors" (Paris 1995, 101). While Paris does not use the word *ubuntu* the meaning of *person* is compatible with that of *ubuntu*. He goes on to draw comparisons between African and African American understandings of *personhood*. He states: "Consonant with the understandings of their African forebears, African American have always known that persons cannot flourish apart from a community of belonging" (Paris 1995, 117). That is to say, they understand personhood as "integrally related to the communal struggle for racial justice. That quest is deeply rooted in the African experience of tribal community, the basic condition for familial and individual life" (Paris 1995, 118). As such, he argues, enslaved Africans in the Americas attended to building community through social bonding (Paris 1995, 118). They demonstrated a spirit of good will toward one another and even toward their slave-owners. The narratives by and about enslaved Africans are "replete with stories pertaining to their many humane attributes that included care, compassion, empathy, and good will primarily to children, especially the children of their slave-owners" (Paris 1995, 119). African Americans have never completely embraced Western individualism from the enslavement period to the present. "Although they developed a more distinctive understanding of person than their African counterpart, the two share much in common with each other... the African American understanding of person exhibits the basic marks of holism that emanates from its traditional African source" (Paris 1995, 120).

African American music comprises one of the most basic expressions of African American philosophy: It reveals the person-community relationship more clearly than anything else, according to Peter Paris. African American spirituals, blues, jazz, rhythm and blues, Gospel, funk, rock, disco, reggae, and rap are all replete with meaningful lyrics of the person-community relationship. Contemporary artists John Legend and Common's Oscar Award winning song *Glory* – which combines ballad and rap music for the movie *Selma* – illustrates Paris's point about African American music that reveals person-community relationship.

African American individualism differed greatly from Western individualism in that the former never separated the individual from the community. African Americans have been alienated from the value system of Euro Americans (Paris 1995, 121). "African-Americans disdain individualism and the cultural spirit it has fostered" (Paris 1995, 126).

Communal belonging and the well-being of the community are at the heart of African American philosophy/ideology that shapes the morality of African Americans. Communal belonging sustained enslaved Africans in North America as they struggled to survive the harsh living conditions on plantations of salve holders as well as their struggle to become free in Canada. The sacrificing of life or property for the good of others is threaded throughout the moral fiber of the African American philosophy/ideology that is also known in the Bantu/South African contexts as *ubuntu*. The sacrificing of life among African Americans is best illustrated by the sacrificial act of Tywanza Sanders who was one of the nine persons slain during Bible study at the Emmanuel AME Church in Charleston, South Carolina on the evening of June 17, 2015 (Petersen 2015). Tywanza, who was 26 years old, was shot and died protecting his mother, Felicia Sanders. She lived to tell of her son's heroic act of saving her life and also struggling while wounded to save the life of his 87-year-old Aunt Susie Jackson. Most importantly, African Americans like Tywanza have woven together an *ubuntu* spirituality of person, family, community, and God (Paris 1995, 126) described in the work of Peter Paris discussed above.

One could assume uniformity of ethical practices regarding connectedness, care, and the community's well-being is compatible to the ideology of *ubuntu*. However, such an assumption would be unwise, given the problem of gender-specific violence among African-descended people, particularly that experienced by African-descended young women. I propose a critical *ubuntu* that takes account of patriarchy and sexism that stymies the practice of *ubuntu* fully. A critical *ubuntu* holds promise regarding patriarch and sexism for young women situated in South Africa and for African-descended girls in the U.S.

What does a critical *ubuntu* look like in practice? If we think of sexism as "a system of advantages that serves to privilege men, subordinate women, and denigrates women-identified values and practices, enforce male dominance and control..." (Adams, Bell and Griffin 2007) then a critical *ubuntu* is shaped by practices that are attentive to the virulence of sexism. Connectedness and care among African-descended peoples is manifest in practices that oppose intimate partner violence against women and girls that is a product of sexism. Men who engage in IPV become aware of their transgressions, confess their sins, and are transformed into advocates against IPV. Women and girls who have internalised sexism will also become aware of IPV and their complicit behaviour that promotes IPV. Their awareness will evolve into postures of confession, transformation and eventual advocacy. Even if conversion of sexist practices among men and women does not evolve into advocacy the transformation that brings emancipatory hope are those persons who become aware of IPV, confess their sins, and begin a new life that does not practice IPV. These men and women champion and model wholesome relationships as well as create a community of well-being that benefits all women, men, and children. They embody emancipatory hope for African American and South African young women who experience the intersection of IPV and HIV/AIDS.

The Christian Methodist Episcopal Church as a case study

Healthy Christian congregations are examples of communities of care where critical *ubuntu* can be practiced. In these congregations men and women work at eradicating IPV among their members and in the greater society. The Christian Methodist Episcopal (CME) Church is a denomination that seeks to practice critical *ubuntu* in its local congregations.

After CME Church clergy and lay advocates lobbied for eight years, the CME Church – a historically black Methodist denomination with congregations in North America, West and Southern Africa – voted in favour of a resolution to establish a policy on Domestic Violence Prevention during the 2014 General Conference in Baltimore, Maryland. The resolution that resulted in the new policy did not come without debate, but nevertheless, General Conference delegates voted in favour of the new policy. The Domestic Violence Prevention Policy requires the minimum of education about IPV and GBV during a special day in the life of the congregation as well as fully developed ministries on the GBV in local congregations across the denomination. As a member of this denomination I take personal interest in the implementation and practice of domestic violence education and prevention within the CME Church. I have proposed an educational model for the Kirkwood Temple CME Church, the congregation where I am a member, to comply with the new policy. Kirkwood already has a fully developed ministry that addresses GBV. The leaders of the GBV ministry have accepted my proposal that specifically addresses IPV and HIV/AIDS prevention. While the case study of the CME Church is open ended in that data is yet to be available about how well the ecclesial practices to end GBV are operating, the case study shows the potential for critical *ubuntu* in the life and witness of an African-descended Christian congregation in the U.S. Below is the proposal offered not only to my congregation but to all African-descended congregations concerned to end IPV and HIV/AIDS as they practice critical *ubuntu*.

My proposal for ecclesial practices in African-descended churches in the U.S. and South Africa for the prevention of IPV and HIV/AIDS is the development of the program "Women and Girls Lamenting and Learning Together." The aim of the program will be critical and transformative education in congregations for men, women, girls and boys about gender-specific violence and the desires of God for them to have good healthy bodies and good healthy relationships. The sequence of the program includes four important steps:

1. *Mourning the pain, suffering and loss of women and girls who have experienced various forms of gender-specific violence.* This step takes serious the need to lament all that a woman has experienced from IVP that includes physical, emotional, and psychological suffering. Healing from IPV is inadequate if opportunity to lament periodically is not given attention. Also, the loss of a partner who was loved by an abused/battered woman requires lamenting.

2. *Learning about gender-specific violence and its impact on the health of women and girls.* The focus of this step is on critical pedagogy that generates critical thinking about IPV and HIV/AIDS as well as critical *ubuntu*. The goal is to create an awareness of IPV and HIV/AIDS and also engage in practices of critical questioning about *ubuntu* in African-descended communities. Critical questioning is a process of teaching learners the skill of raising questions in light of problems that impact the wellbeing of a group, especially those marginalised because of their social location. Learning about gender-specific violence also requires critical Bible study alongside and related to critical questioning about IPV and HIV/AIDS.

3. *Deconstructing patriarchy and sexism among female and male pastors and internalised sexism among women and girls.* Just as congregations engage in critical pedagogy described in step two so will congregation examine and question patriarchy and sexism in biblical texts and in their congregations. Members of congregations will be able to recognise patriarchy and sexism in scripture and in the practices of their members.

4. *Reimagining wholesome relationships within the bounds of a critical ubuntu.* Step four is the constructive phase of step three. Members of congregations will move from deconstruction to the reconstruction of critical *ubuntu* as a corrective to patriarchy and sexism.

The "Women and Girls Lamenting and Learning Together" program starts with a focus on the voices of women and girls in the presence of men and boys in step one but moves to include the voices of men and boys in the remaining steps. While this model must be assessed for its intended goal of empowering a congregation to practice critical *ubuntu* in light of the intersection of IPV and HIV/AIDS, it is not fully applicable for the South African context. More research and collaboration is needed for the model to be applicable in both the U.S. and South Africa. The current research of Beverly Haddad, a South African scholar, and collaboration with her are vital for continuing work on the health of African-descended young women at the intersection of IPV and HIV/AIDS.

The co-occurring health risk for girls who experience IPV and the high potential for HIV/AIDS infections in the U.S. and South Africa can be eradicated when congregations speak out against IPV and HIV/AIDS. Congregations that break the silence about IPV indisputably seek to prevent HIV/AIDS among African-descended young women between the ages of 15 to 24. Congregations in the U.S. and South Africa must be encouraged through theological and financial resources to view the health of young women as equally important as any member in their congregations. Intertwined with this charge, African and African-descended congregations must view their heritage of *ubuntu* as an important theological and practical concept that must be authentically reclaimed among its members who desire the fullness of life that the Triune God has promised.

References

Adams, Maurianne, Lee Anne Bell, and Pat Griffin, eds. 2007. *Teaching for Diversity and Social Justice*. Second Edition. New York: Routledge.

Appiah, Kwame. 1992. *In my Father's House, Africa in the Philosophy of Culture*. New York: Oxford University Press.

Center for Disease Control, National Center for HIV/AIDS, Viral Hepatitis, STD & TB Prevention, Division of HIV/AIDS Prevention. 2014. Atlanta, GA http://www.cdc.gov/hiv/pdf/statistics_surveillance_adolescents.pdf.

Haddad, Beverly. 2013. "The South African Women's Theological Project: Practices of Solidarity and Degrees of Separation in the Context of the HIV Epidemic." *Religion and Theology* 20: 2-18.

Paris, Peter. 1995. *The Spirituality of African Peoples*. Minneapolis, MN: Augsburg Fortress Press.

Parker, Evelyn L. 2003. *Trouble Don't Last Always: Emancipatory Hope Among African American Adolescents*. Cleveland, OH: The Pilgrim Press.

Petersen, Bo. 2015. *The Post and Courier,* July 14. http://www.postandcourier.com/article/20150627/PC16/150629386.

Rogan, Michael. 2010. "The effects of gender and socioeconomic status on youth sexual-risk norms: evidence from a poor urban community in South Africa." *African Journal of AIDS Research* 9 (4): 355-366.

Teitelman, Anne M., Melissa E. Dichter, Julie A. Cederbaum, Jacquelyn Campbell. 2007. "Intimate Partner Violence, Condom Use and HIV Risk for Adolescent Girls: Gaps in the Literature and Future Directions for Research and Intervention." *Journal of HIV/AIDS Prevention in Children & Youth* 8 (2): 65-93.

Women of Color Network, National Advocacy Through Action, Facts and Stats Collection. 2006. Harrisburg, PA. http://www.doj.state.or.us/victims/pdf/women_of_color_network_facts_domestic_violence_2006.pdf

An *ubuntu*-inspired approach to organisational spirituality

Neil Pembroke

Abstract

The main aim of this chapter is to show how the communitarian thrust in *ubuntu* correlates both with important early work on Organisational Spirituality (OS) and with Trinitarian theology. It is argued that theological anthropology suggests choosing *ubuntu* rather than self-actualisation as the cornerstone in a theory of OS. It is further demonstrated that there is a strong connection between the participatory humanism of *ubuntu* and the Trinitarian dynamic of participation. Participation is one of the Trinitarian virtues. It indicates that the divine life is first and foremost an event of mutual indwelling. The doctrine of imago Trinitatis means that human beings were created for participation. In the model of OS developed here, participation is captured in three elements: consensus, dialogue, and good will.

Introduction

There are dozens of books and hundreds of articles on the topic of organisational spirituality (OS). Those who write on OS have a concern for the well-being and flourishing of the agents in organisations. In short, they prize a spiritualised work-place. However, there is a question whether some experiences named by OS authors can legitimately be called "spiritual." It could be argued that to identify positive experiences – such as being part of a good team, having fun at work, and realising individual potential – as "spiritual" is to trivialise the term (cf. Benefiel 2003). One reason that I am attracted to correlating *ubuntu* with a theory of OS is that it presents as a deep spirituality. Another compelling consideration is that *ubuntu*'s communitarian character accords well with central theological anthropologies.

Given that the bulk of the work on OS has come from the North American context in which individualism is strongly emphasised, it is not surprising that some leading approaches virtually ignore a sense of community and concentrate instead on the inner life of individual workers and their experience of self-actualisation. *Ubuntu*, in contrast, is a communitarian ethic. Desmond Tutu captures this well: "Harmony, friendliness, community are great goods. Social harmony is for us the *summum bonum* – the greatest good" (Tutu 1999, 35). The *ubuntu*-inspired model of OS developed below aligns in general terms with proposals by scholars who identify a sense of belonging and experience of togetherness in the workplace as vitally important (McMillan and Chavis 1986; McMillan 1996; Lorion and New-brough 1996; Burroughs and Eby 1998; Ashmos and Duchon 2000; Jurkiewicz and Giacalone 2004).

As already indicated, there are solid theological reasons for supporting a communitarian approach to OS. I hope to show that certain theological anthropologies support choosing *ubuntu* or "participatory humanism" (Mcunu 2004, 34) rather than self-realisation as the cornerstone in a theory of OS.

The model offered here has three elements: consensus, dialogue, and good will. Given that the meaning of the last term is not immediately obvious, a definition is required. The person of good will in an organisation possesses a readiness to engage in discretionary acts aimed at providing help with work-related tasks and problems. Clearly, these are not the only dimensions of OS that one could identify as flowing from *ubuntu*. However, they are central ones, and given the limits of space, it is necessary to be selective. The first step toward developing our model is to clarify the meaning of the term "organisational spirituality."

What is organisational spirituality?

There is no consensus on how to define OS. Quite commonly, the focus is exclusively on the well-being of the individual (e.g. Howard 2002, 231; Graber, Johnson and Hornberger 2001, 39). In a spiritualised workplace, a person finds meaning and purpose, develops her potential, and achieves personal fulfilment. A handful of scholars include the idea that sense of community is important (Jurkiewicz and Giacalone 2004, 129; Ashmos and Duchon 2000, 137).

It is perhaps not surprising that some U.S. scholars pay little or no attention to the vitally important role of community in the workplace. Their thinking is clearly shaped by an individualistic ethos. The *ubuntu* person, on the other hand, construes herself and her way-of-being-in-the-world in terms of togetherness and interdependence. She knows that she is a person because of or through others. As Mbiti puts it: "I am because we are, and since we are, therefore I am" (Mbiti 1970, 141). There is something quite important that follows from this: the recognition that if I am because of other people, I need to act in ways that demonstrate that I value and respect them (cf. Mcunu 2004, 29). With this in mind, I advocate a model of OS built around the principles of harmony, consensus, dialogue, and good will. In order to fill out the details of the model, it is necessary to fill out further the meaning of *ubuntu*.

What is *ubuntu*?

Describing *ubuntu* is not a straightforward task. First, there is no consensus amongst scholars on what the term means. Second, there is no clarity over whether *ubuntu* should primarily be considered a moral quality or a philosophy or world-view. Gade uses the results of analysis of historical discourse and empirical work to show that those who discuss *ubuntu* give answers that fall into both camps (Gade 2011, 2012). Finally, some scholars have argued that intellectual approaches to *ubuntu*, far from representing a straightforward description of a clearly defined traditional African or sub-Saharan African ethic or philosophy, are actually reconstructions or reinterpretations of residual patterns of thinking and behaving from village life carried out at a distance (Van Binsbergen 2001; Bernstein 2002). In the short space available here, I cannot hope to settle these difficult questions.

What I *can* do, however, is capture the major elements in the descriptions one frequently finds in the literature. The starting point is usually a reference to participatory humanness as captured in the Zulu saying *umuntu ngumuntu ngabantu*. Ramose takes this to mean "that to be a human be-ing is to affirm one's human-ity by recognising the humanity of others and, on that basis, establishing humane relations with them" (Ramose 1999, 52). In this philosophy of personhood, relationality is central. Shutte points out that in the *ubuntu* worldview a human self is not something that first exists on its own and then later enters into relationship with others. Rather, it only exists in relationship to others (Shutte 2001, 23).

I further note that some writers use the language of both a philosophy or worldview, on the one hand, and a moral quality a person possesses, on the other. For example, Desmond Tutu refers first to "the African *Weltanschauung*" (Tutu 1999, 34), and then immediately goes on to say: "When we want to give high praise to someone we say, '*Yu, u nobuntu*'; 'Hey, he or she has *ubuntu*'. This means they are generous, hospitable, friendly, caring and compassionate" (Tutu 1999, 34). However, it is much more common in recent literature for a writer to refer to *ubuntu* exclusively as a philosophy or ethic. For example, Venter defines it as "a philosophy that promotes the common good of society and includes hu-manness as an essential element of human growth," (Venter 2004, 149). Shutte suggests that "[t]he goal of morality according to this ethical vision is fullness of humanity…" (Shutte 2001, 30). Finally, Hankela defines *ubuntu* as "an African and South African communal, humane and hospitable philosophy, worldview or lifestyle" (Hankela 2014, 2).

It is a deeply challenging task to answer the question, what is *ubuntu*? The provision of any kind of comprehensive answer is certainly beyond the scope of this essay. It is sufficient for our purposes, however, to propose this working definition: *ubuntu* is a humane and communitarian philosophy or ethic that views persons as interdependent entities whose deepest moral obligation is to become more fully human through expressing virtues such as openness to others, hospitality, generosity, compassion, and care.

Ubuntu, participatory humanness, and *Imago Trinitatis*

In light of this working definition, the next step is to show why it is theologically appropriate to propose a model of OS grounded in the *ubuntu* ethic. We have seen that an *ubuntu*-inspired approach to OS accords well with the earliest work in the literature. It is unfortunate, however, that we have definitions of OS by leading scholars in the field that fail to mention community, a sense of belonging, or connectedness to others (Graber, Johnson and Hornberger 2001; Howard 2002). The participatory humanism that is the foundation of *ubuntu* aligns well with a view of the human person as made in the image of the Trinity. Gabriel Setiloane contends that "the essence of being is participation in which humans are always interlocked with one another. . . the human being is not only 'vital force', but more 'vital force' in participation" (Setiloane 1986, 14, cited in Mcunu 2004, 27). One traditional theological term for Trinitarian participation is *perichoresis*: the three Divine persons mutually indwelling with each other in and through love. There is clearly a strong point of connection here between the theological anthropology undergirding *ubuntu* and the Trinitarian dynamic of participation. Indeed, one notes that South African theologians have also posited an *ubuntu-perichoresis* link (Manganyi 2012; Williams 2013). Given that the human person is created *imago Trinitatis*, it is legitimate to claim that *ubuntu* and Christian theological views of the human correlate. According to this view, we were created for participation; it is a virtue that we need to live out in every domain of our existence.

Cunningham (1998) refers to "participation" as one of the essential Trinitarian virtues. In using this descriptor, he indicates that the divine life is first and foremost an event of mutual indwelling. Furthermore, participation is a virtue that we humans are also called to enact. If the doctrine of the Trinity has anything to teach us about authentic existence, it is that communion rather than individualism is the goal of human life. Participation, then, is a Trinitarian virtue that marks our human existence.

Toward an *ubuntu*-inspired model of organisational spirituality

An approach to life grounded in *ubuntu* is one that highly values harmony and community. Metz (2007) suggests that there are two elements in harmony: solidarity and identity. Solidarity refers to the fact that an individual is morally required to be concerned for the good of others. This concern is expressed both in terms of emotional solidarity (compassion) and in terms of helpful actions. The other element refers to a sense of shared identity that is founded on a common vision of the nature of human life and relations, and of the norms governing these.

If we take a lead from this summary of the nature of harmony or community in building our model of *ubuntu*-inspired OS, there are at least three crucial dimensions that can be identified: consensus, dialogue, and good will.

Consensus

Mangaliso (2001) notes that an approach to decision-making shaped by *ubuntu* differs significantly from one grounded in the Western corporate paradigm. In the latter model, the approach is linear. The steps are: 1) identify the problem; 2) determine the cause(s) of the problem; 3) generate a number of viable solutions; 4) choose the best solution; and, 5) implement the decision. A quick and efficient process is the ideal. The *ubuntu* approach, by contrast, is a circular and inclusive one. The amount of time that the decision-making process takes is not a major consideration. What is important is that sufficient time has been allowed to ensure that all voices have been heard so that a consensus can emerge. The goal is to preserve harmony.

Louw (2001) points out that while inclusivity, a desire to achieve consensus, and a valuing of unity are all laudable, there is also a dark element here. He explains this dark side by using Themba Sono's depiction of the "tyrannical custom" of African culture and its "totalitarian communalism." According to Sono, the role of the group in African consciousness could be "... overwhelming, totalistic, even totalitarian" (Sono 1994, 7, cited in Louw 2001, 19).

In the model of *ubuntu*-inspired OS that we are constructing, it is clearly necessary to correct for this oppressive conformity and forced group loyalty. We want to recognise the importance of inclusivity, a desire for sameness, and seeking to maintain unity through achieving consensus. Yet, we also want to give room for the members of the organisation to appropriately express difference.

When it comes to achieving a balance between sameness and difference in a workplace community, the work of David McMillan is helpful. McMillan (1996) uses the metaphor of "trade" in developing his approach. He observes that "sense of community will be stronger if the community can find ways to juxtapose and integrate the members' needs and resources into a continuous bargaining process" (McMillan 1996, 320). McMillan recognises that while similarity is an important bonding force, over time organisational agents will need to deal with the fact that there are also differences in ideas, outlook, and preferences. It is at this point that McMillan's work offers a helpful corrective to the potentially dark side of *ubuntu*. He uses the metaphor of "trade" in discussing a healthy approach to dealing with difference. Two people cannot trade with each other if they have the same things. A successful trade in a workplace community involves exchanging different ideas, opinions, and criticisms in a way that leaves both parties satisfied.

Social economic trade avoids the threat of "mutual obstructionism" (Mück-enberger 1996, 688) through intelligent, inclusive, and respectful dialogue. Commentators on *ubuntu* have observed that this is precisely the spirit that animates African humanness (see, for example, Louw 2001). This leads us into a discussion of the second dimension in our model: dialogue, in which the particularity and individuality of the other is respected.

Dialogue: Embracing particularity and individuality

Louw (2001) helpfully suggests that respect for the values, beliefs, and practices of others is connected to a less well-known translation of *umuntu ngumuntu ngabantu*. This translation is: "A human being is a human being through [the otherness of] other human beings." In a society that is multicultural and pluralistic – and, of course, a workplace is a micro-expression of this phenomenon – *ubuntu* requires that in order to become human an individual must recognise the otherness of her or his fellow citizens in all its fullness. The other is characterised by her particular beliefs, language, and worldview. I am a human person to the extent that I respect and seek to understand her particularity.

Louw (2001) notes that the respect for the particularity of the other required by *ubuntu* is closely linked to respect for her individuality. He is quick to point out, however, that the notion of individuality that *ubuntu* carries is quite different from the Cartesian interpretation. In fact, the two versions are at odds with each other. In the Cartesian construction, the individual exists prior to, or separately and independently from others in the society. In contrast, *ubuntu* posits that an individual exists only in relationship to others. An individual is, by definition, one who exists through being-with-others. It is not that an individual person comes into existence and then enters into relationship with others. Rather, a human being is always being-in-community. Shutte puts it this way: The Cartesian "I think, therefore I am" is substituted for the "I participate, therefore I am" (Shutte 1993, 47).

There is a striking similarity between the *ubuntu* conception and that of the dialogical philosopher, Martin Buber. Buber's relational philosophy also contradicts Cartesian individualism and that of continental philosophers such as Husserl, Sartre, and Heidegger who followed his ego-centred line. For Buber, the primordial reality is the sphere of the between. "In the beginning," he writes, "is the relation ... as the category of being, as readiness, as a form that reaches out to be filled, as a model of the soul; the *a priori* relation; *the innate You*" (Buber 1970, 78, emphasis in original). A person becomes an I through a You. It is only in the relation that I become a real person.

Louw (2001) notes that this focus on the relation as defining of the human person can lead to a loss of certain valuable characteristics of personhood. He is thinking particularly of freedom and responsibility. Louw argues, however, that these values are not totally suppressed in *ubuntu*. He cites the work of African philosophers who, while celebrating the distinctive African emphasis on collectivism and a collective sense of responsibility, also contend that this emphasis does not mean that individuality is negated. He comes to what I take to be a very important conclusion in relation to our quest to articulate an *ubuntu*-informed vision for organisational spirituality:

An oppressive communalism constitutes a derailment, an abuse of *ubuntu*. By contrast, true *ubuntu* incorporates dialogue, i.e., it incorporates both relation and distance. It preserves the other in his otherness, in his uniqueness, without letting him slip into the distance (Louw 2001, 26).

Contained in this construal of *ubuntu* as dialogical is a principle that is vitally important for any vision of a spiritualised workplace. If the social exchange is to be positive and promote the well-being of the agents, it needs to be founded on relations that are characterised by both closeness and distance. Absent closeness, there is no possibility of community. But a community is oppressive when there is little or no respect for the individuality and particularity of the other. The individual needs space to be the person that she genuinely is; but if all that the organisation provides is distance, there is no possibility that the community that many yearn for will come into being.

I suggest that there is an important correlation here with a Trinitarian conception of the human person, or to be more precise, of persons-in-relation. Space is a key category in Trinitarian theology, as Gunton (1991) shows. He uses the category of space to help shape a relational ontology grounded in the Trinitarian dynamic. This space needs to be correctly defined. If there is too much space in the relational sphere, there is a fall into individualism. Mutual participation in relationships implies nearness. Too little space, on the other hand, is also a problem.

When the other sits on top of me, so to speak, I lose my freedom. She fails to make room for me and so shows a lack of respect for my otherness.

In developing his theological anthropology, Gunton picks up on the notion of Greek theologians that God is a communion of persons. Each person is distinct and yet the Three indwell each other and so share in an essential unity. There is both nearness and space to be. Gunton contends that anthropology needs to be developed along these spatial lines.

We are created in the image of God; therefore, it is to be expected that relationality will be fundamental to our humanity. That is to say, if God is a communion of persons involving mutual participation, we will experience our humanity in our relatedness to others. The structure or *taxis* of human community is relationality that involves both participation (nearness) and otherness (distance). The space between us has to be the right kind of space: we need the space to be. "To be a person is to be constituted in particularity and freedom – to be given space to be – by others in community. *Otherness* and *relation* continue to be the two central and polar concepts here. Only where both are given due stress is personhood fully enabled" (Gunton 1991, 117).

Thus far we have discussed the role of consensus and dialogue in building the experience of community in the workplace. While learning how to talk together is vitally important, more is required. *Ubuntu* is founded on solidarity with others that is expressed through a duty to help them when they are in need. The *ubuntu* person feels compassion and concern for those in her community that are suffering or experiencing some kind of need, and she is ready to do what she can to help out. With this in view, we move to our final dimension in the model we are developing, i.e., good will.

Good will

In constructing his approach to an African moral theory, Metz (2007) posits "good-will" as an essential element. In offering the idea of good-will, he is inspired by *ubuntu*. He defines this virtue as follows:

One...wishes another person well (conation); believes that another person is worthy of help (cognition); aims to help another person (intention); acts so as to help another person (volition); acts for the other's sake (motivation); and, finally, feels good upon the knowledge that another person has benefited and feels bad upon learning she has been harmed (affection) (Metz 2007, 336).

Workmates help each other all the time. "Co-worker support" has been identified as an essential element in the experience of a sense of community (Burroughs and Eby 1998, 512). Often co-worker support is offered because it is part of the job description and/or because there is an expectation of some reward. I contend that such helping behaviour is most efficacious in spiritualising a workplace when it is discretionary. This particular type of co-worker aid is referred to in the literature as "organisational citizenship." It is defined as "individual behavior that is discretionary, not directly or explicitly recognised by the formal reward system, and in the aggregate promotes the efficient and effective functioning of an organisation" (Organ et al. 2006, 3). Ryan (2001) suggests that a good citizen of an organisation engages in actions such as 1) helping others who have heavy workloads; 2) willingly helping others who have work related problems; 3) orienting a new employee to the workplace even though it is not required; 4) considering the impact of actions on co-workers; and, 5) being mindful of how behaviour affects other people.

The Christian love ethic clearly indicates a need to act for the good of the other when and where possible. When others are in need or have a problem, the Christian is required to do what she can to help. However, I contend that in expressing good will in the workplace a follower of Christ is not required to follow an ethic of unrelenting self-denial and self-sacrifice. A Christian *is* called to service of others; she is definitely *not* called to be a doormat for others (cf. Janssens 1977).

In this regard I find the work of the moral theologian Gene Outka very helpful. Outka (1992) first notes that an important starting point in relation to the love ethic is the principle of "equal regard": equal importance is assigned to other-regard and to self-regard (cf. Browning 1987, 150-156; Browning 1992). That is, the protection and advancement of the well-being of the self and of the other are given the same priority. Outka (1992) is prepared to align himself with equal regard to the extent that altruism is not given an endorsement if it is of the radical kind that is dismissive of self-love. However, in taking these two objections seriously, he suggests that it is necessary to go beyond impartiality and incorporate "a practical swerve" away from self and towards the other. Given the fact that we have great difficulty in being even-handed when it comes to balancing our own needs against those of other, we need to build-in a bias towards her well-being.

Outka's proposal is attractive because it acknowledges that the personal needs of an individual committed to *agape* do matter, while offering a way to counteract the deep-seated temptation to selfishness that mitigates other-regard. I contend that it is this principle of universal love, containing as it does both a concern for the legitimate needs of the self and a "practical swerve" to the other, that informs an appropriate understanding of how good will in the workplace needs to be enacted. It is very appropriate for a Christian to take up a stance of solidarity with fellow workers. She needs to be prepared to go beyond the strict demands of her contract and help out where she can. In this way, she contributes to the spiritualising of her organisation. She expresses the other-regarding orientation that is central in the love ethic. But she is also guided by the principle that her own needs are also important and should be balanced against the needs of others.

Conclusion

The communitarian thrust in *ubuntu* aligns at a general level with some of the important early work on OS (McMillan and Chavis 1986; McMillan 1996; Lorion and Newbrough 1996; Burroughs and Eby 1998). It is unfortunate that some leading contemporary approaches focus almost exclusively on self-realisation in the workplace. There are good theological reasons for endorsing a communitarian approach to OS. A positive theological anthropology indicates choosing *ubuntu* rather than self-actualisation as the cornerstone in a theory of OS.

There is a strong point of connection between the participatory humanism of *ubuntu* and the Trinitarian dynamic of participation. Participation is one of the Trinitarian virtues. It indicates that the divine life is first and foremost an event of mutual indwelling. The doctrine of *imago Trinitatis* means that we were made for participation; it is a virtue that we need to live out in every domain of our existence. In the model of OS that was developed, participation is captured in three elements: consensus, dialogue, and good will.

References

Ashmos, Dennis and Donde Duchon. 2000. "Spirituality at work: A Conceptualisation and a Measure." *Journal of Management Inquiry* 9 (2): 134-145.

Benefiel, Margaret. 2003. "Irreconcilable Foes? The Discourse of Spirituality and the Discourse of Organisational Science. *Organisation* 10 (2): 383-391.

Bernstein, Ann. 2002. "Globalisation, Culture, and Development: Can South Africa be More Than an Offshoot of the West?" In *Many globalisations: Cultural diversity in the Contemporary World,* edited by Peter L. Berger and Samuel P. Huntington, 185–249. New York: Oxford University Press.

Browning, Don. 1987. *Religious Thought and the Modern Psychologies.* Philadelphia, PA: Fortress Press.

Browning, Don. 1992. "Altruism and Christian Love." *Zygon* 27 (4): 421-436.

Buber, Martin. 1970 (1937). *I and Thou.* Translated by W. Kaufmann. Edinburgh: T&T Clark.

Burroughs, Susan M. and Lillian T. Eby. 1998. "Psychological Sense of Community at Work: A Measurement System and Explanatory Framework. *Journal of Community Psychology* 26 (6): 509-532.

Cunningham, David. 1998. *These Three are One: The Practice of Trinitarian Theology.* Oxford: Blackwell.

Gade, Christian B.N. 2011. "The Historical Development of the Written Discourses on *Ubuntu.*" *South African Journal of Philosophy* 30 (3): 303-329.

Gade, Christian B.N. 2012. "What is *Ubuntu*? Different Interpretations among South Africans of African Descent." *South African Journal of Philosophy* 31 (3): 484-503.

Graber, David M., James. A. Johnson, and Keith D. Hornberger. 2001. "Spirituality and Healthcare Organisations. *Journal of Healthcare Management* 46 (1): 39-50.

Gunton, Colin. 1991. *The promise of Trinitarian Theology*. Edinburgh: T&T Clark.

Hankela, Elina. 2014. *Ubuntu, Migration and Ministry*. Leiden: Brill.

Howard, Susan A. 2002. "A Spiritual Perspective on Learning in the Workplace." *Journal of Management Psychology* 17 (3): 230-242.

Janssens, Louis. 1977. "Norms and Priorities in a Love Ethics." *Louvain Studies* 6: 207-238.

Jurkiewicz, Carole L. and Robert A. Giacalone. 2004. "A Values Framework for Measuring the Impact of Workplace Spirituality on Organisational Performance. *Journal of Business Ethics* 49: 129-142.

Lorion, Raymond P. and J. R. Newbrough. 1996. "Psychological Sense of Community: The Pursuit of a Field's Spirit." *Journal of Community Psychology* 24 (4): 311-314.

Louw, Dirk J. 2001. "Ubuntu and the Challenges of Multiculturalism in Post-apartheid South Africa." *Quest* 15 (1-2): 15-36.

Mangaliso, Mzamo P. 2001. "Building Competitive Advantage from *Ubuntu*: Management Lessons from South Africa." *The Academy of Management Executive* 15 (3): 23-33.

Manganyi, Jele S. 2012. "Church and Society: The Value of Perichoresis in Understanding Ubuntu with Special Reference to John Zizioulas." PhD dissertation, University of Pretoria.

Mbiti, John S. 1970. *African Religions and Philosophies*. New York: Doubleday.

McMillan, David W. 1996. "Sense of Community." *Journal of Community Psychology* 24 (4): 315-325.

McMillan, David W. and David M. Chavis. 1986. "Sense of Community: A Definition and a Theory." *Journal of Community Psychology* 14: 6-23.

Mcunu, Tobias N. 2004. "The Dignity of the Human Person: A Contribution of the Theology of Ubuntu to Theological Anthropology." Masters' thesis, University of South Africa.

Metz, Thaddeus. 2007. "Toward an African Moral Theory." *The Journal of Political Philosophy* 15 (3): 321-341.

Mückenberger, Ulrich. 1996. "Towards a New Definition of the Employment Relationship." *International Labour Review* 135 (6): 683-693.

Organ, Dennis W., Philip Podsakoff, and Scott MacKenzie. 2006. *Organisational Citizenship Behavior: Its Nature, Antecedents, and Consequences*. Thousand Oaks, CA: Sage.

Outka, Gene. 1992. "Universal Love and Impartiality." In *The Love Commandments: Essays in Christian Ethics and Moral Philosophy*, edited by E. Santuri and W. Werpehowski, 1-103. Washington, DC: Georgetown University Press.

Ramose, Mogobe B. 1999. *African Philosophy through Ubuntu*. Harare: Mond Books.

Ryan, J.J. 2001. "Moral Reasoning as a Determinant of Organisational Citizenship Behaviors: A Study in the Public Accounting Profession." *Journal of Business Ethics* 33 (3): 233-244.

Setiloane, Gabriel M. 1986. *African Theology: An introduction*. Johannesburg: Skotaville.

Shutte, Augustine. 1993. *Philosophy for Africa*. Rondebosch, South Africa: UCT Press.

Shutte, Augustine. 2001. *Ubuntu: An Ethic for a New South Africa*. Pietermaritzburg: Cluster Publications.

Sono, Themba. 1994. *Dilemmas of African Intellectuals in South Africa*. Pretoria: UNISA.

Tutu, Desmond. 1999. *No Future without Forgiveness*. Johannesburg: Rider.

Van Binsbergen, Wim. 2001. Ubuntu and the Globalisation of Southern African Thought and Society. *Quest: An African Journal of Philosophy*, 15 (1-2): 53–89.

Venter, Elza. 2004. "The Notion of *Ubuntu* and Communalism in African Educational Discourse." *Studies in Philosophy and Education* 23 (2-3): 149-160.

Williams, D.T., 2013, "*Perichōrēsis* and the South African ideal", *Koers – Bulletin for Christian Scholarship* http://dx.doi.org/10.4102/koers.v78i1.2118.

"So I lost Africa": Personhood, dignity, and multiple identity politics

Jeanne Stevenson-Moessner

Abstract

Based on field interviews, personal narrative accounts, and artistic expressions, this paper examines multiple identity politics in relation to personhood, human dignity, and injustice. The phrase "multiple identity politics" connotes an individual's distinctive, often dissonant psychosocial identities as impacted or created by political forces in that individual's social and cultural location(s). It is the assumption of my research that cultural consolidation, personhood, and dignity can be attained by those caught up in multiple identity politics. However, this process is often imbued with loss and struggle. Children who are transplanted into a new cultural context face unique challenges in identity formation, and the multigenerational transmission of cultural trauma can also deeply affect identity. Moreover, such uprooting is often caused by an unjust political milieu. For those impacted and for those injured by multiple identity politics, the depth of their cultural sensitivities, awareness, and possibilities for healing is an offering to us as theologians for closing the gap toward dreaming *ubuntu*.

Introduction

"So I lost Africa." Mike[1] said this with such sadness that it seemed he had lost part of himself. Mike was a child of two cultures. Mike was born to Caucasian North American missionaries who founded a small African mission school in Senegal. Mike attended this school in the late 1970s and grew up through his late adolescence with Africans as his closest friends. When he was about seventeen, his parents started to tell him: "You've got to start acting like a white man." According to Mike, he had gradually been elevated to the position of elder in the village, even in a culture where age was usually required for such authority. He was expected "to become 'white' " which implied more responsibility. He was eventually not

---

[1] "Mike" is a pseudonym. I interviewed him in France in 1984. The interview was recorded and transcribed for publication with his permission.

allowed to eat with his Senegalese friends. He became malnourished. He was tormented. "I no longer had the place I had as a child." "So I lost Africa. Up to that point, I always thought I would live in Africa the rest of my life ... I lost Africa."

His parents sent him to a Bible school in France. There, he chose a French girlfriend. Mike's continuing and understandable attempts to locate himself in the culture of this French-speaking country raised the concerns of the American missionary authorities who decided he was "emotionally unbalanced." He was sent to America. Mike: "... I had to come to terms with my American identity. So I went back to America to satisfy my critics once and for all."

Mike tried to go back to Africa once, alone on business. He was working as a liaison between the mission and the Senegalese government, and he had quite a large salary. ".... I became malnourished because of the guilt I had of being able to feed myself when kids I had known as a child were going hungry. I couldn't reconcile my rank. ... here I was. I was twenty, and I could sit where the governor sat. I couldn't take it ... " The Africa he had known no longer existed for him.

Mike was a multicultural child who struggled to retain his identity. In earlier decades, culture was often considered to be an external system of customs, topography, mores, relationships, foods, celebrations, and perspectives that arise out of the shared history of a people (Niebuhr 1951, 52). Today, it is more likely to be acknowledged that culture is often seen as a "porous social reality" (Phan 2003, 13). Culture has been likened to the "humus" of a person's life. I am suggesting that culture is also an internal system that appropriates and absorbs the above. All five senses work to create this internal system which is maintained through interaction and memory. It is the internal cultural system or systems which is my focus today. Injustice will be evident in all my illustrations; I will focus on the impact of multiple identity politics on dignity and personhood. The backdrop to this chapter is the IAPT 2015 conference theme of *ubuntu*. As Desmond Tutu has stated: "A person with *ubuntu* is open and available to others, affirming of others, does not feel threatened that others are able and good, for he or she has a proper self-assurance that comes from knowing that he or she belongs in a greater whole and is diminished when others are humiliated or diminished, when others are tortured or oppressed, or treated as less than who they are" (Tutu 1999, 31).

At the time of the interview, Mike had not reached the *cultural consolidation* that is assumed in traditional identity formation. Erik Erikson described cultural consolidation as a "search for a new sense of continuity and sameness" with the world of skills and tools, with occupational prototypes of the day, with peers, and with the "tangible adult tasks ahead of them" (Erikson 1963, 261). Cultural consolidation is much more arduous for children like Mike, children who have been immersed in multiple identity politics. Their cultural identity can be fragmented into distinct cultural components. At 17, Mike was elevated to tribal elder. Back in the States and upon return to Senegal, he felt *less than a beggar*, for even a beggar can receive. He felt as if he had nothing to give, nor receive. If you are less than a beggar, you have no niche in society.

It is the assumption of my research that cultural consolidation, personhood, and dignity can be attained by those caught up in multiple identity politics. However, this process is often imbued with loss and struggle. For those impacted and for those injured by multiple identity politics, the depth of their cultural sensitivities, cultural awareness, and cultural intimacies far exceeds that in comparison to persons of single identity politics. Mike was in a colonial missionary milieu in the 1970s. However, multiple identity politics appears in other if not all cultures.

"I remember roses": The lost generation[2]

Aboriginal artist Brenda Croft tells how her father, Joseph Croft, like many aboriginal children in the 1920s in Australia, was stolen from his biological family and put in a children's home (Kahlin Compound) in Darwin, Australia. He was moved to a variety of places like the Half-caste Children's Home in Alice Springs. In 1974, now in his fifties, when applying for a birth certificate, he was told by the Northern Territory Government that his biological mother was still alive! Joseph Croft had been told at the Children's Home that his family was dead! His daughter, Brenda Croft, tells his story and that of other Australian children in her photography (Croft 1998).

In the basement level of The Art Gallery of New South Wales, a startling exhibit of Croft's colour ilfochrome photographs titled "In My Father's House" reveal the pain of the dislocation of what is now being called "the lost generation" of Australia. In 1905, the Aborigines Act in Australia legalised the removal of small children from Aboriginal families. The aim was to turn lighter-skinned Aboriginal children into "white" citizens. These children were placed in homes to be adopted by white families (Haebich 2004, 284-285).

"I remember roses" is one Croft photograph from the series, "In My Father's House," that impresses the viewer with the strength of a stolen child's early sensory imprints. It is a collage of fragmentation. In the center and dominating the collage is a white family with an adopted aboriginal child, a boy. The center photo was taken in a lovely garden with roses cascading over a wall. In the lower left corner of the collage, is the aboriginal mother holding the same boy as an infant – again surrounded by wild roses in an earlier garden. A photo of the child peers out from the top of the collage. "I remember roses ... " Are these the roses of both

---

[2]   Portions of this section originally appeared in Jeanne Stevenson-Moessner, *Portable Roots: Transplanting the Bicultural Child,* Cambridge Scholars Publishing, 2014, 102-104.

gardens? Is the child perhaps Brenda Croft's father, remembering his transplanta-
tion from one garden to another, remembering by way of sensory memories!

Brenda Croft fills the whole room with images of displaced and transplanted
children, victims of injurious multiple identity politics. She says of the tragic images: " 'In my Father's House' is a memorial not only to my father and brother but
a memorial to all those children stolen from their families and denied knowledge
of their heritage. This work is about chasing and catching those memories as they
fall" (Croft 1998).

"Don't go kissing at the garden gate" is a memory of a small girl being taken
from her aboriginal parents as the long line of her siblings stand behind the biological mother. The new white mother is beaming in contrast to the doleful expression
of the aboriginal mother who stares sternly forward and away from the severing
of her family. The garden gate is the scene of abandonment.

In an adjacent room at the Sydney museum are black and white films by
Genevieve Grieves showing an aboriginal child being silently removed from a
sibling group. One small child vanishes from the family grouping so subtly that
the viewer is almost unaware – almost.

This is the point where the work of artists Brenda Croft and Genevieve Grieves
and my research as a theologian converge: "The constructed layers of memory
[in Croft's work] reflect the fragmented lives of these children and the ongoing
effects of this through generations as families reconnect. In this process memories become distorted and disparate elements inform one's sense of self, while
questioning the validity of one's thoughts" (Croft 1998). The injustice in multiple
identity politics of transplanting a child can result in not only the fragmentation of
the child's cultural identity, but can negatively impact personhood and dignity as
well. Successful consolidation *can* result in a stronger, more resilient, gifted, creative self. However, some do *not* make it. Some transplanted lives still tackle the
odyssey of consolidation, of finding home, of putting down roots. Violet Bacon, a
Yamatji woman facing her aboriginal history concluded: "What is this thing that
people call identity? What does it mean? It was a long time before I understood
what it was for me. A feeling of togetherness with my spirit, an essence of spirituality, *of Dreaming* that needs to be nourished so it will grow strong and tall.
The tree of identity, that's how I think of it. I picture a tall towering gum tree with
strong branches, a solid trunk and no leaves. Why no leaves? Because then I can
see clearly" (Bacon 2009, 160, emphasis mine).

Tjalaminu Mia, a Nyungar woman in Australia, was placed as a child into
Sister Kate's Children's Home. While there she noted: "something very deep was
missing in my life and it was that deep sense of being connected to my people, my
family, my ancestors and to our cultural beliefs. It was a spirituality that Sunday
School teachers couldn't understand and because of this oppression I started to

lose my sense of being a Nyungar kid" (Mia 2009, 213). She was able to find her "taproot," that is, in her words, the root of the tree that goes the deepest. The taproot for her was the foundation of connection to the spiritual realm of her culture. Identity consolidation can be achieved with an adequate holding environment. A taproot is one such example.

At the University of Iowa Museum of Art, a 1946 oil on canvas titled "Endless Voyage," by Michael Siporin, a Chicago-based artist and the son of immigrants, uses history coupled with his passion for oppressed people to illustrate "injustice, personhood, dignity." In this portrayal of Jewish refugees on a boat with a sail that reads "Land of Israel," a mass of figures fill a tear-drop shaped boat sailing in choppy water and dim light with no land visible. As "Endless Voyage" illustrates, persons who are transplanted into a new cultural context face unique challenges in identity formation, and the multigenerational transmission of cultural trauma can also deeply affect identity. Moreover, such uprooting is often caused by an unjust political milieu or external multiple identity politics. For those impacted and for those injured by such multiple identity politics, the depth of their "tear-drop vessel of pain" summons practical theologians towards heightened cultural sensitivities, social awareness, and possibilities for healing as we theologians seek to close the gap toward dreaming *ubuntu*, even with "no land visible."

Research in Practical Theology will document many types of people whose uprooting has been caused by an unjust political milieu. The varieties of their portable roots will be as numerous as will the forms of "burlap sacks" or holding environments of cultural intimacy. What this research has attempted to show is the following: roots are portable; transplanting roots is a complex process that impacts identity formation; the political climate can harm this development. As the work of human developmentalists, psychologists, and psychiatrists incorporates these and similar findings, children who have been ripped from their roots will cease to be "the lost children" in mainstream developmental theory. Previous research has introduced terms such as double consciousness, multiple consciousness, relational refugees, and spiritual refugees. W.E.B. Du Bois was a pioneer in the understanding of *double consciousness* as looking at one's self through the eyes of the dominant race:

It is a peculiar sensation, this double consciousness, this sense of always looking at one's self through the eyes of others, of measuring one's soul by the tape of a world that looks on in amused contempt and pity. One ever feels his twoness, an American, a Negro; two souls, two thoughts, two unreconciled strivings; two warring ideals in one dark, body, whose dogged strength alone keeps it from being torn asunder.

The history of the American Negro is the history of this strife – this longing to attain self-conscious manhood [or womanhood], to merge his [her] double self into a better and truer self (Du Bois 1903, 16-17).

Archie Smith, Jr., used the concept "spiritual refugees" for those Africans who were uprooted from the ancestral land and brought through force to the shores of America as slaves and black fugitives. The spiritual refugee today shares these characteristics in being "uprooted, homeless, and landless; seeking shelter in another place; losing the protection of one's rights; imprisonment; and deportation" (Smith 1997, 36). Edward Wimberly extends this concept of refugees to those who have cut themselves off from family and past generations. These are "relational refugees" who have severed their ties with community, church, living family members, and ancestors (Wimberly 2000, 22). A "relational refugee" is depicted by Toni Morrison in her novel *Home*. The protagonist Frank Money joins the army to escape the confines and dangers of life for a black man in Lotus, Georgia, in the 1950s. He is forced to return to rescue his little sister, Cee. Like a modern Odysseus, he must meet challenges, especially the memories of brutality and violence in the farm country of Georgia. Unlike the bicultural children interviewed for this research, Frank Money had a distinct sense of his identity from childhood to adulthood (Morrison 2012).

The particularity in my usage of the term "transplanted multicultural child" has to do with the immediacy and physicality of the environment. The bodily interaction with the earthly context and the tactile engagement with caretakers not only imprints the consciousness of the developing child, but makes the "transplanting" a sensory shock. "Transplant shock" is a term from biology and is used specifically when a living organism with a root system is moved into a different soil environment. For example, trees must be transplanted with great care. Transplanting can be a danger to the root system if the "root ball" is not protected and transferred intact. After replanting, it takes an average of three years for the root system to rejuvenate (Burghhardt 2010).

Borrowing language from botany, I have been exploring how a child can be transplanted from one cultural soil to another and avoid transplant shock and stress. How can the "root ball" remain intact? How does a transplanted child maintain its existing growth? How does a child re-root herself socially? What is the optimal climate for roots to rejuvenate? How does such a child live into *ubuntu*, which relies on the relational nature of being and a sense of personal belonging to others?

Transplant shock and stress can be passed down through generations. The following example illustrates such a transmission: "In a "Feelings Release Workshop" in Atlanta, Georgia, in 1992, a participant entered a relaxed state under the expert supervision of trained clinical psychologists. In this relaxed, perhaps regressed state of consciousness, the participant experienced a heaviness on her chest, labored breathing, and constrictions on her wrists and ankles. The two attending therapists crouched by the mat on which she lay. They surmised that what she was experiencing were labor pains; the participant and her husband had just adopted an infant after years of infertility treatments. However, upon regaining consciousness, the patient was adamant: she had experienced the travail of the slave ships. She had felt the shackles on her wrists and ankles and the trauma of being shipped in slavery" (Stevenson-Moessner 2014, 94). Multigenerational transmission of distant cultural trauma is a particular aspect of personhood that begs further investigation as the complexities are realised (Johnson 2013). The generalisability of the cases I have used in this paper point to the undeniable conclusion: developmental theory has not incorporated the intricacies of the child/adolescent exposed to warring subcultures or the recall of distant ancestral memories.

Practical theologians like myself will be challenged now in many ways. 1) What do we have to learn from survivors of injurious multiple identity politics regarding resiliency, personhood, and dignity? 2) In dialogue with them, what is the relevance and meaning of our theological terms such as rebirth, baptism, enlightenment, sanctification, and self-differentiation? 3) How will our trauma theory be further adapted for those uprooted like Mike? Like Brenda Croft's father? 4) For those in pastoral care, what is an adequate holding environment for the uprooted? For those awakening to ancestral memories of brutality? For those injured by multiple identity politics? 5) How will we be challenged to rethink *diaspora*? 6) How do we help those who, in Mike's words, are less than beggars in society, those who have no niche? More importantly, how do we receive from them? When we receive, how is our theology impacted?

In July 2015, my daughter and I attended a national conference in Dallas called Compassionate Friends, a network to support bereaved parents and bereaved siblings. The six-month anniversary of my son's death occurred on the Friday of the conference. The event was held at the Hyatt Regency of Dallas. We had just been there at the Hyatt Regency with him, his fiancée, and her 18-month old daughter at Thanksgiving, eight months earlier. It was a difficult conference, especially occurring in a hotel with such recent memories.

I remembered Mike's cry: "they didn't understand the impact of my experience." How could they understand Mike? Yet I connected with his cry of isolation in my own grief because how could anyone understand what it is to lose a child if she hasn't? That is why 1,500 bereaved parents and siblings congregate each summer, in the pathos of suffering and empathy. Very few attendees are newly bereaved. Some lost children 19 or 20 years ago. They come to help us "beggars," we who are raw and still numb in suffering, we who have nothing to give. We are actually less than beggars. We have no name. We are not orphans or widows (widowers). We can't give, and we can't at first receive; sometimes at first, at the onset of the trauma, we literally cannot even receive food or drink.

First, we are understood, then we receive a name: bereaved parents. We band with others who bear the name. We receive a little broth of kindness, bread and water of understanding. We accept support from those who have survived. We observe they are living beyond the catastrophic loss. We see they are giving. In a long while, perhaps that will be me.

Less than a beggar, unable to receive. How ironic that Mike gave us an image that aptly illustrates the impact of catastrophic loss on personhood and dignity! Mike, the one who had nothing to give! As sociologists, developmentalists, psychologists, educators, anthropologists, and practical theologians rethink the rootlessness we have unearthed in narratives of those violated by unjust multiple identity politics, these courageous stories like that of Mike can only add to the fecundity of the soil of our joint scholarship.

References

Bacon, Violet. 2009. "Joining My Identity Pieces Together," in *Speaking From the Heart: Stories of Life, Family, and Country,* edited by Sally Morgan, Tjalaminu Mia, and Blaze Kwaymullina. Freemantle: Freemantle Press.

Burghardt, Jackie. 2010. "What Happens When a Tree is Moved?" last modified January 5, 2010. http://www.colostate.edu/Depts/CoopExt/4DMG/Trees/movetree.htm.

Croft, Brenda. 1998. Wall plaques from "In My Father's House." Exhibited in The Art Gallery of New South Wales, Sydney, Australia.

Du Bois, William. 1968. *The Souls of Black Folk.* New York: Fawcett Premier Books.

Erikson, Erik. 1963. *Childhood and Society.* New York: W.W. Norton.

Haebich, Anna. 2004. " 'Clearing the Wheat Belt': Erasing the Indigenous Presence in the Southwest of Western Australia." In *Genocide and Settler Society: Frontier Violence and Stolen Indigenous Children in Australian History.* Edited by A. Dirk Moses. New York: Berghahn Books.

Johnson, Cedric C. 2013. "Globalisation, Cultural Trauma and the Reconstruction of Diasporic African Identities." Paper presented at the Society for Pastoral Theology's Workshop on Postcolonialism, Globalisation, and Pastoral Care, Decatur, GA, June 14, 2013.

Mia, Tjalaminu. 2009. "Boorn – Taproot." In *Speaking From the Heart: Stories of Life, Family, and Country,* edited by Sally Morgan, Tjalaminu Mia, and Blaze Kwaymullina. Freemantle: Freemantle Press.

Morrison, Toni. 2000. *Home.* New York: Random House.

Niebuhr, H. Richard. 1951. *Christ and Culture.* New York: Harper and Row.

Phan, Peter C. 2003. *Christianity with an Asian Face.* Maryknoll, NY: Orbis Books.

Siporin, Michael. 1946. *Endless Voyage.* Oil on Canvass. Iowa City, Iowa: University of Iowa Museum of Art.

Smith, Jr., Archie. 1997. *Navigating the Deep River: Spirituality in African American Families.* Cleveland, OH: United Church Press.

Stevenson-Moessner, Jeanne. 2014. *Portable Roots: Transplanting the Bicultural Child*. Newcastle upon Tyne: Cambridge Scholars Publishing.

Tutu, Desmond. 1999. *No Future Without Forgiveness*. New York: Doubleday.

Wimberly, Edward P. 2000. *Relational Refugees: Alienation and Reincorporation in African American Churches and Communities*. Nashville, TN: Abingdon.

Echoes of *ubuntu*: Common good ethics and the struggle for life with justice and dignity

Raymond J. Webb

Abstract

The diaconal aspect of practical theology rightly concerns itself with the theory of how groups and individuals relate and flourish. The question is especially acute when a significant number of persons have limited resources. *Ubuntu* stresses our interconnectedness as constitutive of our very identity as persons. Awareness of inter-relationship is the only path to knowing who we truly and paradoxically "can be." By considering the common good, solidarity, and subsidiarity, this chapter offers a complementary path to the realisation of *ubuntu's* triad of justice, personhood, and human dignity. Then three courses of action are elaborated: practicing a preferential option for the poor, facing into structural violence, and accompaniment. I draw on the work of ethicist David Hollenbach and community health scholar and practitioner Paul Farmer.

At the heart of *ubuntu*

The use of the term *ubuntu* in post-apartheid South Africa offers an opportunity to draw on *ubuntu*'s rich, multivalent meanings and nuances to explore the relationship between the individual and the community. While *ubuntu* will be explored in much more complex ways throughout this volume, it may be useful to draw on additional complementary sources to investigate how persons are and should be in relationship, especially in the more poorly resourced and more exploited parts of our world. At the core of the interest in *ubuntu* is the struggle to seek justice, to understand personhood, and to promote human dignity for all. What this leads to is that my humanity is bound up with your humanity and with the common humanity of all. We all affect each other. Your need is my need. A person is a person through other persons. My joy should be your joy. Generous concern for the next person is a living out of *ubuntu*. We are beings-with-others, but we do not take away their otherness, their individual rights, their differences (cf. Louw 2001). There is no common mold for all. A self-centered individualism is the opposite.

Under the gaze of *ubuntu*, one must address the questions posed by those who have and those who do not have, or the widening gap between rich and poor, or the billions who do not have access to fundamental human rights and an adequate share of the world's resources (even in countries with significant natural riches). There is a struggle to be found in broadly implementing the vision of *ubuntu*. As anti-apartheid martyr Steve Biko (1978, 47) foreshadowed: "We believe that in the long run the special contribution to the world by Africa will be in the field of human relationship. The great powers of the world may have done wonders in giving the world an industrial and military look, but the great gift still has to come from Africa – giving the world a human face."

The perspective offered here also attempts to avoid the possible pitfalls of provincialism or intra-group "tyranny."

Practical theology's conversation is with resources from our religious traditions, with other disciplines, and with specific situations in our world. This chapter offers a complementary structure in light of *ubuntu*. It offers a way for any community, including the global community, to analyse, even structure its understanding of itself in pursuit of *ubuntu* values. Toward a framework for the struggle for justice for all, for recognition of the inherent dignity of each person, I will propose a consideration of "the common good" and its particular aspects of solidarity and subsidiarity. My consideration of the common good is shaped by the work of ethicist David Hollenbach. Next, in light of *ubuntu* and common good ethics, I will offer three courses of action: 1) practicing a preferential option for the poor; 2) recognising and working against structural violence; and 3) encouraging accompaniment. In this, I am following the suggestions from Paul Farmer's achievements in community health theory and practice, which is anchored in the pursuit of justice and respect for the dignity of every person. Following this route, this paper hopes to expand the conversation based on *ubuntu* values.

David Hollenbach is a social ethicist who has written at length on the common good, solidarity, subsidiarity, and situations with an African context. Currently at Boston College, he has held university positions in Kenya, the Philippines, and Vietnam. Paul Farmer, Harvard Professor of Social Medicine, is an epidemiologist and community health expert, the co-founder of Partners-in-Health, who lives in Haiti. He has done extensive work in Rwanda, Russia, and Peru, as well as Haiti, to bring comprehensive health care to people of very limited financial means.

My own context includes more than five years spent in Palestine, over the course of the past forty years. I have waited for full citizenship for all, for an end to the occupation, and for a dignified and just work situation for all. I have hoped and cried. Since 2007, my journey has also included forty visits to El Salvador, which survived a 1980-1992 war that extinguished 75,000 lives (Wood 2003, 8), only to be succeeded by a "peace" with a new dreadful "occupation" by murderous Salvadorean gangs of extortionists who impact most lives.

Background

In the interplay of principle and action, practical theology describes specific practices of principled living for the sake of justice and in respect for the dignity of the others who share their earth with us. It is theory and practice, much like medicine is theory and practice. Some of the earliest practical theology of solidarity is to be found in Acts 2: 44-45 (echoed in Acts 4: 32-35): "And all that believed were together, and had all things common; and they sold their possessions and goods, and parted them to all, according as any man had need."

Another related dimension of the principles and action germane to practical theology is the work of theologian Gustavo Gutierrez (1988, 162-173), a pastor who has been significant in developing a theology of liberation, a return to base Christian communities meditating on the scripture and their own lives toward greater agency and an end to oppression. The Exodus and the Paschal Mystery of the saving death and resurrection of Jesus are the primary scriptural guides to the emergent possibilities. According to the Christian tradition, human persons have a dignity received from their Creator. Every person is equally created in the image of God. These religious insights of creation and redemption evolve into an insistent focus on a preferential option for the poor.

There are parallels to *ubuntu* found in Western philosophical analysis related to the individual, community, justice, personhood, and dignity. The distribution of rights and duties, of available goods, is governed by distributive justice. While distributive justice depends on the law, one must also bring to the fore social justice, which derives from the solidarity of the human community. All have the right to what is needed to live a life fitting with their dignity as human persons, including water, food, hygiene, health care, safety, and work opportunities, especially for members of the human family who live at the margins. Paul Farmer contends that the healthy thriving of the poor will also be determined by the level of fulfillment of their social and economic rights (equity), which in turn affects their civil and political ones (Farmer 2005, 9, 75).

Three ethical principles promoting justice, personhood and human dignity

In this section, I will review complementary ethical principles, flowing from the goal of our interconnectedness, consistent with *ubuntu*, which support the ideal of all human persons enjoying lives that befit their dignity as members of the human community. The dignity is not conferred by others; it comes from being a human person. The problem comes when the dignity is not recognised by others, when all are not "equal" persons; when distributive justice and social justice are not operative. I consider the notion of the common good, as well as solidarity and subsidiarity (which are two aspects of the common good). They are elaborations, from a Western philosophical-theological perspective, of the *ubuntu* concept of one's humanity coming from other humans. Then, in the following section, I move to three areas of practice which draw on our principles – promoting the preferential option for the poor, addressing structural violence, and encouraging accompaniment. In a sense we are looking at a kind of *ubuntu* for the larger community.

The common good

David Hollenbach (2002, xiv) contends that growing but unequal global interdependence calls for a revitalised understanding and commitment to the common good. I would describe the "common good" as a humanly created national and international order that promotes social justice. John XXIII in *Mater et Magistra* called for all economic activity to be conducted not merely for private gain but also in the interests of the common good (John XXIII 1961, 38-40). He argued that there should be a balance between different elements of society or the economy: owners and workers, individual freedom and civil authority actions [even in regard to property] (John XXIII 1961, 92, 53-58, 116-117). Economic progress and social progress should balance, leading to a reducing of inequality (John XXIII 1961, 73).

Hollenbach (2008) says:

I like to understand this commitment to the common good as actualised both in deeds and in words, both by citizens acting together to create a common life and by deliberating together about what their action should be when they at first disagree on what their society should do. I call these forms of interaction the *social solidarity* that enables peoples to participate actively in social life and the *intellectual and imaginative solidarity* that connects people to each other in discussion, conversation, and debate about how they should live together and helps them imagine what it is like to be in another's shoes.

The common good is a way of looking at what can also be called a common morality or a global ethic. While it may seem to be very difficult to describe the common good, certain documents indicate that a consensus is possible. The United Nations' Universal Declaration of Human Rights (General Assembly of the United Nations 1948) showed that considerable agreement on the common good is possible (Hollenbach 2003, 233). The United Nations Millennium Declaration (General Assembly of the United Nations 2000, 1-9) built international consensus on specific areas for global improvement, such as specific support for the nations of Africa and "development for all the peoples of the world, the fight against poverty, ignorance and disease; the fight against injustice; the fight against violence, terror and crime; and the fight against the degradation and destruction of our common home" (General Assembly of the United Nations 2000, 27-29).

We can briefly note two other philosophical perspectives on the common good. Michael Ignatieff (2001, 56) says that the common good stands opposite what he would call the "insufferably, unarguably wrong." Wanting to avoid foundationalism, he claims that the harms all people want to avoid can be identified (Ignatieff 2001, 88-89). Hollenbach notes that one can also look for the common good under the rubrics of what John Rawls calls an "overlapping consensus (Hollenbach 1987, 240; Rawls 1987, 1). For Rawls, understanding the common good begins to be built from values that few would deny, such as freedom from slavery and serfdom, liberty (but not equal liberty) of conscience, and the security of ethnic groups from mass murder and genocide (Hollenbach 2003, 251). Interlocutors discover grounds from their own perspectives for affirming a set of basic moral principles that others can agree with.

Solidarity

Solidarity is the recognition by, and action of, persons and groups according to the principle that "we are all in this together." We are at the heart of *ubuntu* – the one community, in mutual support, "defining" the humanity of all the others. We have a relationship to every other human being and an obligation to pursue their well-being, especially in situations where they are not able to take actions on their own. Solidarity is a recognition of interdependence and the duty to act for the common good, that common good ultimately stretching to all who inhabit this planet. This principle encourages the strong to work for the weak, while not encouraging passivity. To take one definition, John Paul II defined solidarity as "a firm and persevering determination to commit oneself to the common good; that is to say to the good of all and of each individual, because we are all really responsible for all" (John Paul II 1987, 38). Hollenbach comments that many people in Africa and other areas do not have the resources to become involved in the markets that are supposed to be the engines of economic development (Hollenbach 2003, 227). Economic marginalisation leads to political disenfranchisement, a gap between rich and poor and the opportunity dictatorships and entrenched elites. This is the opposite of solidarity. In contrast, Louw sees in South Africa's *ubuntu*-inspired societal transition "the emergence of an ethos of solidarity" (Louw 2001, 27).

Subsidiarity

Simply put, subsidiarity advocates that action and control be exercised at the lowest level possible. Governments should not do or decide what individuals can do or decide. Although elders sometimes receive more attention, *ubuntu* argues that all voices are to be heard, all gifts used, every contributor matters, humility is in order.

In 1931, Pius XI, developing the Catholic social teaching tradition, stated that "just as it is gravely wrong to take from individuals what they can accomplish by their own initiative and industry and give it to the community, so also it is an injustice and at the same time a grave evil and disturbance of right order to assign to a greater and higher association what lesser and subordinate organisations can do" (Pius XI 1931, 79).

Richard Esenberg notes that subsidiarity focuses on the freedom and empowerment of individuals and local community groups toward solidarity of protection of the weak, the promotion of the common good, and the limitation of individualism (Esenberg 2010). Subsidiarity gives the opportunity for creativity and responsibility. Elizabeth Schiltz asserts, "Solidarity without subsidiarity, in fact, can easily generate into a 'Welfare State,' while subsidiarity without solidarity runs the risk of encouraging forms of self-centered localism" (Schiltz 2009).

Economist William Easterly wary of imposed global solutions, argues that sustainable development, after so much failure, requires learning from history rather than acting as if all is a blank slate; not shorting individual judicial and political rights for the sake of the nation/people/group; and favouring the spontaneous solutions of the local people involved rather than the grand design by outsiders (Easterly 2013, 24-25). These aspects seem to be active features of subsidiarity.

From *ubuntu* and ethics to action

Beginning with inspiration from *ubuntu,* with its promotion of justice, personhood, and human dignity, we have looked at the values of the common good, solidarity, and subsidiarity. Now we consider three specific areas of implementation. Paul Farmer points us toward three principled initiatives, which, I believe, engage the principles of the common good, solidarity, and subsidiarity: the preferential option for the poor; facing into structural violence; and accompaniment. The preferential option for the poor is a movement toward equal sharing of resources, an *ubuntu* concept. The common good does in fact become common to all when the needs of the poor have a priority, so that they become part of the "common." Facing into structural violence lays bare a shadowy threat to community solidarity and to appreciation of each individual. Accompaniment provides unity, empathy, and a certain warmth and is at the heart of *ubuntu*. It is a "walking with," not an expert/novice relationship. Each person involved contributes something. I draw many examples from Farmer; they are also analogues or examples of ways to use our principles and applications, hopefully useful for faith communities and other non-governmental organisations.

Preferential option for the poor

Gustavo Gutierrez has influenced Farmer's thinking about the poor, through their conversations and work on a joint project in Peru (Farmer 2003, 121). From Gutierrez' theological perspective, "God has a preferential love for the poor not because they are necessarily better than others, morally or religiously, but simply because they are poor and living in an inhuman situation that is contrary to God's will" (Gutierrez 1987, 313). For Gutierrez, "Preference implies the universality of God's love, which excludes no one. It is only within the framework of universality that we can understand preference, that is, 'what comes first' " (Gutierrez 2013, 13).

Gutierrez has made known the preferential option for the poor and lived it in his parish in the slums of Lima. But there is a rich, prior background. The Second Vatican Council's *Gaudium et Spes* echoing Pope Leo XIII from 75 years earlier, stated that "to possess superfluity is to possess the goods of others" (Vatican Council II 1965, no. 69). Everyone has the right to possess a sufficient amount of the world's goods for themselves and their families. Amplifying this line of teaching, the U.S. Catholic bishops in *Economic Justice for All*, which Hollenbach helped craft, have stated:

The needs of the poor take priority over the desires of the rich; the rights of workers over the maximisation of profits; the preservation of the environment over uncontrolled industrial expansion; the production to meet social needs over production for military purposes ... The obligation to provide justice for all means that the poor have the single most urgent economic claim on the conscience of the nation ... The prime purpose of this special commitment to the poor is to enable them to become active participants in the life of society. It is to enable all persons to share in and contribute to the common good (United States Catholic Conference of Bishops 1986, 86, 88, 94).

Solidarity is realised when all of us have the chance to attain a minimum standard of human well-being, hence the preferential option for the poor, a focus on everyone "catching up." As one specifies the contextual effect of being poor, one notes that the poor are simply more vulnerable to persistent outbreaks of infectious diseases (e.g., HIV-AIDS, drug-resistant tuberculosis, Ebola, Zika) or to earthquake death from vulnerable housing (e.g., Haiti and Nepal). So Farmer argues that, for example, in regard to infectious diseases we must move beyond weak prevention programs to allocating sufficient resources for serious research and effective prevention and treatment programs (Farmer 1999, xxiii-xxvi). We can no longer accept whatever we are told about "limited resources." Better use of certain monies budgeted for armaments as well as increased taxation of extreme income could improve the situation of the world's seven hundred million extremely poor people. Cost effectiveness cannot mean that only the rich can afford to be cured. Disease prevention in developing countries must include a social-justice component, the shape of which only local people immediately involved may be able to point to, in keeping with the principle of subsidiarity.

Facing into structural violence

Adam Burtle has described structural violence as systematic ways in which social structures harm or otherwise disadvantage individuals and populations (Burtle 2010). It is structural and social because it is embedded in the political and economic organisation of the social world. It is violent because it causes harm and even death to people. As Farmer notes, structural violence is the result neither of culture nor of individual will, but rather of historically and economically driven processes which constrain individual agency (Farmer 2005, 40). Structural violence costs those who do not have the social status to benefit from scientific and social progress. It includes many and varied assaults on human dignity: extreme and relative poverty, social inequalities ranging from racism, classism, and social stratification to gender inequality. Given these conditions violent acts will result as these forces come together through routine, ritual, or the "hard surfaces of life" to limit the actors choices, with structural violence ensuing. Farmer notes that it is sometimes impossible to treat a patient who doesn't get enough food to eat (Farmer 2013, 242). He then names five pitfalls in thinking which may account for the largely structural causes of the continuation of this and other structural violence: conflating structural violence and cultural differences, minimising the role of poverty, exaggerating patient agency, romanticising "folk healing," and persisting in insularity (Farmer 1999, 257-260). In another reflective investigation, Farmer traced the path from dubiously legal confiscation of land for a dam in Haiti, which led to former farmers having no means of employment. As a result, men and women went to Port au Prince for employment, increasing the risk of HIV-AIDS and loss of life in a health resources deprived country.

I would want to argue that the growing rich-poor gap is at least destabilising but can become a kind of structural violence. Self-interested tolerance by other governments of dictatorships, totalitarianism, and corruption is likely to be a contributor to structural violence. There is somewhere a line between structural violence and social inequity. Farmer would say that social inequalities can be measured, but we are not able to measure their total social cost, which moves toward the designation of "structural violence" (Farmer 2006, 532-537). If ethical dilemmas are de-socialised – seen as simply the result of personal agency rather than being significantly under the influence of societal structures – we have an epistemological problem and also compound the ethical dilemma.

It must be noted that Farmer does not accept the argument that what are obvious assaults on human dignity may be highly valued cultural institutions (Farmer 2005, 47-49). One must be wary of conflating structural violence and cultural difference, so that the former hides behind the latter. The common example is certain discourse around female genital circumcision. Every culture cannot be a law unto itself, answerable to nothing other than itself. Farmer asserts: "The role of cultural boundary lines in enabling, perpetuating, justifying, and interpreting suffering is subordinate to (though well integrated with) the national and international mechanisms that create and deepen inequalities. 'Culture' does not explain suffering; it may at worst furnish an alibi" (Farmer 2005, 49).

Accompaniment

Farmer was buoyed up by Gustavo Gutierrez' remark, "I think the first person is 'you are,' and after we have recognised that you are, we can say, 'I am' " (Farmer and Gutierrez 2013, 187). Farmer adds that the implied accompaniment is a long term commitment (Farmer 2014).

Accompaniment is becoming involved in a situation (of others), supporting them, sharing their journey, and perhaps their fate for a while, learning from them, and then staying with them and the situation until the partners are able to deliver services and provide long term livelihoods and they feel that the task is completed. Forster asserts: "As a person participates with others and the environment, the person's identity (who the person is in society, who the person sees him or herself to be and the community's relation to the person) changes" (Forster 2010). Accompaniment is a form of solidarity, in the spirit of *ubuntu*. Like *ubuntu* accompaniment recognises the gifts of the person, values being together, recognises that all contribute in some way, and does not fall back on class or "expert/novice" distinctions. Accompaniment supports *ubuntu* "coping" qualities elaborated by Broodryk, such as kindness, generosity, harmonious family-like living, modesty, humility, helpfulness caring, sharing, respect, and compassion (Broodryk 2006).

Farmer sees that in difficult settings, everyone needs accompaniment, including those who accompany (Farmer 2013, 234). One group that accompanies is community health workers, who weave together a context of acute medical care and the community social and economic environment necessary for ultimate well-being. For Farmer the goal is to build effective systems for economic development and healthcare delivery, which must include members of the local community.

Accompaniment-approach principles, in the spirit of subsidiarity, would include: favour institutions that the poor identify as representing their interests; make job creation a benchmark of success; buy and hire locally; apply evidence-based standards of care that offer the best outcomes (Weigel, Basilico, and Farmer 2013, 294-296).

As Farmer has said, the goal is not personal efficacy but giving people a chance to do good in their own world (Farmer 2014). It is "over" when people there say that it is "over." "Solve, deliver, and leave" builds no future. It is interesting that, when asked why he has been able to stay in community health work for so long, under often discouraging circumstances, Farmer answered, "We are still in Haiti and Rwanda because there is a we" (Farmer 2014). As Gutierrez states, "If there is no friendship with them [the poor] and no sharing of the life of the poor, then there is no authentic commitment to liberation, because love exists only among equals" (Gutierrez 1988, xxxi). The common good, solidarity, and subsidiarity are evident here.

Conclusion

A strategic practical theology will carefully observe the situations of poor people in the world. We will see the ongoing effects of the disgusting history of apartheid in South Africa. We will see that around the world to be a woman and poor means deficient healthcare and a shorter life. We will see the need for clean water and adequate sanitation for billions of people. We see the rich-poor divide: 85 people control as much wealth as half of the world's population, according to Oxfam (Hutchins 2014).

We need to note that without solidarity we have "no skin in the game." The exercise would fade into the abstract. There would be no common good. We cannot feel the human "we." Without subsidiarity, we may be "know-it-all" outsiders imposing our grand plans. We would be colonisers, in effect, who may well not know what we are doing. There would be no local voice.

Ubuntu may have grown out of a village context, but the world has become the village. We cannot arrive at common good unless all have the possibility of developing to a minimum standard of human life, hence the preferential option for the poor. The notion of structural violence is the hidden secret. It says that a convergence of negative societal factors (intended or not) can severely limit human agency. Unless one is careful and reflective, there can be a quick leap to "blaming the victims." Accompaniment is coming and staying, in other words – solidarity. We need to listen carefully, respect our interlocutors as our equals, realise that most people are expert in something, be it agriculture, monetary systems, or deep humanity (subsidiarity). We are in a continual becoming human through our sisters and brothers – *ubuntu*.

References

Biko, Steve. 1978. *I Write What I Like*. New York: Harper and Row.
Broodryk, Johann. 2006. "Ubuntu: African Life Coping Skills, Theory and Practice." Paper, CCEAM Conference, October 12-17. http://www.topkinisis.com/conference/CC EAM/wib/index/outline/PDF/BROODRYK%20Johann.pdf.
Burtle, Adam. 2010. "Structural Violence." http://www.structuralviolence.org/structural-violence/.
Easterly, William. 2013. *The Tyranny of Experts*. New York: Basic Books.
Esenberg, Richard M. 2010. "Never Let a Good Crisis Lead You Astray: The Lessons of Christian Realism and Subsidiarity for Public Policy." *University of St. Thomas Law Journal* 7 (2). http://ir.stthomas.edu/ustlj/vol7/iss2/7.
Farmer, Paul. 1999. *Infections and Inequalities: The Modern Plague*. Berkeley, CA: University of California Press.
Farmer, Paul. 2005. *Pathologies of Power: Health, Human Rights, and the New War on the Poor*. Berkeley, CA: University of California Press.
Farmer, Paul. 2006. "Rich World, Poor World: Medical Ethics and Global Inequality." In *Partner to the Poor: A Paul Farmer* Reader, edited by Haun Saussy, 528-544. Berkeley, CA: University of California Press.
Farmer, Paul. 2013. *To Repair the World: Paul Farmer Speaks to the Next Generation*. Berkeley, CA: University of California Press.
Farmer, Paul. 2014. "Paul Farmer on Liberation Theology." Video, Harvard Divinity School, posted on March 3, 2014. http://www.bing.com/videos/search?q=Paul+Farm er&FORM=HDRSC3{#}view=detail&mid=6C1ECEFE5E60BD65617D6C1ECEF E5E60BD65617D.
Farmer, Paul and Gustavo Gutierrez. 2013. *In the Company of the Poor: Conversations with Dr. Paul Farmer and Fr. Gustavo Gutierrez*, edited by Michael Griffin, and Jennie Weiss Block. Maryknoll, NY: Orbis Books.
Forster, Dion. 2010. "A Generous Ontology: Identity as a Process of Intersubjective Discovery: An African Theological Contribution." *HTS Theological Studie*s 66 (1). doi:10.4102/hts. v66i1.731.
General Assembly of the United Nations. 1948. The Universal Declaration of Human Rights. Resolution 217A. http://www.un.org/en/universal-declaration-human-rights/i ndex.html.
General Assembly of the United Nations. 2000. United Nations Millennium Declaration. A/Res /55/2. http://www.un.org/millennium/declaration/ares552e.pdf.
Gutierrez, Gustavo. 1987. *On Job: God-Talk and the Suffering of the Innocent*. Maryknoll, NY: Orbis Books.
Gutierrez, Gustavo. 1988. *A Theology of Liberation*. Maryknoll, NY: Orbis Books.
Gutierrez, Gustavo. 2013. *Essential Writings*. Edited and with an introduction by James B. Nickoloff. Maryknoll, NY: Orbis Books.

Hollenbach, David. 2002. *The Common Good and Christian Ethics*. Cambridge: Cambridge University Press.

Hollenbach, David. 2003. *The Global Face of Public Faith: Politics, Human Rights, and Christian Ethics*. Washington, DC: Georgetown University Press.

Hollenbach, David. 2008. "Faith and Politics: Christian Spirituality and Working for the Common Good." Lecture, Sacred Heart Church, Detroit Michigan. September 18. el ephantsinthelivingroom.com

Hutchens, Gareth. 2014. "Richest 85 Boast Control Same Wealth as Half the World." *The Sydney Morning Herald: Business Day*. January 21, 14. http://www.smh.com.au/bus iness/richest-85-boast-same-wealth-as-half-the-world-20140120-314vk.html.

Ignatieff, Michael. 2001. *Human Rights as Politics and Idolatry*, edited with an introduction by Amy Gutmann. Princeton, NJ: Princeton University Press.

John XXIII. 1961. *Mater et Magistra* [On Christianity and Social Progress]. http://w2.vatican.va/content/john-xxiii/en/encyclicals/documents/hf_j-xxiii_enc _15051961_mater.html.

John Paul II. 1987. *Sollicitudo Rei Socialis* [The Social Concern of the Church]. http://www.vatican.va/holy_father/john_paul_ii/encyclicals/documents/hf_jp-ii_enc _30121987_sollicitudo-rei-socialis_en.html.

Louw, Daniël J. 2001. "Ubuntu and the Challenges of Multiculturalism in Post-apartheid South Africa." *Question: An African Journal of Philosophy* 15 (1 & 2): 15–36. http: //michiel.ipower.com/Quest_2001_PDF/louw.pdf.

Pius XI. 1931. *Quadragesimo Anno* [Forty Years After]. http://www.vatican.va/holy _father/pius_xi/encyclicals/documents/hf_pxi_enc_19310515_quadragesimo-anno_ en.html.

Rawls, John. 1987. "The Idea of an Overlapping Consensus." *Oxford Journal of Legal Studies* 7 (1): 1-25. http://www.jstor.org/stable/764257?seq=1{#}page_scan_tab_ contents.

Schiltz, Elizabeth R. 2009. "Subsidiarity and the Financial Crisis." *First Things*. http: //www.firstthings.com/web-exclusives/2009/04/subsidiarity-and-the-financial.

United States Conference of Catholic Bishops. 1986. *Economic Justice for All: Pastoral Letter on Catholic Social Teaching and the U.S. Economy*. http://www.usccb.org/uplo ad/economic_justice_for_all.pdf.

Vatican Council II. 1965. *Gaudium et Spes* [Pastoral Constitution on the Church]. www. vatican.va/punkte{}/vat-ii_cons_19651207_gaudium-et-spes_en.html

Weigel, Jonathan, Matthew Basilico, and Paul Farmer. 2013. "Taking Stock of Foreign Aid." In *Reimagining Global Health: an Introduction*, edited by Paul Farmer, Jim Yong Kim, Arthur Kleinman, Matthew Basilico, 287-301. Berkeley, CA: University of California Press.

Wood, Elisabeth Jean. 2003. *Insurgent Collective Action and Civil War in El Salvador*. Cambridge, UK: Cambridge University Press.

The authors

NADINE BOWERS DU TOIT
is a senior lecturer in Theology and Development, Department Practical Theology & Missiology, Faculty of Theology, University of Stellenbosch, South
Africa.

LYNN BRIDGERS
is a licensed mental health counselor. She also teaches in the Religious Studies
Program at the University of New Mexico.

JOHAN CILLIERS
is Professor in Homiletics and Liturgy at the Faculty of Theology, University
of Stellenbosch, South Africa.

PAMELA COUTURE
is the Jane and Geoffrey Martin chair of Church and Community at Emmanuel
College of Victoria University in the University of Toronto, Canada.

FRITZ DE WET
was (until his death in 2015) Professor in Practical Theology and Director of
the Unit for Reformed Theology and the Development of the South African
Society, Faculty of Theology, University of the North West, Potchefstroom,
South Africa.

WILHELM GRÄB
is Professor of Practical Theology at Humboldt-University Berlin and Director of the Institute of Sociology of Religion and Community Development at
Humboldt-University Berlin. He also serves as an Extraordinary Professor at
Stellenbosch University, South Africa.

HANS-GÜNTER HEIMBROCK
is Professor emeritus in Practical Theology and Religious Education, Faculty
of Protestant Theology, Goethe-University Frankfurt, Germany.

DAVID HOGUE
is Professor of Pastoral Theology and Counselling, Garrett-Evangelical Theological Seminary, Evanston, Illinois U.S.A.

SIMANGALISO KUMALO
   is Associate Professor in Practical Theology, University of Kwazulu-Natal and
   Seth Mokitimi Methodist Seminary, Pietermaritzburg, South Africa.

DANIËL LOUW
   is Professor emeritus in Practical Theology, Faculty of Theology, University
   of Stellenbosch, South Africa. He also serves as an Extraordinary Professor,
   University of the North West, Potchefstroom, South Africa.

VHUMANI MAGEZI
   is Senior Lecturer Pastoral Care and Counselling, Faculty of Humanities
   School of Basic Sciences, Vaal Triangle Campus, North-West University, Van-
   derbijlpark, South Africa.

MAAKE MASANGO
   is Professor emeritus in Practical Theology, Department of Practical Theology,
   Faculty of Theology, University of Pretoria, Pretoria, South Africa.

JOYCE ANN MERCER
   is Professor of Practical Theology and Pastoral Care, Yale Divinity School,
   New haven, CT, U.S.A.

JOHANN-ALBRECHT MEYLAHN
   is Professor in Pastoral Care and Congregational Studies, department of Practical Theology, Faculty of Theology, University of Pretoria, Pretoria, South
   Africa.

IAN NELL
   is Professor in Practical Theology, Department of Practical Theology and Missiology, Faculty of Theology, University of Stellenbosch, Stellenbosch, South
   Africa.

EVELYN PARKER
   is the Susanna Wesley Centennial Professor of Practical Theology, Perkins
   School of Theology – Southern Methodist University, Dallas, TX, U.S.A.

NEIL PEMBROKE
   is Associate Professor in the School of Historical and Philosophical Inquiry,
   University of Queensland, Brisbane, Australia.

JOHN MOHAN RAZU
   is Adjunct Professor at Clark Theological College, Mokokchung, Nagaland,
   North-East India. He is also Professor of Social Ethics and currently coor-
   dinating the Research Unit of the Indian Social Institute (ISI) based at Ben-
   galuru.

FRIEDRICH SCHWEITZER
   is Professor and Chair of Practical Theology / Religious Education, Protestant
   Faculty of Theology, University of Tübingen, Germany.

JEANNE STEVENSON-MOESSNER

is Professor of Pastoral Care at Perkins School of Theology – Southern Methodist University, Dallas, TX, U.S.A.

ROGER TUCKER

is an emeritus minister of the Uniting Presbyterian Church in South Africa, and Research Associate, department of Practical Theology at the University of Free State, Bloemfontein, South Africa. He is also a staff member of the post graduate Department, South African Theological Seminary, Johannesburg, South Africa.

WENTZEL VAN HUYSSTEEN

is the James I. McCord Professor of Theology and Science Emeritus, Princeton Theological Seminary, Princeton, NJ. U.S.A. He is also an Extraordinary Professor, Faculty of Theology, Stellenbosch, South Africa.

RAYMOND WEBB

is Chair and Professor of Pastoral Theology, University of Saint Mary of the Lake, Mundelein, IL. U.S.A.

TRYGVE WYLLER

is Professor, Faculty of Theology, University of Oslo, Oslo, Norway. He is also an Honorary Professor, School of Religion, Philosophy and Classics, University of Kwazulu-Natal, Pietermaritzburg, South Africa.

International Practical Theology

edited by Prof. Dr. Chris Hermans (Nijmegen), Prof. Dr. Maureen Junker-Kenny (Dublin), Prof. Dr. Richard Osmer (Princeton), Prof. Dr. Friedrich Schweitzer (Tübingen), Prof. Dr. Hans-Georg Ziebertz (Würzburg) in cooperation with the International Academy of Practical Theology (IAPT), represented by Heather Walton (President) and Robert Mager (Vice-President)

Pamela Couture
We Are Not All Victims
Local Peacebuilding in the Democratic Republic of Congo
Bd. 18, 2016, 392 S., 39,90 €, br., ISBN 978-2-643-90796-7

Pamela Couture; Robert Mager; Pamela McCarroll; Natalie Wigg-Stevenson (Eds.)
Complex Identities in a Shifting World
Practical Theological Perspectives
Bd. 17, 2015, 284 S., 29,90 €, br., ISBN 978-3-643-90509-3

R. Ruard Ganzevoort; Rein Brouwer; Bonnie Miller-McLemore (Eds.)
City of Desires – a Place for God?
Practical theological perspectives
Bd. 16, 2013, 216 S., 29,90 €, br., ISBN 978-3-643-90307-5

Edward Foley (Ed.)
Religion, Diversity and Conflict
Bd. 15, 2011, 312 S., 29,90 €, br., ISBN 978-3-643-90086-9

Heid Leganger-Krogstad
The Religious Dimension of Intercultural Education
Contributions to a Contextual Understanding
Bd. 14, 2011, 288 S., 29,90 €, br., ISBN 978-3-643-90085-2

Annemie Dillen; Anne Vandenhoeck (Eds.)
Prophetic Witness in World Christianities
Rethinking Pastoral Care and Counseling
Bd. 13, 2011, 248 S., 24,90 €, br., ISBN 978-3-643-90041-8

Hans-Georg Ziebertz; Ulrich Riegel (Eds.)
How Teachers in Europe Teach Religion
An International Empirical Study
Bd. 12, 2009, 408 S., 34,90 €, br., ISBN 978-3-643-10043-6

Gordon Mikoski; Richard Osmer
With Piety and Learning
The History of Practical Theology at Princeton Theological Seminary 1812–2012
Bd. 11, 2011, 256 S., 29,90 €, br., ISBN 978-3-643-90106-4

Hans-Georg Ziebertz; William K Kay; Ulrich Riegel (Eds.)
Youth in Europe III
An international Empirical Study about the Impact of Religion on Life Orientation. With a preface by Silviu E. Rogobete
Bd. 10, 2009, 272 S., 19,90 €, br., ISBN 978-3-8258-1579-0

Hans-Georg Ziebertz; Ulrich Riegel (Eds.)
Europe: secular or post-secular?
Bd. 9, 2008, 216 S., 19,90 €, br., ISBN 978-3-8258-1578-3

LIT Verlag Berlin – Münster – Wien – Zürich – London
Auslieferung Deutschland / Österreich / Schweiz: siehe Impressumsseite

Mechteld Jansen; Hijme Stoffels (Eds.)
A Moving God
Immigrant Churches in the Netherlands
Bd. 8, 2008, 248 S., 24,90 €, br., ISBN 978-3-8258-0802-0

Wilhelm Gräb; Lars Charbonnier (Eds.)
Secularization Theories, Religious Identity and Practical Theology
Developing international Practical Theology for the 21st Century. International Academy
of Practical Theology Berlin 2007
Bd. 7, 2009, 424 S., 39,90 €, br., ISBN 978-3-8258-0798-6

Theo van der Zee
Religious ideas, feelings and their interrelationship
Research into the effects of religious education in parables on 10- to 12-year-olds
Bd. 6, 2007, 192 S., 17,90 €, br., ISBN 978-3-8258-0530-2

Hans-Georg Ziebertz; Friedrich Schweitzer (eds.)
Dreaming the Land
Theologies of Resistance and Hope. International Academy of Practical Theology Brisbane 2005
Bd. 5, 2007, 224 S., 19,90 €, br., ISBN 978-3-8258-0082-6

Hans-Georg Ziebertz; William K Kay (eds.)
Youth in Europe II
An international empirical Study about Religiosity. With a preface by Cardinal Josip Bozanić, Vice-President of the European Bishops' Conference
Bd. 4, 2009, 376 S., 29,90 €, br., ISBN 978-3-8258-9941-7

Richard R. Osmer; Kenda Creasy Dean (Eds.)
Youth, Religion and Globalization
New Research in Practical Theology. Preface by Friedrich Schweitzer
Bd. 3, 2007, 312 S., 19,90 €, br., ISBN 978-3-8258-9766-6

Hans-Georg Ziebertz; William K Kay (eds.)
Youth in Europe I
An international empirical Study about Life Perspectives. With a preface by Lambert van
Nistelrooij (MEP)
Bd. 2, 2009, 280 S., 24,90 €, br., ISBN 978-3-8258-8718-6

Elaine Graham; Anna Rowlands (eds.)
Pathways to the Public Square
Practical Theology in an Age of Pluralism. International Academy of Practical Theology,
Manchester 2004
Bd. 1, 2005, 328 S., 39,90 €, br., ISBN 3-8258-8423-6

LIT Verlag Berlin – Münster – Wien – Zürich – London
Auslieferung Deutschland / Österreich / Schweiz: siehe Impressumsseite